A
Shepherd
in
Combat Boots

Chaplain Emil Kapaun
of the 1st Cavalry Division

by
William L. Maher

BURD STREET PRESS
SHIPPENSBURG, PENNSYLVANIA

In respect for the scholarship contained herein, the acid-free paper used in this book meets the guidelines for permanence and durability of the Committee on Production Guidelines for Book Longevity of the Council on Library Resources.

For a complete list of available publications please write

Burd Street Press
Division of White Mane Publishing Company, Inc.
P.O. Box 708
Shippensburg, PA 17257 USA

Library of Congress Cataloging-in-Publication Data

Maher, William L., 1928–
    A shepherd in combat boots : Chaplain Emil Kapaun of the 1st
Cavalry Division / by William L. Maher.
        p.   cm.
    Includes bibliographical references and index.
    ISBN-13 978-1-57249-069-7 ISBN-10 1-57249-069-1 (alk. paper). --
    ISBN-13 978-1-57249-305-6 ISBN-10 1-57249-305-4 (pbk.)
    1. Kapaun, Emil, 1916–1951. 2. Korean War, 1950–1953—Prisoners
and prisons. 3. Prisoners of war—United States—Biography.
4. Prisoners of war—Korea (North)—Biography. 5. Chaplains,
Military—United States—Biography. 6. Catholic Church—United
States—Clergy—Biography. I. Title.
DS921.M225   1997
282'.092—dc21
[B]   97–19800
                                                                          CIP

 PRINTED IN THE UNITED STATES OF AMERICA

DEDICATION

To my dear wife, Lee, for her encouragement, help, and patience; to Maureen, Vince, Greg, Sue Ellen, Christopher, John, Emily, Jay and all persons, young and old, who are inspired by the story of a good man.

CONTENTS

ILLUSTRATIONS

ACKNOWLEDGMENTS

Several years ago I decided to write the biography of a 20th-century American Catholic who might become a saint. I read a newspaper story about Chaplain Emil Kapaun in June 1991 and reached the conclusion that he met all the qualifications for the story. As I gathered facts about his life as a soldier, I became pleased that this book also gave me an opportunity to honor some of the men who suffered with him. Whether Chaplain Kapaun is worthy of beatification must be left to other judges, but he undoubtedly led an exemplary life.

Dozens of individuals and organizations have helped me in the preparation of this book, some without realizing the purpose of my research. Eugene and Helen Kapaun, the brother and sister-in-law of my subject, were always cooperative. Monsignor Arthur J. Tonne, the author of *The Story of Chaplain Kapaun: Patriot Priest of the Korean Conflict*, whose book was a valuable starting point, supported my efforts from the beginning.

Colonel Cletus J. Pottebaum, USAF (ret.) put extraordinary enthusiasm and energy into compiling facts from sources in Kansas. Two men who were prisoners of war with Chaplain Kapaun, Dr. Sidney Esensten and Walter L. Mayo, Jr., provided extensive accounts about living in a Communist prison camp.

Assistance and information came from various sources, including many of Chaplain Kapaun's friends from Kansas and his former comrades in arms, Reverend Quentin Kathol, O.S.B., archivist of Conception College in Missouri, Sister Jacinta of the Diocese of Wichita, Sister deMontfort of Kapaun-Mt. Carmel High School in

Wichita, Dr. William J. Hourihan of the Army Chaplain Center, Matt Newhouse of the Marion County (Kansas) *Record* and the staffs at the public libraries at Jericho, New York and Syosset, New York. Some of the pictures were made available through the courtesy of photographer Leslie Broadstreet of Wichita.

The staff at the White Mane Publishing Company, especially Dr. Martin Gordon, Dr. Diane Gordon, and Harold Collier, assisted significantly in bringing this project to successful conclusion. My agent, Bruce E. Matter, Esq. deserves mention for his continuous support. Antoinette Bosco provided a helpful hand in reviewing the manuscript and Bishop Francis X. Roque of the Archdiocese of the Military Services, USA always encouraged me to move forward with the book.

To the other helpful men and women who pitched in to help, and there are many, I am sorry if I overlooked naming you. To everyone who contacted me during the last six years in regard to Chaplain Emil Kapaun, the story of his life could not have been accomplished without your participation.

Many thanks to all of you.

William L. Maher

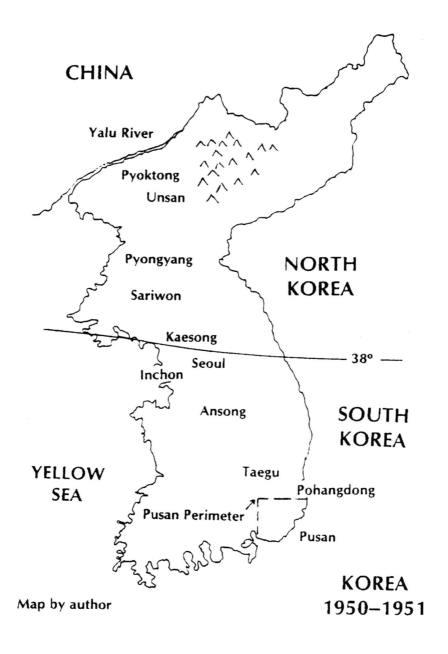

CHINA

Yalu River

Pyoktong

Unsan

Pyongyang

Sariwon

NORTH KOREA

Kaesong

Seoul

38°

Inchon

Ansong

SOUTH KOREA

YELLOW SEA

Taegu

Pohangdong

Pusan Perimeter

Pusan

Map by author

KOREA
1950–1951

ONE

Captured by the Communists

Chaplain (Captain) Emil Kapaun never knew about the midnight meeting in Beijing, China, yet it became a milepost on his journey into a Communist prison camp.

In that darkened capital, at the beginning of October 1950, Chou En-lai, the premier of the People's Republic of China, summoned Kavalam Panikhar, the Ambassador from India, to the Ministry of Foreign Affairs.[1] Chou intended no dialogue with Panikhar. Instead, the Chinese leader had decided to dispatch a warning to the Western world and had chosen the Indian Ambassador as the courier of the message.

Communist China had expressed its views frequently on the subject of the Korean War. But now, as the slender 34-year-old Kapaun and other American soldiers advanced against the forces of Communist North Korea, Chou had reached the conclusion that a more precise warning was necessary.

If any U.S. troops crossed the border into North Korea, Chou bluntly informed Panikhar, Chinese troops would intervene in the fighting on the side of their Communist allies.

That same day, October 3, Panikhar flashed the ultimatum from Beijing (then called Peiping) to Delhi, India. The Indian government forwarded the message westward to London, and British officials notified Washington. Until then it had seemed that American and other United Nations (U.N.) forces soon would bring the hostilities to a quick and successful conclusion. Now, a new fear of global warfare, perhaps even the dreaded atomic confrontation with the Soviet Union, suddenly overshadowed all expectations of peace.

The very act that Chou had warned against, however, was about to happen. Troopers of Kapaun's unit, the 1st Cavalry Division, an historic U.S. Army unit which in the 20th century had been transformed into a motorized infantry force, were moving northward. The 38th parallel, the official boundary between Communist-ruled North Korea and the U.N.-supported Republic of South Korea, was almost in sight of American forces.

Barely two weeks earlier, the North Korean armies had severely battered all of the American and U.N. units and cornered them above the port city of Pusan in South Korea. But then a daring landing of American troops behind enemy lines at Inchon surprised the Communist forces. Within a few days the 1st Cavalry forged ahead toward Seoul, the South Korean capital which had been occupied by the North Koreans immediately after the war began.

That was a welcome change for Kapaun, an energetic, almost six-foot-tall Catholic priest from the farmlands of eastern Kansas. Together with the youthful American soldiers, he had suffered through the frenzied retreats and steaming summer days since the 1st Cavalry landed in Korea a few months earlier.

"We had a tough time lately and were trapped. I still wonder how we got out alive," he wrote to his brother Eugene and his sister-in-law Helen at the beginning of October. "No food for two days, no water supply for one day. Luckily it rained at night and I caught a drink in my slicker. Now we are running fast ahead."[2] What Kapaun left unsaid was that he had been trapped four times, once in the open during an enemy artillery barrage.

"The Reds are on the run and we are hot after them. By the time you get this letter the war may be over," Kapaun predicted in a hopeful note to his Aunt Tena. As the rapidly moving U.N. forces rumbled through the valleys and low hills in pursuit of the retreating North Koreans, the 8th Cavalry, one of the regiments in the 1st Cavalry Division, paused on October 2 to bivouac for a short time at Ansong in South Korea.

The exhilarating advance had carried the American troops, commonly called GIs, more than 100 miles. It was still a savage conflict, even though the U.S. Congress had never declared war, and the memories of bloodshed and breathtaking escapes were fresh in the soldiers' minds. "Something saved us besides our efforts," Kapaun remarked in a letter to his bishop, Mark Carroll of Wichita, Kansas, "for many of us are convinced that we are living only on borrowed time."[3]

Foot soldier and priest; he excelled in both capacities. But for a few days in the battered village of Ansong, about 40 miles south of Seoul, his role as a chaplain clearly took precedence.

The vanguard of the 1st Cavalry suddenly rolled into that small South Korean community in the afternoon of October 1. The North Koreans had seized the village earlier in the war, and signs of their Communist ideology were everywhere—pictures of Soviet leader Joseph Stalin and posters depicting supposed atrocities by U.S. troops.

The American GIs surprised the North Koreans just as they were about to sit down to their mid-day meal. As the U.S. vehicles screeched to a halt in front of the city hall and the police station, the startled enemy soldiers leaped out of the windows and raced away, leaving their afternoon servings of rice still warm on their platters.

Several Christian churches had served the residents of Ansong before the war. As soon as the shooting stopped, Kapaun left the other Americans and hurried off to find the Catholic parish. A red cross identified the local hospital and he inquired there: Where is your church? However, the now-liberated South Korean nurses did not understand English, and he could not speak their language.

However, individuals who grow up on farms learn resourcefulness, and Kapaun found a way to communicate. He showed the Koreans his rosary beads and his stole, the long narrow cloth that priests wear around their necks when they perform religious functions. Just to make sure, he pointed to the white cross on the front of his helmet and then blessed himself. The women knew instantly that Kapaun was a Christian clergyman.

The overjoyed Koreans led their American visitor through narrow dirt lanes between mud houses until they reached the Catholic compound. A wrenching sight awaited Kapaun. The enemy had ransacked the building. The statues and crosses were shattered and in disarray; paper, wood, and debris of all kinds were scattered around. Surprisingly, however, the altar was intact.

The Catholic residents of Ansong had not heard Mass since the Communists captured their community several months earlier and scattered their priests. Kapaun decided that he should conduct religious services to celebrate the liberation of the town. He instructed his interpreter to tell everyone. Word quickly circulated among the residents that a U.S. Army priest planned to say Mass at 9 A.M. the following day.

At last free to worship publicly again, the citizens of Ansong hurriedly tidied up their disheveled church and joined some of the American soldiers at Mass. To Kapaun's profound joy two Korean youths served as altar boys and recited the traditional prayers in Latin in front of the altar.

Saying Mass before those devout Koreans stirred the young chaplain. "As I said the prayers at the foot of the altar I could not help but think I could not speak the language of these people nor could they speak mine, but at the altar we had a common language. I imagine the people felt the same way," he wrote to Bishop Carroll.[4]

The Koreans who came to the church were overwhelmed by gratitude. When the Mass ended they surrounded Kapaun, tugging at his garments, crying, kissing his feet. Embarrassed, his eyes filling with tears, he blessed the joyful congregation.[5] Later, his experiences at Ansong led Kapaun to summarize the life of a military chaplain: "It has its rough days when a person is face to face with death, and it has its days of tenderness and love as we found out in Ansung [sic] City, Korea."[6]

Ironically, immediately next to the church the American military police had established a prison compound which held some 300 Communist prisoners. The Catholic choir in Ansong reorganized quickly and its joyful hymns carried into the jail. When Kapaun returned from conducting religious services for other units he heard about the North Korean prisoners and reported to Bishop Carroll, "They were the ones who said they would not let anyone believe in God, yet now, right in the building next to them a free people was worshiping God in a free way, and the Reds were in prison."[7]

The re-emergence of the Catholic faith in Ansong after the Communists had suppressed religion there profoundly affected Kapaun. Captain Joseph O'Connor, who later became a POW with the chaplain, recalled that "[h]e told us to let that be an example to us that we should never lose our faith. Little did I realize that later I would be put in a position where, had it not been for his example and teachings, I could easily have lost faith in God and mankind."[8]

Many of the American soldiers knew little about the background of this clerical warrior who was about to accompany them into North Korea. Kapaun's ancestry was German and Czech. When anyone asked how to pronounce Kapaun, he compared the sound of his family name to a capon and replied "Remember a chicken."

Born in 1916 as the first child of a poor farming family in Pilsen, Kansas, Kapaun occasionally was as mischievous as most youngsters, but more often he was serious-minded. Caring for his chickens and tending his garden were a normal part of growing up on a farm in the 1920s. However, not long after Kapaun entered the local public school his teachers recognized that this quiet lad was a superior student.

Kapaun took his first steps in the direction of the priesthood when his parents sent him to Conception, Missouri to complete high school and attend a Catholic college. Then he enrolled at a seminary in St. Louis, Missouri for further training. During his college and seminary years Kapaun spent several steamy summers with the grain harvesting crews on the farms near Pilsen. Hard work never bothered him after that experience.

Ordained a Catholic priest in 1940, Kapaun returned to his home parish of St. John Nepomucene where he assisted the pastor, Father John Sklenar, who had helped to finance his education. The newly titled Father Kapaun discovered that living again among his family and friends was a satisfying experience, but ministering to many single-minded Bohemian neighbors in Pilsen was an unexpected challenge.

The United States entered World War II late in 1941, and suddenly the lives of all Americans were changed. Kapaun was no exception. He volunteered to become an Army chaplain, but his bishop at that time, Christian Winkelmann, refused permission. Persistent by nature, Kapaun kept asking. At first he became a part-time civilian chaplain at a nearby army base in Kansas. Finally, Bishop Winkelmann relented and in 1944 he allowed Kapaun to enter military service, where he served as a chaplain in Burma and India for two years.

Although Kapaun became a parish priest again in 1946, he never lost his taste for the rigors of military life. He earned a master's degree in education, but that did not change his mind. Bishop Carroll, who had succeeded Bishop Winkelmann, eventually allowed Kapaun to leave his parish and he returned to uniform in 1948. "It is a rough life—but I like it rough," he admitted to a friend, Fred Tuzicka. "That makes the priesthood more interesting."[9]

Throughout his short military career Kapaun's courage, humanity, and religious fervor endeared him to the troops whom he served in peacetime, on the battlefield, and as a prisoner of war. The prevailing attitude of many veterans of the Korean War was summed up in these words: "Father Kapaun, in my opinion, is one of the finest men who ever lived. If he had fear of anything in combat it was only fear for the lives and well-being of our soldiers and none for himself."

And so in October 1950 the young chaplain, who had once told his brother that Communism was the United States' most dangerous enemy, was on the verge of crossing the border into a Communist country. After joining in the recapture of the battered South Korean capital, the rejuvenated 1st Cavalry moved across the Imjin River and approached the 38th parallel. All along the route Kapaun conducted religious services for his soldiers, not only Catholics, but GIs of all beliefs. He devoted particular attention to the officers, stressing that their leadership would be tested in the uncertain days that lay ahead.

Premier Chou's forces had not yet passed across the border from China into North Korea when General Douglas MacArthur, the leader of the American and U.N. armies, broadcast a message early in October 1950. He demanded that the enemy commanders lay down their weapons and surrender. But the North Korean government said nothing, simply ignoring MacArthur's ultimatum.

At the same time many miles away, and unknown to the advancing American soldiers, elements of Communist China's armed forces, which numbered an estimated 5,000,000 men, were massing in Manchuria on the opposite side of the Yalu River from North Korea. Chou intended to fulfill his threat. His troops would enter North Korea by mid-October.

Late in the afternoon of October 7, the lead vehicles and troopers of the 8th Cavalry Regiment and other units of the 1st Cavalry Division started moving across the invisible line of the 38th parallel. Their target was the North Korean capital of Pyongyang. As he had done many times before, Kapaun celebrated Mass out in the open that day. His church was a grain field south of Munsan, his altar the hood of a jeep. Mass often ended with his fatherly words of caution to the congregation of grimy GIs: "Take good care of yourselves."

Kapaun shared the wishful thinking of many Americans when he wrote from Kaesong, near the border with North Korea, that the killing probably would end soon. However, the bloodshed was far from finished. That was evident when the chaplain witnessed the death of an ambulance driver who was transporting wounded off the battlefield. Kapaun immediately grabbed the wheel and drove the vehicle through mortar and machine gun fire to safety. "That was just another day's job for him and he became a legend to the men of the Eighth Cavalry Regiment," reported Frank Noel, an American newspaper correspondent who later became a prisoner of war with Kapaun.[10]

By early October the mosquitos and stifling summer heat which had characterized combat conditions in Korea several weeks earlier had given way to the first frosts of autumn. Many soldiers still wore their lightweight summer uniforms because shipments of heavier clothing had not caught up with them. Huddling in their foxholes under two or more blankets at night, they grumbled about shortages of food and cigarettes.

A different pattern of battle was emerging. No longer conquerors but now defending their homeland, the North Korean forces had heavily mined the dirt roads over which the American troops were moving northward.[11] As narrow and muddy as they were the roads nevertheless had to be shared with thousands of beleaguered North Korean refugees who were streaming south away from the combat areas. Even the countryside had changed. The hills were higher in North Korea, the valleys more confining.

The North Koreans retreated grudgingly and fiercely resisted the invading U.S. troops along the road to Sariwon. Even clearly marked American ambulances attracted enemy gunfire. Captain John P. Gannon remembered one incident:

> The Koreans fired on anything that moved. A cloud of dust coming from our rear revealed a jeep coming fast. It stopped and out jumped Father Kapaun and his friend, a Protestant chaplain. I said, "Hello Father. It's pretty hot here, so take to the ditch and keep low." He smiled and thanked me, but said: "I'll be all right." He was smoking a pipe. We left and I moved to the road as a hill gave us cover at this point.

> For some reason I turned and looked back to see how Father was doing. It was funny afterwards but a mortar shell seemed to land exactly on the spot where he and the other chaplain were walking. The blast was terrific and I started back toward them but didn't have far to go. Out of the cloud of dust, gravel and other debris, I saw legs and arms really moving as the two of them, apparently unhurt, high-tailed it for the ditch.[12]

At about the same time Bishop Carroll learned that the army had awarded Kapaun the Bronze Star. The medal resulted from his heroism in rescuing a wounded soldier early in August. The bishop mailed a congratulatory note which said "...that the Recording Angel has written down in the book of life your courage and your sacrifice for your men."

The sometimes impassive Kapaun was chagrined when he found out that Bishop Carroll had published one of his letters in a Wichita newspaper. He remarked about his newfound status as a celebrity: "I better be careful or the sheriff will be looking for me."[13] Kapaun nevertheless decided to risk further publicity. He sent the bishop some Communist posters, arm bands, and other war souvenirs, together with his final letter to his religious superior. "God has been very good to us," Kapaun summarized his experiences.

Maintaining a regular correspondence with Bishop Carroll was typical of Kapaun. Whenever there was a lull on the battlefield he found some paper and wrote to his friends and family. He addressed one of his last letters before being captured to Fred Tuzicka, a young Kansan who was soon to be ordained a priest. His words revealed Kapaun's concern for the young soldiers under his wing.

"I have no difficult dogma to study or any classwork to do. Nothing to do but take care of my boys," Kapaun quipped to Tuzicka. Then reflecting more seriously, and repeating the observation that he made to Bishop Carroll, he added, "God has been very good to me. He chose me for some reason or another to be with the soldiers in this war. The work is always gratifying, but to see so much destruction of lives and property is heartbreaking."[14]

Strong memories about this priest-turned-infantryman lingered for years after he died. Kapaun was self-confident, but also humble. Many men remembered his down-to-earth holiness. Even though as a chaplain he wore a captain's bars on his shoulders he felt as much at home with the enlisted men as with other officers. Kapaun knew how badly those young soldiers needed his help. Equally important, they also felt at ease with him. His uniform usually was rumpled and muddy; no one ever accused Kapaun of being a spit-and-polish parade ground officer.[15]

Of all of his enduring characteristics Kapaun's love of his pipe was among the best remembered. He mentioned it prominently in his last letter to his brother and sister-in-law. Using an old map as his stationery, Kapaun wrote from Kaesong in the middle of October:

> On Monday and Tuesday this week we had another slaughter. Several of our soldiers got killed and many wounded. My pipe got wrecked as a Red machine gunner sprayed us with lead and we had to hit the ditch. It is funny how a fellow can jump so fast into a ditch. This time it did not have water in it. The last couple of times the ditch had water in it and you can imagine how we looked. We do have a few laughs in spite of the evils of war.[16]

What Kapaun had failed to disclose was the heroic part of his story. He was crawling to reach a wounded soldier when North Korean gunners spotted him. Their bullets missed him, but whizzed past near enough to shatter his pipe as he scrambled for shelter. The close call apparently did not deter Kapaun. He remained on the battlefield; later his jeep driver found him alone and reported, "There he was, quite calm, under machine gun fire."[17]

The resourceful chaplain went to the medics at that point. He was not hurt, but he needed some adhesive tape (in his words "mighty handy stuff") to repair his beloved briarwood pipe. Indeed, Kapaun's pipe was so important that on another occasion he puffed on the broken stub until he had a chance to whittle a new bamboo stem.[18]

In mid-October, as the U.N. forces closed in on Pyongyang, American military and political leaders continued to worry about Communist China. Intelligence reports during September had predicted that the Chou's ground forces might enter the conflict. However, MacArthur disregarded them, certain that the opportune time for Chinese intervention had passed. When he met with President Harry Truman at Wake Island on October 15, MacArthur assured the President that there was little chance that the Chinese Army would attack.

On that same day, however, officials in Beijing ordered units of the Chinese 4th Field Army, reputed to be the largest and most battle-tested in Asia, to cross the Yalu River. Chou had told Soviet dictator Stalin that his armies would be four times larger than the forces opposing them.[19] Their orders were to hide until they received instructions to engage American and South Korean forces which were moving northward. During the next two weeks, some 180,000 Chinese troops entered North Korea. That massive array of military strength moved into the chilly hills well above the 38th parallel, where they lay in wait for Kapaun and the other American soldiers.

Meanwhile, the troopers of the 1st Cavalry were still battling North Korean units. The Americans won a fierce fight at Kumchon and then captured Sariwon. Those achievements earned for the 1st Cavalry the right to lead the U.S. forces which were attacking Pyongyang.

South Korean soldiers, however, sought the honor of being the first U.N. unit to enter the city, which previously had been the capital of all Korea. South Korean General Paik Sun Yup wanted that distinction badly. The commanding officer of the 1st Republic of Korea (ROK) Division, he had grown up in poverty in Pyongyang and had fled his homeland a few years earlier.[20] The race was on, with the 1st Cavalry hurrying northward and the South Koreans advancing from the east.

From MacArthur on down to the youngest GI, the Americans were unaware that overwhelming Chinese Communist forces secretly had marched into North Korea. The U.S. soldiers' spirits soared as the 1st Cavalry reached the outskirts of Pyongyang on October 19. Clanging bells from Christian churches greeted the liberators.[21] They expected to be back in Tokyo by Thanksgiving, resplendent in their bright yellow scarves as they paraded in triumph along the Plaza. Victory, then returning home, seemed so near.

The first question, however, was who would win the race into the North Korean capital. With their national pride at stake, the South Korean units promptly claimed that honor. They even erected a wooden sign at the outskirts to Pyongyang to welcome the U.S. forces.[22] The 1st Cavalry, however, had built a pontoon bridge over the Taedong River and argued that its troopers entered the city hours ahead of the South Koreans.

The Americans found that rubble-strewn Pyongyang was a city almost smothered by Communist ideology. What Kapaun saw was disturbing. Almost every street corner displayed pictures of Stalin and his North Korean counterpart, Kim Il Sung. Copies of a Communist magazine called *Crocodile* filled a new college building which the Russians had constructed.

Although political posters were everywhere, the some 500,000 occupants of Pyongyang were not. Thousands had escaped into the fields beyond the city, abandoning the quiet Communist capital to the invading American and South Korean troops.

As soon as it established control of Pyongyang, the 1st Cavalry moved into bivouac in the outlying areas. The 8th Cavalry Regiment, the unit to which Kapaun was attached, relocated to the northern outskirts and began carrying out its task of rounding up hundreds of North Korean prisoners.

The military situation had settled down, at least temporarily. American supply units even started issuing the yellow scarves which traditionally identified cavalrymen.[23] Shining combat boots became important again. Kapaun had more opportunities to say Mass. Then a familiar face from home appeared in Pyongyang. Comedian Bob Hope and a troupe of USO entertainers staged a show for the 1st Cavalry.[24]

At about that time Captain Joseph O'Connor noticed that frequently no one could locate Kapaun. He even failed to show up for his meals. The chaplain was doing something important. That was his only explanation, but he refused to disclose any details. O'Connor wrote:

> Shortly after, I found him in a dilapidated and abandoned Korean hut adjacent to the large building the Battalion occupied. He had an old ammo crate for a desk and an ammunition box for a seat.
>
> He had approximately five to six hundred cards of men who were killed or who had died while in combat. Also, on each card he had the address of the next of kin and a notation as to whether or not he had administered the last rites to the individuals. He was writing a personal letter to each of the next of kin.
>
> This, to the best of my knowledge, is definitely not required of an army chaplain. Father Kapaun and the Protestant Chaplain, Captain Carter, were taking it upon themselves to do this so as to better ease the minds of friends and relatives of the deceased. The building Father used had holes in it and was extremely cold.[25]

The weather notwithstanding, MacArthur was determined to chase the disorganized North Korean armies northward all the way to the Yalu River. But during the last week in October, unexpected resistance developed when U.N. forces, including the ROK 1st Division, encountered Chinese Communist soldiers for the first time.

The prospect of battling their historic foe frightened the South Koreans, especially after the first Chinese prisoners informed them that tens of thousands of their countrymen were hiding in the countryside ahead of the U.N. forces.[26] When the South Korean units showed signs of becoming demoralized, the 1st Cavalry's relatively easy life at Pyongyang ended abruptly. On October 28 the division was ordered northward to bolster the South Korean regiments. Progress was slow because heavy rains had turned the roads leading out of Pyongyang into stretches of mud.

Although the first snowflakes of the season already had fallen, many American infantrymen still were not equipped with sleeping bags, overcoats, and heavy boots. The army's supply system was stretched to the limit and food and ammunition took priority. As the nights grew colder, Kapaun remembered that he had told Tuzicka that he liked the rough army life. Now he changed his mind. Living outdoors was great, but only for those who liked it. Nevertheless, Kapaun and other American soldiers started moving toward the rugged rises of the Taeback range in North Korea.

The slopes concealed not only the Chinese, but also movements of U.N. units. While South Korean forces retreated southward along a mountainside road, on the other side of the same mountain the 1st Cavalry traveled in the opposite direction toward the massing Chinese Communist armies.

The enemy troops differed from their American foes in many important ways. Political commissars instead of chaplains provided guidance for the Communist soldiers. While the Chinese government punished anyone who deviated from Godless Communism, Kapaun and most of the men to whom he ministered believed not only in God, but also in the democratic principles of the United States.

Even though those Chinese soldiers were peasants, many had been hardened by years of fighting their own former Nationalist government. They wore quilted cotton uniforms and canvas shoes and marched almost endlessly.[27] In contrast, too many of the Americans had become accustomed to traveling in trucks which transported their supplies. Each Chinese soldier carried his own food, a four- or five-day supply of rice, corn or bread.[28] Some had World War II American rifles, yet many entered battle without any weapons.

As the U.S. soldiers would soon learn, stealth, surprise, and nighttime troop movements were hallmarks of Chinese military tactics and compensated for some of their deficiencies in equipment.

When they crossed the Yalu and headed south toward the 38th parallel, the Chinese marched in darkness through the valleys and over the hills until just before dawn. During daylight hours they hid in the villages and wooded regions. Cooking meals was restricted in order to conceal the fires from searching reconnaissance planes. In this manner thousands of Chinese soldiers positioned themselves ahead of the 1st Cavalry without being detected.

Major General Wu Xinzhan, the commander of the Chinese forces, described his plans in an ominous tone: "As a warning to the imperialists we shall destroy the most vulnerable advance units."[29] Although Wu may not have realized it, he was talking about the fast-moving 8th Cavalry.

The regiment had penetrated 19 miles ahead of other units of the 1st Cavalry. It crossed the Chungchon River and led the American forces toward Unsan, a small crossroads town which was within 50 miles of the North Korean-Chinese border.

A mining area, Unsan was located in a broad valley, but it also was ringed by hills which offered maximum concealment. Near the freezing Nammyon River were a few mud houses, but not much else.[30] When the 8th Cavalry arrived at Unsan, "It was just dead," recalled an American officer. "Anytime you encounter that kind of atmosphere it arouses a feeling of apprehension."[31]

By October 31 elements of the 8th Cavalry, relieving the 12th ROK Regiment, had dug in near the town. A full moon illuminated the landscape that Halloween night. The nearby South Korean units continued to fall back[32] and a feeling of isolation hung over the Americans.

It was cold and quiet near Unsan; a sentry strained to hear the unexpected notes of a bugle call in the distance.[33] Although North Korean refugees had warned that thousands of enemy soldiers were approaching through the surrounding hills, the 8th Cavalry officers shrugged off intelligence reports that they should be prepared to fight a new foe.[34]

When the 8th Cavalry reached Unsan, Kapaun and another chaplain, Donald Carter, a Progressive Brethren minister, decided to exchange assignments. The 3rd Battalion of the 8th Cavalry had been placed in a reserve position. Kapaun transferred to that unit while Carter moved to the forward positions with the regiment's two other battalions. The idea, according to Chaplain Carter, was that his friend could "...enjoy a day or so away from the tension where the heaviest attack was expected."[35]

Kapaun was no stranger to combat. He had participated in several battles in Korea even before the 3rd Battalion arrived there.

With its officers and noncommissioned ranks drawn from other units, the battalion had been organized hastily soon after the fighting started. The army rushed it to Korea from Fort Devens, Massachusetts, where Kapaun had first entered military service in 1944.

Even though the 3rd Battalion had entered the war zone more than a month after other elements of the 8th Cavalry, it went into battle quickly. By mid-September the soldiers had suffered a devastating toll. There were 400 casualties from wounds and sickness among its roster of 703 men.

The battalion took positions in a cornfield south of Unsan. The temperature was falling toward 20 degrees and wind-driven snow flurries settled into the shallow foxholes. During the period since they had broken out of the Pusan perimeter the now-confident GIs had become unaccustomed to digging more deeply.[36] Their mission was to protect a bridge at Camel's Head Bend on the Nammyon River,[37] the escape route for the entire regiment if one were needed. However, the location offered scant protection from a nighttime assault. The battalion commander received a warning to relocate to higher ground, but he ignored the advice.

The next day, November 1, was All Saints Day. Kapaun was extraordinarily busy, offering four Masses for his soldiers. But something else unusual happened that day. The cavalrymen counted ten forest fires in the hills immediately north and west of their position.[38]

The Americans were puzzled over what had caused the fires. No one thought to blame a hidden enemy. Layers of smoke and cinders drifted between the snow-capped hilltops and over the entrenched U.S. infantrymen. Visibility was reduced to hundreds of yards. Even more worrisome was the fact that the smoke prevented U.S. reconnaissance planes from detecting troop movements on the ground.

For the widely dispersed and understrength 8th Cavalry the situation was rife with the potential for disaster. And disaster arrived in a hurry. Chinese troops, principally the 116th Division and the 347th Regiment, pushed into positions on three sides of Unsan. By midnight the South Korean units on the fourth quadrant caved in to a heavy attack and became totally disorganized.[39] Suddenly, Kapaun and everyone else in the 8th Cavalry were in danger of being surrounded.

A frightening cacophony late in the moonlit evening of November 1 heralded the Communist attack, the first battle between U.S. and Chinese forces.[40] The blare of bugles, the shrill chirps of whistles, English language curses shouted in Chinese accents, bells and horns all sounded out of the surrounding darkness. "My God! A Chinese funeral," someone described the scene.[41]

Down from their hiding places in the shadowy hills charged hundreds of Chinese soldiers, looking much like mechanized stuffed dolls in their padded uniforms.[42] Enemy horsemen riding Mongolian ponies joined the assault.[43] To one American combatant the Communists moved ahead like a swarm of locusts.

Wreaking havoc with grenades, bayonets, and rifle fire, the Chinese began to infiltrate among the startled GIs. The Americans heard a distant yell, "Hey, stop shooting, we're Charlie Company."[44] The voice, however, belonged to an oncoming Communist soldier who probably had learned his English in a Christian school.

Facing overwhelming odds, it became apparent quickly that the outnumbered 8th Cavalry had to pull back from Unsan. At first, Major General Hobart R. Gay, the commanding officer of the division, refused permission for the regiment to withdraw. Finally, a message came through at 11 o'clock that night. The orders read: Pull back and take the ford which led to the Kuryong River. From there the road to safety headed toward the walled city of Yongbyon.[45]

As the 1st and 2nd Battalions of the 8th Cavalry began their withdrawal, the 3rd Battalion assumed the role of rear guard. Up to that point it had not been involved in any fighting near Unsan. In fact, Kapaun had set up his pup tent in a corn field and had gone to sleep early in the evening of November 1. However, his rest was interrupted before midnight. The suddenly enveloping battle forced the chaplain and his assistant, Private First Class Patrick J. Schuler, to load their jeep hastily in anticipation of joining the withdrawal.

"But we ran into a Communist roadblock up ahead and had to turn the vehicles around," reported Schuler. "Father and I picked up a lot of wounded, put them on the jeep and trailer and came back to the Third Battalion C.P. 'Stay with the jeep and say your prayers' Father Kapaun told me." Then Kapaun went off into the darkness to find more of his "boys." Schuler later burned the jeep so that the enemy would not capture it.[46]

Chinese infantrymen, however, already had sneaked in behind the 3rd Battalion and blocked the escape route. To make matters worse, an American two and a half ton truck which was hauling a howitzer had overturned on the only road leading south out of the town, preventing other vehicles from getting around it.[47] At 2:30 A.M., finding themselves encircled in the darkness, the survivors of the 3rd Battalion began to pull together into a small defensive perimeter in the flat farmland between the Nammyon and Samtan Rivers.

"We were completely surrounded and everyone knew it," said Sergeant Ernest J. Ritter of the 3rd Battalion. "Thinking of our loved ones back home, of ourselves. Would we live to see daylight again?

No one knew, but everyone prayed, and prayed hard, hoping that God would help us out. Little by little the enemy was closing in on us. We had to do something, but what?"[48]

Throughout that hectic night the 8th Cavalry's determined chaplain hurried from one foxhole to another, sharing a brief prayer with one frightened GI, whispering an encouraging word to the next grim-faced trooper. One worried GI promised Kapaun that he would attend church every Sunday if he survived. Unsan was fast becoming another testing ground for Kapaun's courage and leadership skills.

There was an elevated dirt road leading through the valley floor where the American were feverishly reorganizing themselves. Late that night a column of about 200 Asians appeared out of the blackness, moving briskly in the direction of an American road block and on toward the center of the 3rd Battalion's defensive area. The leader of the oncoming group announced, "Sixth ROKs" and kept marching ahead.[49] The freezing 3rd Battalion sentries assumed that these soldiers were South Korean and allowed them to pass.

The column continued quickly along the road toward the battalion command post. Some of the American wounded were there and Kapaun was helping to provide medical treatment in the comparative protection of the dimly lighted shelter. Suddenly the crisp notes of a bugle sounded in the darkness. It was a signal to "The Sharp Swords," the group of Chinese commandos who had deceived the U.S. soldiers and penetrated their defenses.[50] The infiltrators immediately started firing in all directions. The attack caught some of the startled GIs asleep in their foxholes. The battle of "Bugle Valley," as the survivors called it, was under way.

"I was at a Battalion command post," Lieutenant W. C. Hill told a war correspondent. "I thought I was dreaming when I heard a bugler sounding 'taps' and the beat of horses' hoofs in the distance. Then, as though they came out of a burst of smoke, shadowy figures started shooting and bayoneting everybody they could find."[51]

Kapaun once again risked his life to help his comrades. "....suddenly everything opened up," recalled Sergeant Alfred J. Paternode, another member of the 3rd Battalion. "We went back about 500 yards and crossed the river. Father Kapaun and Dr. Anderson came across, too, but when somebody said that he'd seen one of his buddies getting hit, Father Kapaun said he was going back in. Dr. Anderson went with him. That was after 3 o'clock in the morning."[52]

Peter V. Busatti prepared an account of that fearful night and called it "My Chaplain Was A Saint." Busatti, who was trying to reach one of the 3rd Battalion positions, later wrote:

As I was lying in a large fox hole getting ready to go, someone came flying into my fox hole. This was my first meeting with Father Kapaun. He asked me my name and how I felt. I told him my leg was stiff and my back hurt; an old shrapnel wound in my back had reopened. He ripped open my shirt and put some liquid on it.

I asked him if he was a Catholic Chaplain, and he said 'Yes.' He said an Act of Contrition with me and blessed me. He told me I was about 50 yards from the G. I. perimeter and that I had better get out of there fast. A few minutes later I made a run for it and jumped over the sandbags which encircled the area.[53]

The Chinese attackers captured Kapaun for a few moments during the firefight. Fortunately, as they hustled him into the darkness, one of the cavalrymen looked up and yelled, "There goes the chaplain." The Americans quickly directed their gunfire at his captors. The shots distracted the Chinese and gave Kapaun a brief opportunity to escape, but only for a short time.

The hand-to-hand combat at Unsan was so close that the Americans worried that they would shoot each other. Kapaun was in the middle of the fracas. He had assembled about 30 of the wounded U.S. soldiers that night in a 20 foot square log and straw dugout which the North Koreans had constructed to hide their vehicles from U.S. planes.

One of the GIs was attacking a machine gun when, in his words, "...my mind sort of snapped." He awoke in the log dugout and learned later that Kapaun had arranged for him to be carried there. As the fighting swirled around them the chaplain and Dr. Clarence Anderson also brought another wounded soldier into the relative safety of the crude structure. Meanwhile, those troopers who were still unscathed clustered around three American tanks and after half an hour of intense fighting drove away the Chinese attackers.

The first glimmer of daybreak on November 2 revealed how badly the 3rd Battalion had suffered. Dead bodies were scattered around the floor of the valley. The chaplain and Bill Mayer stacked up more than 100 corpses and there were others that they could not reach.[54] Kapaun had not been hurt, but more than 170 wounded Americans lay among the wrecked vehicles and debris.[55] Many were in no-man's land between the opposing forces.

All day long, within easy range of Communist weapons, Kapaun crouched on a parapet and scanned the battlefield. A powdery snow covered dead bodies and damaged vehicles. Whenever he spotted someone who was wounded the chaplain crawled out and dragged him into the battalion's defensive positions.[56] For others he dug shallow trenches to keep them out of the line of fire.[57] By the end of the day Kapaun had saved 15 soldiers.

Anyone venturing out to help was likely to be shot, and some rescuers were. Lieutenant Willard Latham shouted in exasperation, "Stay down, Chappie, they'll shoot you, too." Kapaun was fearless. There was no other word for it.[58] Despite the danger he worked ceaselessly to help the stricken GIs. They had become, in the chaplain's words, "his wounded flock."

Some two hundred 8th Cavalry troopers who had not been wounded began to draw together into a defensive enclave barely a couple of hundred yards wide.[59] The setting was reminiscent of the fate many years earlier of Colonel George Custer and the 7th Cavalry Regiment who were surrounded and annihilated by the Sioux Indians in the battle of Little Big Horn. However, the shrunken perimeter which the 3rd Battalion still held at Unsan no longer included the wooden dugout. Dozens of wounded men there were outside the battalion's lines and unprotected.

Daylight brought vigorous efforts to help the beleaguered 3rd Battalion. Attacking aircraft kept hundreds of Chinese holed up in their bunkers and gave the remaining American soldiers an opportunity to dig new defensive positions. Other planes dropped medical supplies. A rescue helicopter even attempted to land and evacuate a few of the wounded, but Chinese gunfire drove it away.[60]

During the afternoon, a small liaison plane swooped in over the perimeter and the pilot threw down a message. The words were encouraging: A relief column, I and L Companies of the 5th Cavalry Regiment, was trying to break through the Chinese positions and reach the battalion.[61]

As the day waned, however, and darkness curtailed the supporting air strikes, the encircled men knew that the attacks were certain to resume that night. Then heartbreaking news reached them. Their rescuers were miles away and could not pierce the Communist lines.[62]

Frank Peljae, a radio operator who was ordered to evacuate, told how he was haunted for years by the forlorn and exhausted looks of the cavalrymen who stayed behind to defend the wounded.[63] Kapaun finally forced Schuler, his assistant, to take his last chance to escape.

The chances of leaving alive were decreasing rapidly. Survivors remembered that Kapaun had chances to flee.[64] One soldier screamed at him to get away, but he refused. The chaplain was well aware of how badly the North Koreans treated prisoners, yet he decided to allow himself to be captured so that he could remain with the wounded Americans.[65] "I can't imagine his leaving when there were wounded men there," Chaplain Carter commented later.[66]

Teen-aged Private Tibor Rubin phrased it differently, "Knowing Father Kapaun he wouldn't just take off and leave us young people holding the bag."[67] In fact, the chaplain had several opportunities to get away, according to Warrant Officer John Funston, but he declined to take advantage of them.[68]

Kapaun explained his actions to another GI. "He told me they needed his help and the only way to assist them was to stay and worry about the consequences later. He knew that he would either be killed or taken prisoner and at the same time he thought perhaps the enemy would not separate him from those soldiers who needed him." Kapaun confirmed his decision by confessing later to Joseph Ascue that he had volunteered to stay behind.[69]

The dugout which held the wounded at that point was about 150 yards outside the 3rd Battalion's positions. Still, as dusk came down over the valley, Kapaun left the main force, dashed across the battlefield and leaped into the shelter.[70]

The Chinese bombarded and then rushed the battalion's defensive perimeter again and again in the darkness, six times in all. When some of the soldiers ran out of ammunition William Bryant recalled that they threw rocks at the oncoming enemy.[71] Each time the outnumbered Americans repulsed the Chinese.[72]

The few defenders in the dugout were not as successful. The Chinese hurled grenades and killed some of the cavalrymen. Then the enemy infantrymen began an assault. By that time close to 50 freezing and wounded GIs huddled in the makeshift shelter.[73] No able-bodied soldiers remained there to protect them.

Finally, Kapaun was the only unharmed officer in the dugout. The men reluctantly requested that he arrange their surrender.[74] The chaplain asked a wounded Chinese officer in the shelter to persuade the Communists to stop shooting. As the Chinese soldiers warily entered the shelter, Kapaun stepped forward and somehow convinced them not to hurt the wounded who were under his care.

The Chinese decided to remove Kapaun and about 15 other American prisoners who were still able to walk. When the troopers emerged from the dugout their path was blocked by the bodies, in some places piled three high, of the Chinese soldiers who had attacked them only hours earlier. The GIs stepped over the corpses and were hustled out of the battle area.[75]

In a shallow ditch nearby lay Sergeant Herbert Miller, wounded in the ankle and leg. A enemy infantryman approached Miller, raised his rifle, and prepared to shoot him in the head. Kapaun saw what was about to happen. He rushed forward and pushed aside the startled Chinese soldier. Then the chaplain lifted Miller to his feet and carried him away. For several days thereafter, as they trudged almost 100 miles through snow-covered mountains, Kapaun continued to support his wounded comrade.[76]

The rescue effort, led by Colonel Harold Johnson, who later became Vice Chief of Staff of the U.S. Army, and who only a few weeks earlier had commanded the 3rd Battalion, was unable to dislodge the Chinese troops who had blocked the escape route. The division reluctantly terminated plans to relieve the stricken unit and urged any of the surrounded troopers who were still fit to evacuate in any way that they could. As a consequence, the 3rd Battalion became known in military history as "the Lost Battalion."

About 250 wounded Americans had to be left behind. "Not a man cried," the history of the 3rd Battalion reported. "Instead they told us to come back with reinforcements soon and get them out."[77]

For a short time the smoke from Chinese gunfire drifted back into their own lines. Some of the battalion's survivors seized the moment to organize an escape.[78] However, the Communists rounded up most of them in a matter of days.[79] Of the 800 men of the 3rd Battalion who marched into Unsan, approximately 600, including Kapaun, either had been killed or captured by the Chinese Communists.

Two

Growing Up on a Farm

Emil Kapaun was born in eastern Kansas on a chilly spring day in 1916. The hardships of growing up on a farm helped to prepare him for his ordeal in a North Korean prison.

At that time a few scattered families lived on the windy prairies surrounding Pilsen in Marion County. Among them was the recently married couple of Enos and Elizabeth ("Bessie") Kapaun. Life for the Kapauns and others on the mid-American farm required long, tough, often financially risky work. Men and their horses supplied the muscle-power to till the rich alluvial soil. Only when Emil was growing up did tractor-drawn combines become available to perform the heaviest tasks.[1] Even grade school children such as Emil learned to do their share.

Winters were bitter and confining, the drabness broken every day by the freezing chores of caring for the farm animals. Spring brought threats of tornadoes, or thunderstorms which could wipe out emerging crops. The summers were brutally hot and severe winds often swept in from the western prairies, accompanying the droughts that the farmers feared so much.

Although the bluestem grasses in the Flint Hills region near Pilsen provided some of the finest grazing lands in the country, the twin crops of corn and wheat actually gave the state its agricultural identity.[2] In the early years of the 20th century wheat became king in Kansas. Even when grain and livestock prices were beginning to decline, ambitious farmers across the state increased their crops by a million and a half acres within the two years after Emil was born.

If the Roaring Twenties were a prosperous period elsewhere in the United States, that was not true in many farming areas. The price of a bushel of wheat plummeted between 1919 and 1923. Later, during the national depression in the 1930s, corn became so cheap that sometimes it was burned in place of coal for household heating.[3] Defaults on mortgage loans increased sharply and caused more than 100 banks to fail throughout Kansas.

Providing the limited necessities of daily life was a struggle for many rural families and Emil's parents were no exception. They butchered their own hogs and fed their family with the meat. Enos and Bessie also brought the eggs and cream from their farm some eight miles to Marion, the seat of Marion County. They sold their products there, using the receipts to purchase food and clothing for themselves and their infant son.[4]

Farmers such as Enos Kapaun had to be jacks-of-all-trades, as varied as mechanics, bookkeepers, and carpenters, among others. Faced with cruel weather and inadequate capital to maintain their businesses, many were unable to save their crops and were wiped out. As a result of their struggles to earn a living, Kansas farmers usually were viewed as sober individuals. In fact, a female politician advised them to raise less corn and more hell.[5]

Enos Kapaun certainly was not a hell raiser. He, his wife and Emil never prospered, but they survived a rural existence which was difficult in many ways. The roads that linked households and communities were narrow and alternately covered with dust or mud. Farm parcels in the eastern part of the state were small by Kansas standards, usually 100 to 200 acres, barely enough to produce a living for the residents.

Many wood-framed houses near Pilsen lacked electricity well into the 1930s. Until that time kerosene lamps provided a minimum amount of lighting. Most often the only sources of heat in such houses were a pot-bellied stove and another cooking stove in the kitchen, which burned either firewood or coal.

The Kapaun home, which was built in 1913, was no fancier than the others. A two-story structure, it contained a couple of small unheated bedrooms upstairs and one on the ground level.[6] The farmstead, which also included a chicken coop, a barn, and an outhouse, was located in the flat countryside about two and a half miles from the small community of Pilsen.

The land where Enos, Bessie, and their son lived consisted of 160 acres, the average size farm for that part of Kansas. They farmed under a Scully lease,[7] which was named for an Englishman who owned large tracts in Kansas during the 19th century. The Scully arrangement allowed the Kapauns to own the buildings and use the land as long as they made payments to their landlord. Enos rented additional land, some from Jacob Klenda, who was Emil's sponsor at his confirmation,[8] and 80 acres from Joseph Meysing.

Situated north of Wichita, Pilsen was the center of a farming district which yielded at least two grain crops annually. The community had no railroad and was tiny in every sense. It was just a rural crossroad with a couple of general stores, two gas stations, a post office and about 20 weatherbeaten wooden houses. Except for Marion County's weekly newspaper, Pilsen at the beginning of the 20th century had little contact with the outside world.

In the middle of the small village stood the 120-foot high, silver-colored spire of a neo-Gothic structure which was the focal point of Emil's early life. The parish church of St. John Nepomucene had been named after the patron saint of Bohemia, a Christian martyr from the 14th century.

The building's European architecture featured stained glass windows which had been imported from Munich, Germany. The sounds of its bells carried across the countryside. The interior of the church was sizeable, described as large enough to seat 650 husky Bohemians. It was Bohemian not only in size, but also in its decor. One of the windows depicted King Wenceslas being taught by his grandmother.

Those Bohemian-Americans were hardy individuals, a strong, Catholic, family-minded element in a state where other influences predominated. Kansas in the early part of the 20th century included factions among the Republicans and party weaknesses among the Democrats, a noticeable presence of the Ku Klux Klan, and a fundamentalist-oriented Protestant ministry which opposed pleasures as diverse as playing cards and participating in a baseball game on Sunday afternoon.

The vigorous roots of the handful of Catholics in Pilsen drew them together and helped to fend off the problems that divided other residents of that region. In 1874 their forbearers had begun to travel from the Czech and Slovak regions of Europe to Chicago and later onward to the lonely plains of Kansas.

By the end of the 19th century, many Czechs and Germans, including seven-year-old Enos Kapaun, had crossed the Atlantic Ocean to seek new opportunities in the heartland of America. Within a generation after the first arrivals, 46 Bohemian families had decided to settle in and around Pilsen. As they purchased land from the Santa Fe Railroad their newly erected homes became numerous enough to assume the character of a community.

In the beginning there were too few Bohemians to support their own church. Determined to perpetuate their Catholic faith, they gathered regularly in the "Beauty of the West" school to read the Bible and to train their offspring in their religion. Once a year, at Easter, one of their number, Jacob Rudolph, drove his team of horses 60 miles to Emporia, Kansas and returned to Pilsen with a priest who conducted religious services.

Before many years passed those farm families had their own spiritual leader, Father John Sklenar. Conscientious, impatient, with the same Czech heritage as many of his congregation, Sklenar was a follow-the-book pastor.[9] He openly espoused the European tradition in which a social and educational barrier usually existed between the priest and his parishioners.

The culture of St. John Nepomucene was equally old-fashioned. Despite the objections of younger members who preferred sermons and readings at Mass in English, Sklenar ordered that they be recited in Bohemian. As much as anyone he mapped the path which eventually led Emil to the priesthood.

Sklenar laid the cornerstone of St. John Nepomucene church in 1914,[10] the year after Bessie Hajek moved into Marion to work as a housekeeper for a local family. Although Bessie's ancestry was Bohemian, she was the Kansas-born daughter of a railroad worker. Before long, the teen-age girl had met a local farmer named Enos Kapaun, whom she married on May 18, 1915.

While Enos was taciturn, Bessie, who was about 15 years younger than her husband, was short, plump and more animated. She became upset occasionally, but her anger quickly faded into laughter.[11] Those who knew the family reached the conclusion that while Emil looked more like his thin-faced, stoop-shouldered father, the boy more closely resembled his mother in personality and temperament. No doubt it was her quiet influence that ultimately convinced Emil to learn how to speak and write the Bohemian language.

On April 20, 1916, Enos moved his wife's bed close to the warmth of their wood-burning stove and she gave birth in her kitchen to their first child, Emil. The day was Holy Thursday, which commemorates the ordination of the first Catholic priests.[12] The following month, with Uncle John and Aunt Cecilia Melcher standing by as godparents, Father Sklenar baptized the first son of Enos and Bessie Kapaun.

From his earliest years Emil's Catholic faith strongly affected the course of his life. Sklenar kept his eye on Emil, hoping that this boy might be a local candidate for the priesthood. Everything about the Kapaun household encouraged that possibility. It was a loving home, the perfect place to nurture any inclination toward a religious vocation. Emil and his mother recited prayers in both

Bohemian and English. Holy pictures adorned the walls, and books with spiritual stories were always available.[13]

Emil was quiet, but nevertheless full of boyish enthusiasm. He spent much of his energy playing at the creek behind his parents' house. Winters were for ice skating, and summers were not only the time for fishing, but also swimming from a homemade diving board.

There were bullheads in the stream, but it was most thrilling for the six-year-old boy to catch a five-pound catfish. The excitement one day proved overwhelming. No sooner had Emil hauled his fish out of the water than he laid down his fishing pole and catch at the shoreline. Then he raced across the fields to summon his parents to admire his prize.

But the eager lad had forgotten something—he had not secured his pole. By the time the proud family returned, the catfish had freed itself and jumped back into the stream. Emil learned from his disappointment. In later years more seasoned fishermen, with better equipment, watched unhappily while he surpassed their best efforts.

In September 1922 Emil started the first grade in District School No. 15. By then he also was big enough to be given responsibility for handling some of the chores on the farm.[14] Chickens, including some of Emil's own birds, needed care, and cows had to be milked. Bessie usually attended to the animals, but one day she asked Emil to do the job.

A cow that Emil was trying to milk refused to stand still. The boy sensed that the animal missed Bessie's presence. The problem stymied him until he finally realized that he could solve it by wearing his mother's dress. The familiar sight quickly calmed the cow, and the earnest young farmer successfully completed the procedure.

While playing along the edge of the creek one day Emil saw a kingfisher, but he confused the bird with a stork. The boy thought that he already knew the truth about storks: They fly into the neighborhood and deliver babies. "I told the stork to bring me a little brother," he reportedly announced to his mother.[15] His wishes came true not many months later when the second Kapaun child, Eugene, was born in 1924.

Emil enjoyed grade school almost as much as fishing. His intelligence delighted his teachers, who were nuns from the Sister Adorers of the Precious Blood of Wichita, Kansas. The local school district had contracted for them to teach in the public school in Pilsen. Emil's aptitude impressed the sisters so much that they selected him to explain difficult subjects to other students. Indeed,

Eugene Kapaun, *left*, and Emil Kapaun

Photo property of Eugene Kapaun

one of his schoolmates recalled that Emil made perfect grades without any apparent effort.

His attendance records in the early grades were equally good. Despite the long daily walks over rutted roads, often muddied from rain and snow, he was almost never absent or late. Except for one period when he missed two weeks of classes, the teachers issued certificates for his attendance year after year. "If we had not kept sending him [to school], he would have been lost," Enos said about his young son.

The boy had not been in school very long before the influences which surrounded him—devout parents in a religiously oriented home, the nuns who taught him, and the attentive example of his pastor—produced their combined effect. Enos asked his son what he wanted to do when he became older. No one was surprised when Emil replied that he wanted to be just like Father Sklenar.

Accepting Sklenar's invitation to become an altar boy was one of Emil's first steps toward following his pastor's career. He took the assignment seriously, as he did most situations throughout his life. His mother noticed that after Emil returned from school every day he hurried out of the house into the backyard. Then he knelt down in the dirt and practiced again and again the Latin prayers that were expected of an altar server.

Notwithstanding all of his commendable attributes Emil nonetheless sometimes got into trouble. He demonstrated that side of his personality one summer when he was too young to help the men who were harvesting wheat on the Kapaun farm. As was the custom, Emil's mother and the families of the other workmen were expected to prepare and bring a hot meal to his father and his helpers. At noontime Bessie and her friends began to carry the food across the fields to the workers.

Emil remained in the house with the children of the other workers, or so his mother thought. However, there was a new car in the Kapaun garage and the boy's imagination took a leap. Why not take the other kids for a ride? So Emil and his friends jumped into the car. They started the engine and managed to back the vehicle out of the garage—where it promptly stalled.

The conspirators tried frantically to return the car to its starting point. Alarm turned into panic when the youngsters learned that Bessie and the other women were crossing the fields again and returning to Kapaun's house.

No matter how hard the children tried, the car would not start. The knowledge that certain punishment awaited everyone, especially Emil, finally lifted their desperation to a new level, so strong that they succeeded in pushing the vehicle back into the garage, only moments before Emil's mother arrived on the scene.[16]

Emil even occasionally behaved mischievously toward his parents. His father was husking corn one day and had taken his lunch out into the fields. Emil and a friend went looking for Emil's dad. They did not see Enos, but instead found his lunch. Being young, devilish and most of all hungry, the boys succumbed to temptation. Enos arrived shortly for what he expected would be his mid-day meal, only to discover that the youngsters were finishing the last few mouthfuls of food.[17]

The school year in farming communities such as Pilsen was determined by more than strictly educational requirements. Practical considerations were foremost. The families needed their children during the warm-weather months to help attend to the crops. "He would come home from school and change his clothes and take the hoe and go out and chop weeds," said Emil's mother. "He wasn't always begging to go here and there." Only in late September could the farmers release the youngsters to begin their classes. Schooling continued until early in the spring when once again chores at home took precedence over textbooks.

The classes were small. In fact, in some rural schools in Kansas there was one teacher and only one pupil. In Emil's case, he and another child constituted the entire class in Pilsen from the sixth through the eighth grades.[18] In those circumstances the students and teachers got to know each other very well.

Years later, when his former schoolmates heard that Emil had died a hero in a cruel prisoner of war camp in North Korea, many recalled his character and achievements in school. He learned so easily that he finished grade school in six years. "If you were lucky enough to be on his debating team, you were sure to win," recalled Martin Klenda, a classmate from Pilsen.[19] Emil also was a fledgling poet, much to the delight of his teachers.

When winter arrived and the creeks froze, many boys fell prey to the temptation to skip classes and go ice skating. Emil was wiser, and more cautious, so he also avoided the punishment which awaited his friends upon their return to school.[20] Yet he was not a sissy. "He was a real boy," one of the nuns declared, "ever ready to tease and joke, an extremely clever mimic, imitating his teachers and classmates, but always inoffensively." Perhaps the sister had not heard about the time when her prize pupil gave an electrical shock to one of the girls in his class.

Pictures of young Emil showed wide-set eyes, a thin nose, a ready grin, a noticeable cleft in a determined chin, and dark blond hair parted in the middle like his dad. Emil's temperament was typically Bohemian: quiet and retiring, with a good sense of humor. But the boy could be emotional. He showed his anger after Bessie bought him a new pair of knickers. Emil's dislike for his old trousers was so intense that he and a friend grabbed a pair of scissors and promptly cut them into several pieces.[21]

Father Sklenar frequently assigned Emil to serve as his altar boy at weekday Masses. After a while Bessie and Enos realized that there must be an easier way for their son to reach church than walking into Pilsen early in the morning, so they bought him a bicycle.

Emil soon was seen hunched over the handlebars, his peaked cap pulled over his brow, skinny legs pedaling furiously, guiding his two-wheeler over the rutted roads into town. Once in a while a neighbor offered Emil a ride in his Model T Ford car, but the youngster usually turned down the opportunity.[22]

It was a tiring trip because, in addition to his school books, Emil sometimes carried a handful of freshly picked wild flowers. When he arrived at school he hurried into the church and placed the bouquet at the altar of the Blessed Virgin Mary before going to his first class. Years later grateful soldiers in Korea remembered more hectic rides as Emil doggedly drove a shaky bicycle to visit them on the battlefield.

Cycling to school was hardly more comfortable than walking during the wet winter months. Fortunately for Emil, his cousin and close friend, Emil Melcher, solved the transportation problems. Emil Melcher came to live with the Kapaun family at the time that both boys began the two-year high school in Pilsen.

The Melcher family owned a two-wheeled cart and a clumsy looking horse called Bally. The animal hauled the two Emils to and from their classes. Even though Bally was only a horse, when the weather turned dreadful the boys put its comfort first. They sheltered Bally in George Vinduska's barn and then trudged the last two blocks to the schoolhouse.[23]

The two youths were a contrast in several ways. Emil Kapaun was a superior student, but his cousin was closer to average. On many afternoons the boys began their homework in the kitchen of the Kapaun house. Bessie Kapaun checked on them later in the evening. She often found her son busily writing in his science notebook and Emil Melcher slumped over the kitchen table, sound asleep.

Emil Melcher was a tall, hefty lad while Emil Kapaun could be described as scrawny. The difference in their appearances was so striking that they acquired the collective nickname of "Pounds and Ounces."[24] There were always friendly jibes and private jokes between them, characteristics of a strong friendship that continued into their adult years.

Many years later in the Communist prison camp Emil had opportunities to apply some of the manual skills which he had developed as a child. For example, when Eugene was eight years old he told his older brother that he wanted a threshing machine. Emil agreed to construct one, but he warned Eugene not to pester him until he was finished.

When Emil completed the model, his younger brother complained that it would not work. Emil decided to show off his craftsmanship by loading the device with sand. Eugene finally was reassured when the sand came out the other end, just like grain passing through real farm equipment.

On an earlier occasion the school sponsored a contest to choose the best handmade birdhouse. The two Emils sawed and hammered and built a 22-room miniature house, but that was only the first part of the job. Then they found an old telephone pole, cut off a 12-foot section and nailed the birdhouse on top. The last step was to install the finished project in the school yard. When the teachers announced the prize winners, the unusual entry from the team of Emil and Emil won first place.

The boys often played among the cottonwood and elm trees along the stream behind the Kapaun house. They enjoyed the location so much that they decided to build a rock dam.[25] However, Enos Kapaun was skeptical. He thought that the dam might divert the water from where he needed it for farming. But his son convinced him not to worry.

Emil recognized that the creek was more than a place for his boyhood fun. It was where he, the same as some farm boys of that era, conducted his business of catching muskrats. All year long, rain or shine, the young entrepreneur regularly went out to check his traps.[26] Emil often found dead animals and sold their pelts to a store in St. Louis.[27]

One morning, however, Emil trapped the wrong animal. Without realizing his mistake he continued to school that day. His classmates detected immediately that their friend had come too close to a skunk. The teacher caught a whiff, too. She quickly ushered Emil and his smelly clothing out of the building, homeward bound.[28]

As Emil approached teenage his character began to reveal itself in the diary that he kept for several years. The entries showed that he was quiet, hardly a leader and nervous about appearing before the other pupils. "It was pretty ticklish," he wrote at age 13 when he was chosen to speak to the entire student body.

The Catholics in Pilsen already had marked Emil as a devout youngster, one who sometimes attended Mass twice on Sundays. "Always close to God," was how Bessie described her son. Yet there was also a different, inner side to Emil, a secret, sometimes roguish attitude. That was obvious from the opening page of his diary. It posted the following warning: "No Trespassing. Please Keep Out If You Don't Want To Be Killed. Signed. X. Y. Z."[29]

Having scared off most intruders on his privacy, he recorded some common occurrences in the life of a farm boy: Arising at 4:30 A.M. on a mid-November day intending to husk corn with his father, only to find that snow was falling and it was impossible to work in the fields; careful observations about wind direction and the prospects for rain; constructing a motor from plans which he found in his science textbook; and writing early in December, "Yesterday I read that Santa Claus was coming to Kansas City already. It seems rather soon to me."[30]

He began to consider becoming a priest during his first year in high school. His thoughts were apparent in his diary entry for February 17, 1930, "Lord of the harvest is choosing his followers. Many are called, but few are chosen, few hearken to His call. Is he calling you?"

Emil responded to the call to a religious life. He had been corresponding with the St. Columban's Mission Society for some time, and he asked that religious order to educate him in its seminary without charging tuition.[31] Father Sklenar heard about what Emil was planning and became upset. He acted quickly to quash the idea.

Sklenar told Enos and Bessie that their son should become a parish priest, not a missionary. He reminded them that St. John Nepomucene church never had produced a vocation and, if necessary, he would pay for the young man's training at a different seminary. Sklenar did not say it, but clearly he wanted Emil to succeed him some day as pastor of the church in Pilsen.

Sending their first child away to school would have imposed an enormous financial burden on Enos and Bessie Kapaun. The 1930s witnessed the slide into a national economic depression, and in a rural farming community, the Kapauns were among the poorest. Even at Christmas time they had little available for gifts. Yet Enos and Bessie would not oppose Sklenar's wishes, and they recognized that the only way that Emil could prepare for the priesthood was to accept the help of their pastor.

Emil was alert to the circumstances which were beginning to shape his life. Deep within his diary, almost as though he were whispering to himself, he wrote:

> We are getting a catalogue from the Seminary where
> Father wants you to attend—and knows it is a good place.

Father is willing to help you—if your parents let you go and you want to go. This place is at Conception, Missouri. Don't mention this to anyone for a while until we get it, etc. Pray hard, receive the sacraments frequently, above all give good example. "God will do the rest in time."[32]

| THREE |

Becoming a Priest

"Gosh! Gee, Whillikers and criminy jacks if today isn't a nice day."[1] The enthusiasm jumped off the pages of Emil's diary in April 1930. The boy was still full of teen-age energy that summer when he left home for Conception, Missouri, where he was to complete the last two years of high school.

Emil was a studious and serious-minded youth and neither characteristic diminished at Conception Abbey, an all-male high school and college. Although some of its graduates had become Catholic priests, the school was not a seminary at that time.[2] The high school was important for Emil because it offered courses in Greek and Latin. While the youngster may not have realized it, Father Sklenar had chosen the school so that his protege could do the groundwork to prepare for the priesthood.

For a 14-year-old, life at Conception Abbey was full of new experiences. The Benedictine monks were farmers, but they also chanted hourly, and celebrated High Mass every day in the basilica at the Abbey. At least the routine of schoolwork was familiar to Emil. But life in a dormitory proved to be far different from the farm. Before long Emil became homesick. He missed his mother's cooking, and he awaited eagerly the first visit from his father a few weeks after the first term of high school started.

Yet as quickly as Emil accustomed himself to the boarding school schedule his interests began to broaden. He won the role of a fugitive in "The Lord's Prayer," a play which Conception presented in a state-wide dramatic contest. Later, in a performance given at the University of Missouri, he participated in "The Brink of Silence," a story about life at the South Pole.[3]

32

Students and teachers who knew Emil during 1930 through 1932 identified him as quiet, self-reliant, devout, and unusually well-balanced. A teacher recalled, "He was a great guy. Although he didn't try hard for it, everybody liked him. He didn't stand out as a leader and wasn't much interested in football, but in the intramural games (e.g., softball, bowling, etc.) he certainly played his part."

Small for his age, underweight and skinny, Emil was nevertheless persistent and competitive. His letters spoke of playing sports in the mud and more than once he crawled out from under a pile-up of football players. The school newspaper reported his third place finish in the 220 yard dash.[4] Yet he excelled in one category. His diary recorded an appetite that only a teenager could satisfy at one sitting: two bottles of soda pop, two beers, two dishes of ice cream and five hamsausage sandwiches. "Man. Oh Man. I feasted," he wrote.

"It is raining and cloudy and lonesome today. I wish I were at home," Emil's diary noted forlornly in October 1931. But then the 15-year-old thought about food and his mood brightened, "Received my overalls today and also some smashed bananas and some good suckers and other candy and 5 oranges. Mom is sure good to me."

The diary served as the reservoir of Emil's innermost thoughts. He understood that someday a stranger might scan this summary of his youth and judge him by what he had said. So one day during his early years at Conception he wrote "...if you, dear diary, ever fall into somebody else's hands don't give them a bad example for I am personal with you."[5]

One of the happiest events that Emil described was going home for Christmas in 1931. His travels started at 2 A.M. a couple of days before the holiday. Ahead lay a long ride on the railroad. He took a wagon to the local station, then different trains to Topeka, Florence, and Marion, the closest stop to his home.

The trip was worth it, for the Christmas-New Year's holiday was not only a spiritual period for the reunited Kapaun family, but also a fun-filled occasion for Emil. He enjoyed everything, from outdoor activities such as touch football and ice skating on the stream in his backyard to card games of poker and ten point pitch.

The festive holiday gatherings sometimes featured violin music and always included appealing foods. There were roasted goose and duck, chicken noodle soup, vegetables for every taste, angel food cake and, of course, the familiar *kolache*.[6] However, when the beverages were served everyone turned down Enos Kapaun's homemade beer. While he was a good farmer, his reputation as a brewmaster left something to be desired.[7]

The Christmas presents that Emil received were hardly lavish. They were mostly little items that a teenage boy needed, such as a knife, chewing gum, a few dollar bills, a picture of Aunt Tena. The handful of gifts only reinforced the fact that even on this happiest of days money was scarce in the Kapaun household. His brother remembered one lonely Christmas when Enos and Bessie could not afford to bring Emil home from school for the holidays.

Conception high school proved to be more rigorous academically than the country school at Pilsen. Still, Emil consistently received grades in the mid and upper 90s.[8] He was chosen for the honor roll in his junior and senior years,[9] much to the delight of Father Sklenar and his former teachers at St. John Nepomucene parish.

High school was a blend of activities for Emil: rabbit hunts, unnecessary worries about his marks, interclass basketball games, a farm boy's continual eye on the weather ("This morning it was 6 $\frac{1}{3}$ degrees above zero," his diary noted. "Well, that was not so bad."), the joy of learning that a skunk that he had caught had sold for ten cents and watching Shirley Temple in "Baby Take a Bow" with the biggest movie audience in the history of the school.[10] William Lorenz, a fellow student, remembered how Emil admired one of his teachers who was "a magician with the fungo bat" that baseball players use to hit balls high in the air.[11]

Emil remained at Conception Abbey after high school graduation in 1932 and started college there in the autumn of that year. At about that time he began smoking cigars. Buying them required a trip to "Dog Town," the students' name for the nearby community. Occasionally Emil also planned to enjoy a beer, and he wanted to keep it a secret. How could the young collegian avoid being detected? He settled on the idea of eating some butter before heading into town, figuring that it would mask the odor of the beer.[12]

While many teachers and students at college regarded Emil as unobtrusive he also was covertly mischievous. On one occasion another student needed some help in chemistry class. The problem occurred when Father Benedict Villager, their white-haired science professor, prepared a test tube of chemical reagents for each pupil. He instructed them to identify the contents by the end of the week. Using his own unique set of shorthand symbols, the professor drew up a list of the answers. However, he made the mistake of tacking the paper inside the closet containing the chemicals.

Can you read Father Benedict's shorthand? the other student asked Emil hopefully. Emil promptly deciphered the description of his friend's formula. Many years later the former classmate remembered Emil's assistance, "He agreed that this way of speeding up the work would be quite effective, without the ethical problem of doing any great harm."[13] If Emil lied it was only to tease someone. He shocked a friend by announcing in the mail that Conception was becoming a co-ed school, then he ended the letter by adding that he was joking.

Resourcefulness was one of Emil's strong points and he demonstrated it again when he and his father were driving to Conception in a model T Ford. When the car headed up an incline the flow of gasoline into the engine stopped. Emil figured out if they backed the car up the hill the fuel would pass in the opposite direction. Gravity worked in their favor and they continued on their way.[14]

Emil nevertheless got into trouble once in a while during his college days. An enviable array of beer and whiskey bottles filled a bookshelf in his room at Conception. All of them were empty, but that made no difference when the prefect of discipline saw the line-up of glass containers. Emil failed room inspection that day and was ordered to get rid of the bottles. The disciplinarian reminded Emil that if he wanted a collection, he should select something more worthwhile.[15]

He must have followed the advice, for on one occasion he collected a group of visitors to the grounds at Conception. The school paper's gossip column reported the event: "We noticed Kaupan [sic] strolling around the campus with four young maidens recently. We had better keep an eye on that small but mighty Kaupie boy."[16]

Writing, one of Emil's favorite pastimes, was one of the extra-curricular activities which occupied his time at college. He joined the student publicity committee and distributed stories about the Conception College Bluebirds athletic teams to local newspapers.[17]

Religion also remained a serious matter for Emil, and he composed a prayer for the members of the Sodality of the Blessed Virgin Mary. Finishing third of 22 entrants in a public speaking contest was commendable, but one place short of earning Emil a trip to Kansas City, Kansas for a regional competition.

When each college year ended, Emil returned to Pilsen for the summer. The vacation period was hardly an opportunity to relax. He helped his dad repair the binder, planted muskmelon seeds for his mother and, most importantly, farmed in the same way as any teen-age boy in rural Kansas. Instead of employing outsiders, many farmers relied on their families to handle the first stages of the wheat harvest: severing the stalks with a binder, tying the pieces into 30-pound bundles about three feet long, then forming a shock of about eight bundles.

Farming was dusty, sweltering, day-long labor for Emil, his father, and his young brother, Eugene. The workers enjoyed well water on a hot summer day, and Emil never forgot the little girl who brought him a cold drink. He promised to do something special for her and he did. She was an attendant when he offered his first public mass as a priest.[18]

Threshing the wheat took several additional steps that required the Kapauns and the other farm families to supply a tractor, at least three teams of horses and wagons, a threshing machine and a crew of between eight to ten workers. The Kapaun family provided one of the bundle wagons and the labor of Enos and his two sons.

Harvesting demanded teamwork, loading bundles of wheat on to wagons and scooping them into each farmer's granary. The job required the combined efforts of the Kapaun, Meysing, and Reznick families. Emil operated a wagon and also helped as a grain loader. The crew managed to clear about 25 acres a day, going from one farm to another until the task was completed.[19]

No wonder that Emil's hands were heavily calloused by the time he returned to school in the autumn. How much his religious convictions influenced his actions became clear when another worker asked Emil why he refused to wear work gloves. "I want to feel some of the pain our Lord felt when He was nailed to the cross," he replied.

The homecooked dinner—fried chicken, potatoes, gravy, tomatoes, apple or peach pie, plus a local favorite, *kolache*—was a welcome mid-day pause. The harvesting machines were shut down, and the hungry, dirty workers washed themselves with buckets of water. The crew took another break when lunch, which featured lemonade, was served about 4 P.M. Work continued until early in the evening, the end of a tiring 12-hour day.[20]

The farm families near Pilsen knew each other well, and one day Emil benefited from his friendship with his neighbors. He had delivered a load of wheat to the grain elevator and was on the return trip when the black model T Ford truck that he was driving began to overheat. Some friends lived in the vicinity, so Emil simply pulled into their driveway, filled the radiator with water and was on his way again.[21]

The workers on the harvesting team felt confident about their safety when Emil was with them. One time thunderheads in the northwest signaled that a storm was approaching. Emil and the others quickly unhitched the horses and led them into the protection of a nearby barn. The workmen believed that with an obviously religious person among them both the men and the animals surely would be safeguarded from threatening weather.[22]

Perhaps because everyone regarded Emil as a serious person no one suspected him when he played a prank on his co-worker, an employee on the Kapaun farm. The man prized his model T Ford car, but Emil secretly shut off the gas line. No matter how often the owner cranked the engine, the car refused to start. Emil barely concealed a smile when he sauntered over to the man and suggested that maybe he was not feeding enough gas to the motor.

In addition to farming, summer vacations gave Emil some added opportunities to improve his manual skills. He became more proficient at woodworking, a talent that he used again in the prison in North Korea. When Eugene complained about the condition of his bicycle, big-brother Emil spruced it up with a coat of red paint.[23]

Despite Emil's help during the summertime, Enos and Bessie realized that sending their son to college in Missouri would continue to be a constant financial burden. During Emil's second year the family could not pay his railroad fare home for Thanksgiving. He was forced to remain at school for the holiday, but he entertained himself by reading Sherlock Holmes stories.

Tuition, room and board at Conception College cost $190 a semester, more than Emil's parents could afford. However, Anna Luska, his aunt, helped by contributing the funds to cover his tuition for one year.[24] Another time the school granted him a $125 scholarship, but with an unusual condition attached: He could not occupy a private room in the dormitory.

The determined youth wanted to avoid any possibility that he might not complete his education. Emil wrote to Bishop Augustus Schwerter of the Diocese of Wichita and asked whether the diocese would pay the tuition if the College failed to grant him a scholarship. His reasons were very sensible; drought and poor crops had limited his family's ability to support him. Emil knew as well as anyone that the price at which Kansas farmers sold their wheat had dropped from 99 cents a bushel in 1929 to 33 cents a few years later.[25] Besides, it was important to have the opportunity to continue studying Bohemian and there was a professor at Conception College who taught that language.[26] In the end, however, a lack of money never interrupted Emil's education.

Other students recognized that as Emil was growing older he was becoming more serious. His contemporaries saw him as an involved and studious individual. Among the best-remembered descriptions was "...one of the most normal men."[27] Emil seldom complained, not even when his mother asked him to make an unplanned drive to transport an acquaintance to Missouri.

Yet, beneath an outward calmness, Emil held strong feelings. A college soccer game between the Irish and the German students at Conception College one Saint Patrick's Day brought his European heritage forcefully to mind. "You know none is as good as a

German," he wrote in his diary. "But to hear Downs talk you would think the Irish are 'the Stuff'."

While he was seldom a leader or a winner, Emil continued to join in many activities during his college years: a semi-finalist in the student bowling tournament, a participant on a team in the softball championship, a cast member in the morality play, "The Great Theatre of the World," the treasurer and leader of a group of Sodality members who recited the Rosary prayers, and an avid handball player.

He also worked as a waiter in the faculty dining hall and, after one of the meals, he confessed to his diary, "I got some of the priests' wine—did it make me groggy—....". Emil also gained a nickname when he took part in igniting a ceremonial fire on May Day. In that role the student newspaper called him "Runner Kapaun."[28]

Emil was reluctant to attract attention to himself. "I don't want to be a leader so I am going to cut up and try to get low grades, but I certainly will study and try to learn," he noted in the diary during his second year at Conception College. However, Emil did achieve one recorded first—he was first bass in the polyphonic choir.

Yet, while Emil tried to avoid becoming notorious, he could not shirk in his school work. His records disclosed that he was at the head of his Greek class and had earned the best grades in the course in logic. Emil's reputation for educational achievements was so solid that his classmates assembled in his dormitory room before philosophy class and asked him to review the subject with them.

By the time Emil graduated from Conception College in June 1936 almost all of his grades were Superior or Excellent. He was labeled "The Brain" by friends whom he tutored in Greek and Latin. "Others were more flashy and brilliant," said one of his professors, "but in the long run he seemed to work himself to the top like a large stone in a bucket of sand."

Father Sklenar continued to encourage Emil's aspirations. He still wanted his protege to become a priest in the Diocese of Wichita instead of serving in a foreign mission. When a diocesan official asked Sklenar if the young man was sufficiently frivolous to be disqualified from entering the seminary, the pastor dismissed the idea. After all, he pointed out, plenty of hard work around the Kapaun house would keep Emil out of trouble.

Money for his education still was a serious concern, in more ways than one. In the first place, the Kapaun family could not pay for any further education. The second problem was the Bohemian attitude toward how a man established his status in the community. Many Bohemians believed that owning 1,000 acres or a sizeable bank account was a sure sign of God's approval.

Some of Emil's relatives and acquaintances tried to convince him to become a lawyer or a doctor. They assured him that then his education would yield a big income. Those advisors reminded Emil that an assistant pastor received only $50 monthly. The salary of a pastor was $125 per month, but he had to pay a housekeeper. They tried to make the young student understand that after he trained for 12 years and was ordained a priest, from a material standpoint he would be a failure.

Despite such practical arguments, Emil seemed destined for the priesthood. While he was friendly to both boys and girls, he never attended dances. In fact, Eugene remembered that his brother never had a date.[29] Friends recalled one summer evening when they gathered on the steps of the Marion County courthouse. Emil wondered aloud whether he had a vocation to a religious life.

His pals insisted that he was worthy of such a calling. They saw that Emil was thinking carefully about his future. The nation was suffering from a financial depression and remembering Emil's student years, one of his teachers, Father Luke Becker, O.S.B. said, "It forced even a young man to decide what really was important in life."

Still, Emil gave conflicting signals about his intentions. When Sister M. Virgilia Winter asked him if he planned to study for the priesthood, Emil answered flippantly, "When the sun rises from the west."[30] Soon afterward he surprised everyone by disclosing that he planned to enter the seminary in the fall of 1936.

Nevertheless, Emil's doubts persisted. One of his teachers at Conception Abbey finally persuaded him to continue his quest toward a religious vocation. "His piety was of such depth and yet such simplicity that I was convinced the little difficulties would not stand in the way of reaching his goal," recalled Father Bede Scholz, O.S.B.[31] Emil's jobs in college, cleaning the chapel and keeping the priests' vestments in order, clearly had strengthened his desire to serve God.

Although Conception College offered courses in church history and the New Testament it did not provide the intensive theological education that was necessary for men to enter the Catholic clergy. The next step was enrollment in Kenrick Seminary in St. Louis. Father Sklenar already had attested that his young friend was a "...fit subject for an ecclesiastical calling."

Before being admitted to Kenrick, Kapaun had to survive a tense interview with Bishop Schwerter, who was known for his authoritative demeanor and deep bass voice. The Diocese of Wichita had little money for Kapaun's seminary education, and the bishop suggested that he wait a year before starting. Sklenar pleaded that the delay might snuff out Kapaun's religious vocation. If necessary, the pastor offered to pay for his protege's first year in the seminary.

Bishop Schwerter authorized Kapaun to start at Kenrick in the fall of 1936. However, the diocese notified him that he must pay for his transportation and textbooks. A former teacher also contributed toward Kapaun's expenses. Despite those helpful arrangements, Enos and Bessie Kapaun had to agree that if their son voluntarily left the seminary or was dismissed they would refund to the diocese the tuition of $187.50 for each semester that he attended.

Kenrick stretched Kapaun intellectually. Although most of his grades were A's and B's he occasionally needed help from some of his classmates.[32] Kapaun never whined, even though the daily schedule was demanding. He normally arose at 5:15 A.M. and went to classes six days a week. Some students could rest on Saturday evenings, but Kapaun and others who were studying Bohemian had to attend the two-hour course at 8 P.M. that night. He worked hard, yet other students agreed that Kapaun remained even-tempered, pious, and friendly. In short, everyone liked him.[33]

St. Louis was too far from Pilsen for Enos and Bessie to visit their son, but he was too busy to be lonely. Emil's schedule of classes notwithstanding, the young seminarian found time to write a history of the Diocese of Wichita. He also supervised other students who corrected test papers in Kenrick's correspondence course about the Catholic religion.

Kapaun relaxed by doing what he did as a child, fishing in the lake at the seminary. He brought his catch into the kitchen where the fish could be cooked and served to the other students. As part of his seminary training, Kapaun went to Caldwell, Kansas one summer where he participated in street preaching. The population was largely Bohemian and he could address them in their own language. "They flocked around him so as not to miss a word," the local pastor reported.

During his years in St. Louis Kapaun kept in touch with Emil Melcher, who continued to be his best friend. Kapaun was 20 years old when he entered Kenrick, and the letters to his cousin from the seminary disclosed the gradual changes in Kapaun's personality during that time.

At the beginning the correspondence depicted one old pal kidding another. "Dear Emilio," Kapaun wrote from Kenrick, "Well, here comes more of the old stuff. Roll up your pants legs and put on your boots—she's going to be deep."[34] The signature often read, "Hairless, bashful Joe Greenslough."

Then the news that Melcher was about to be married in February 1938 elicited a happy comment from his cousin, "I can't help but think of all the 'dogs,' *kolaci, rohlicky, knedlicky, pivo, vino,* a *mozna koralku* that will be consumed that day. Take a drink for me, but don't get drunk."[35]

Recalling how they had enjoyed their boyhood together Kapaun apologized that he could not get permission from the seminary to return to Pilsen for his cousin's wedding. He offered some advice, "Since God has called you to the married life, He is expecting you to do your duty in that life that you might save your soul..."[36]

The serious tone in Emil's correspondence with the newlyweds soon wore off. In a couple of months the old nickname that each Emil had applied to the other appeared again in their letters. Emil and Victoria Melcher had become Mr. and Mrs. Greenslough.

The correspondence between the cousins opened a window into Kapaun's four years at Kenrick. His letters were simple and chatty. Kapaun knew that many of his friends had finished their education in grade school, and he refused to show off his college training. His writings told how he mourned the loss of another student who had died of appendicitis, how he rooted for the Chicago Cubs in the World Series, and how his golf score one day was 47 strokes—for nine holes. One letter regretted that he could not listen to a heavy-weight championship fight because the staff at Kenrick turned off the students' radios at 7:30 P.M. each night.[37] Kapaun's correspondence with Alice Klenda, his schoolmate at St. John Nepomucene who had become a nun, noted a coincidence. He had mailed an Easter greeting to his friends, and she had sent the same card to him.

The country boy from Pilsen was awed by a visit to the Anheuser-Busch brewery in St. Louis. He told Emil and Victoria, whom he now called both Vicki and Vicky, that the plant covered some 71 city blocks. Cases of beer could be loaded onto 130 freight cars—all at the same time![38] The enormity of the facility overwhelmed Kapaun. Yet despite the abundance nearby, he boasted that he had not enjoyed a beer in almost a month.[39]

Some subjects, however, contained no surprises for a farmer. Corn, for example. One of Kapaun's letters to the Melchers commented wryly, "But anyway some dumb guy from Iowa said that where there is corn there is hoosch! Can you imagine anything so dumb. Schucks, he hasn't been around. He ought to come to Kansas where we raise (I mean you, the Melchers and the Charley Klendas) corn and still have no hoosch. No, but we got something better, we got the Republicans—and how!"[40]

As Kapaun approached the time of his ordination he wondered whether he was spiritually or intellectually strong enough to become a Catholic priest. However, Aloysius F. Preisner, a contemporary at the seminary, expressed the consensus about Kapaun: "...there is a good egg who will be a good priest."[41] The religious aspects of Kapaun's personality slowly were becoming more pronounced.

After he had delivered a practice sermon to more than 200 students and faculty at Kenrick, Kapaun remarked exuberantly to Vicki and Emil, "That was a feeling, but man, it wasn't half the feeling I'll have someday giving a sermon in Pilsen church. Boy, will I give you guys the d———l."[42]

Midnight Mass at Christmas 1939 was Kapaun's first opportunity to preach at St. John Nepomucene parish. Familiar faces filled the church while he spoke the sermon in Bohemian. When Kapaun had finished talking, the ordinarily taciturn but obviously pleased Father Sklenar hurried to the front of the church and patted the proud seminarian on the back.

The references to Mr. and Mrs. Greenslough gradually disappeared from Kapaun's correspondence. The closings to his letters became more formal, usually "Yours sincerely in Christ." Kapaun asked Emil and Vicki to pray for him, for 1938–39 was a stressful period in his training. "Yes, Emil," he wrote, "this is my year and if I don't come thru I will be blowed up so bad that it won't even be funny."[43]

Despite Kapaun's foreboding, the seminary elevated him to the rank of deacon in 1939. The bishop scheduled what Kapaun called his "Big Day" for June 9, 1940, the date of his ordination. As the preparations for the ceremony neared completion Kapaun never could have guessed that one day he would be named his alma mater's most distinguished alumnus.

The soon-to-be Father Kapaun expressed his thoughts on his future responsibilities in a letter to the Melchers in mid-April 1940:

> You know, Emil & Vicky, I feel like the dickens. Maybe you do not realize fully what it means to be a priest, but I tell you—after I have studied all these years I am more convinced that a man must be a living saint in order to dare to take that step. And that is where my worries come in. Gee whiz, I have a feeling that I am far, far from being a saint worthy to receive the Priesthood.
>
> Think what it means!! To offer up the Living Body and Blood of Our Savior every day in Holy Mass—to absolve souls from sins in Holy Confession and to snatch them from the gates of hell in which they would suffer for all eternity.
>
> These and a hundred or more duties and responsibilities make a person realize that the Vocation to the Priesthood is so sublime that the angels in heaven were not given

a vocation to the Priesthood, no, not even the Blessed Mother who was never stained with sin—not even she was called to be a priest of God—and here I am called!![44]

By that time Bishop Christian Winkelmann had succeeded Bishop Schwerter as the head of the Diocese of Wichita. Described by his subordinates as "a very princely man," Bishop Winkelmann had selected the spacious St. John's Chapel at Sacred Heart College in Wichita for the ordination to the Catholic priesthood of Kapaun and four other seminarians. Kapaun arrived on Saturday for the rehearsal and spent that entire night kneeling and praying about the career which lay ahead of him.[45]

The next morning Enos, Bessie, and Eugene sat in the front row of the chapel and watched joyfully as Bishop Winkelmann extended his hands over Kapaun and ordained him a priest. The ceremonies were conducted in Latin, but the bishop had arranged for the prayers to be explained to the congregation in English.

After a breakfast celebration with the bishop, the new Father Kapaun and his happy family returned to Pilsen. Kapaun had expected to live at home until Bishop Winkelmann assigned him to a parish somewhere in the Diocese of Wichita. The new priest now was subject to the authority of the Catholic Church and Father Sklenar insisted that he stay at the rectory of St. John Nepomucene parish.

The people of Pilsen at last had seen one of their own become a priest. Local pride and joy reached their zenith when Kapaun said his first public Mass at St. John Nepomucene church on June 20, 1940.

The holy event was a family affair. Kapaun's parents donated the vestments and his uncle, Emil Melcher's father, provided the chalice. Eugene was the crossbearer leading a colorful procession into the overcrowded church. Following him were two local bands, members of the Knights of St. George and the Catholic Workmen Societies, and 14 Catholic clergymen. There even was a connection in the ceremony to the founding of Pilsen generations earlier. Margie Krotz, the great-granddaughter of Jacob Randolph, the first settler in the community, was one of the flower girls in the procession.

More than 1,200 friends and relatives then proceeded to a banquet in the church hall. The festivities featured a Hawaiian duet, a film of "The Little Flower," happy songs, speeches and, of course, the best of Bohemian foods.[46] Enos Kapaun was hardly wealthy, yet he, and not the parish, paid for the ordination reception for his son.

Kapaun's new status as a priest and his earlier days as a student did not prevent him from developing strong convictions about

Emil Kapaun at his ordination

Photo by Les Broadstreet, Wichita

international affairs. Some of his views were uniquely prophetic. More than three years before the surprise Japanese attack on Pearl Harbor Kapaun had told Emil Melcher that he was concerned that Japan might attempt to pull the American people into war. "I am afraid that our government is going to fool around till we get mixed up in another bloody struggle," he predicted to his cousin.

Because his father's background was German and his mother's was Czech, Kapaun focused most of his attention on happenings in Europe. He believed that England and France had deceived the United States into fighting Germany in World War I so that they could retain control over their territories around the world.

The Treaty of Versailles had unjustly deprived Germany of its rights and foreign possessions, Kapaun argued when he wrote to Emil Melcher in 1939. "The real danger to us Americans is England, France and Russia." he declared. "By propaganda they are trying to fool the American people again. The controlled newspapers picture one side of the question and the other they leave."[47]

Kapaun fretted that once again the United States might be drawn into a bloody conflict on the European continent. "Hitler seems to be getting his 'share of the cake' and he takes it without anybody doing anything about it," he complained to Emil and Vicki Melcher.[48] However, by the time that the United States entered the war against the Axis powers in 1941 and Eugene went into the army, Kapaun had re-evaluated the situation in Europe. He cautioned his brother, "You don't have to worry about Hitler. We'll take care of him. Your biggest trouble is going to be Communism."[49]

In mid-1940 Kapaun's immediate concern was not the European war, but instead to which church the bishop would assign him. The new priest possessed all of the attributes for an appointment to his home parish: he was one of only three priests in the Diocese who could speak Bohemian, he knew most of the parishioners, and Father Sklenar was an older man who could use some help.

Just the same, Kapaun expected to be sent elsewhere. Sklenar was away when the letter announcing Kapaun's first assignment was delivered to the rectory of St. John Nepomucene church. The surprising news was that he had been instructed to remain in Pilsen as assistant pastor to Sklenar.

Throughout the 49 years of his priesthood Sklenar always had lived alone. Hard of hearing, cranky, and outspoken, he believed that a pastor should remain aloof from his flock. During several decades at St. John Nepomucene church Sklenar never had an assistant pastor. Visitors to his rectory were confined to a room adjacent to the front door. The pastor discouraged idle chatter; his parishioners were expected to state their business and depart immediately.

Kapaun's new boss at St. John Nepomucene parish would not tolerate anyone being late. In fact, a bride and groom were fined one dollar for each minute that they were not on time for the nuptial ceremony. Excuses and friendship did not matter. When a blizzard made roads impassable and a nephew of another priest appeared at the church ten minutes late on his wedding day, Sklenar nonetheless assessed the required penalty.

In contrast, the new assistant believed in a cordial, open relationship with the people of his home parish. Being friendly to everyone while under Sklenar's supervision required tact and flexibility. Fortunately, Kapaun possessed a considerable supply of both. One day the young cleric performed a double wedding, the next day he taught students in the parish school to play soccer and then refereed the match,[50] and on another occasion he addressed the graduating class. The children idolized Kapaun. Equally important, the teachers appreciated that he supervised the school playground at noontime so that they could enjoy their lunch in peace.

In addition to his religious duties, Kapaun also became the parish janitor, gardener, and all-around handyman. Tasks such as painting classrooms and cutting the grass around the church cemetery were part of his job. No matter what work the new assistant was doing, or how hot the day was, Sklenar insisted that Kapaun wear his clerical collar. In the old pastor's mind, any clergyman who appeared without it was a "cowboy priest."

The vow of obedience which Kapaun had taken a few weeks earlier was often put to the test. One warm afternoon Kapaun was in a dilemma. He was working outside the rectory with an old wheelbarrow equipped with a steel-rimmed wheel. Whenever he moved the wheelbarrow it screeched loudly enough to disturb Sklenar's nap. He knew that if he awakened Sklenar, the pastor was not one to keep his displeasure to himself.

Kapaun pondered over how he could complete the work without incurring the wrath of his religious superior. Growing up on a farm taught him that there was usually a solution. He walked across the street and found an old bicycle tire. Kapaun cut it into pieces, wired them around the previously noisy steel rim and, much relieved, he silently finished the job.[51]

Their son's assignment to his home parish overjoyed Enos and Bessie. The new assistant pastor ("Father Emil" as his mother proudly called him)[52] occasionally had time to go home and help his mother milk the cows. But he concentrated on becoming a careful clergyman, meticulous about saying Mass. When Kapaun worried that his work was becoming lackadaisical he asked Father Bede Scholz, O.S.B., to correct the way that he performed religious services.

The young priest's sermons were well-organized. He typed the talks in English, with a few handwritten afterthoughts at the end, even though sometimes he delivered them in Bohemian. Kapaun's parents sat in their usual seats in the fourth row on the right hand side of the church. No matter what language her son used Bessie beamed whenever he spoke at Mass. On the other hand, Enos was nervous and squirmed in his pew while watching his son preach to their neighbors among the congregation.[53]

Father Sklenar completed 50 years as a priest in June 1941. He loved being honored at parties. In fact, elaborate celebrations occurred each year before he departed for a vacation in Europe and again when he returned. A huge party was planned for the golden anniversary of Sklenar's ordination, and Kapaun took charge of all of the arrangements.

Among the highlights at the festivities for Sklenar were several special cakes. The bakers formed them in the shapes of objects which were associated with the celebration of Mass, among them a missal, a chalice, and a bunch of grapes to depict wine. The baked goods were displayed at the church and appeared so realistic that one of the guests walked over to the missal-shaped cake and tried to open it. When Kapaun heard what had happened he burst into laughter.

Continuing the habit which he had started as a teen-ager Kapaun maintained a meticulous diary and notes about his activities at St. John Nepomucene church. He described some of the routine events in the life of a rural parish priest; for example: "September 12. Grandma Vinduska died. Monsignor tolls the small bells, first in a rolling tone, then a pause, then about seven distinct tolls, a pause, then a rolling toll, pause, distinct tolls, etc., about four or five times."[54]

Christmas in 1940 was special for Kapaun because now that he earned a salary he could join in the spirit of giving. His notes reported gifts to the children in the parish school: a missal for one, candy for another, holy water for some, and occasionally a knife for one of the boys. The presents for his father one year were both material and spiritual: pipe tobacco and rosary beads.

However, the Christmas season the following year, 1941, was unexpectedly different. On December 7, Kapaun was listening to the radio broadcast of the "Catholic Evidence Hour" from Salina, Kansas. The station interrupted the program with an announcement that Japanese airplanes had attacked the United States base at Pearl Harbor. Kapaun recalled later that at Mass the next day, the feast of the Immaculate Conception, the parishioners were greatly disturbed over the horrifying news.[55]

Before long, men who were Kapaun's age started to leave Pilsen for service in the army. Well aware of his obligations to Father Sklenar, Kapaun nevertheless began to think that he should join thousands of other young Americans in uniform. Then 25 years old, Kapaun notified Bishop Winkelmann that he wanted to become a military chaplain.[56] But the bishop refused, writing Kapaun in February 1942 and instructing him to remain as the assistant to Sklenar.

In that same month, Kapaun offered the funeral Mass for a young woman who had been a member of St. John Nepomucene parish. He based his sermon on a story from the Second Book of Maccabees, the martyrdom of the seven brothers who refused the king's order to abandon their faith in God. The monarch forced their mother to witness their painful executions, one at a time.

As the last of her sons was about to be murdered, the woman spoke:

> I implore you, my child, observe heaven and earth, consider all that is in them, and acknowledge that God made them out of what did not exist, and that mankind came into being in the same way. Do not fear your executioner, but prove yourself worthy of your brothers, and make death welcome, so that in the day of mercy I may receive you back in your brothers' company.[57]

No one among the congregation that day nor Kapaun himself appreciated the long-lasting impact that the tale of the seven courageous brothers would have on his life. Years later, as he lay dying in a squalid Communist prison camp, Chaplain Kapaun tearfully repeated the same story. It was part of his final instructions to a group of heartbroken American officers who huddled around him.

Although Bishop Winkelmann had barred him from joining the army, Kapaun was determined to assist the war effort in other ways. He prepared a list of Pilsen men who had entered the military services and wrote to them about news from home. Kapaun typed as many as five letters a night. Had he done them all by hand, he joked that his arm would be in a sling. To Private Gerald Franta Kapaun commented, prophetically, "Be true to God and to your country, and you will be a good soldier."[58]

The possibility of joining the armed forces was never far from Kapaun's mind. "They called recently for 4,000 chaplains," he wrote in March 1943. "Looks like we young priests will get a chance for some army action." His desire to put on a uniform was more emphatic in another letter: "When I read your letter, Gerald, I just about felt like pulling up my anchor and enlisting in the air corps."[59]

By that time the U.S. government had opened a military airfield at Herington, Kansas. The rapid arrival of hundreds of soldiers made it necessary for civilian clergymen in the area to serve as auxiliary chaplains. The priest who lived near Herington was too old to handle the additional assignment so Kapaun volunteered in a part-time capacity in January 1943. On Sunday afternoons and twice during the week for the next year and a half Kapaun and one of his friends from Pilsen drove to Herington, which was located about 16 miles away.

Bessie Kapaun was certain that these frequent trips to the army base had convinced her son to enter military life. Father Sklenar reached the same conclusion: "I had always figured he would take my place but after he had been to Herington, his ambition was with the soldiers. So I said 'God bless you' and sent him off."

The facility where Kapaun said Mass at the Herington base was hardly conducive to religious services. It was just a recreation room filled with cigarette butts and the odor of tobacco smoke. Later, when Kapaun reported to Bishop Winkelmann that conditions had improved, he added, "I enjoy the work with the men very much," a veiled reminder to his superior that he still wanted to enter military service.

Even though few of the Catholic troops at Herington attended Mass and some of the fervent ones became disheartened, Kapaun was not discouraged and devoted all of his energy to his task. He heard confessions, visited patients in the base hospital and prisoners in the jail and supplied religious magazines, all in addition to his Sunday work at St. John Nepomucene church.

His congregation at Herington consisted almost entirely of soldiers so Kapaun's sermons focused on the military part of their lives. To one group he preached, "...a Catholic soldier will have his heart set on obedience and faithfulness to duty to service of his country and through that service, to the honor and glory of God." He ended another sermon on October 24, 1943, with this thought: "Faith is worth dying for. It is worth living for. Let us be worthy of the name—Catholic."[60]

Throughout 1943 and into 1944, Kapaun continued to help at the Herington base, but his primary task of parish work demanded most of his time. With 135 families and five church buildings under the care of Father Sklenar and himself, Kapaun was busy from dawn until dusk.

One of Kapaun's most enjoyable projects was teaching in the school. He believed that recitation was an important element of education and awarded two-thirds of the children's grades for how well they spoke in his classes. Just to be sure, Kapaun reinforced his lessons by giving each child a copy of the New Testament for Christmas in 1943. His advice to his students was direct; if someone was intentionally doing something wrong they should "...give them a good piece of your mind and stay away."[61]

A few months later, in March 1944, Kapaun was rushed to St. Francis Hospital in Wichita for an emergency appendectomy. It was the only significant interruption in his busy schedule that year. Although convalescing, Kapaun still was a priest and, when requested, he left his hospital bed to hear a confession.

Father, now Monsignor, Sklenar, retired as pastor of St. John Nepomucene parish in November 1943. Kapaun knew the congregation so well that no one was surprised that he was appointed temporary administrator of the church later that month. The Bohemian parishioners wanted to be certain that their permanent pastor was not Irish or German. They preferred Kapaun or someone else from their own background. Less than a week later, a committee of laymen from Pilsen asked Bishop Winkelmann to designate the hometown priest as their new pastor.

"There are peculiar circumstances and needs of our community that require proper handling of our people," wrote the delegation from St. John Nepomucene. Bishop Winkelmann accepted their recommendation. It was not long before Kapaun understood how his parishioners' references to "peculiar circumstances" and "proper handling" would influence the direction of his life.

Four

Into the Army

A setting which appeared ideal—a clergyman serving among the families and within the small town where he had grown up—was not what it seemed. Several circumstances in St. John Nepomucene parish in 1944 troubled both Kapaun and his parishioners.

The educated child of a farm family was uncomfortable ministering to older folks who had known him as a boy. Some Bohemian members of the parish were equally uneasy with him.[1] Old-timers in the church rejected the young priest's guidance. They could not forget that Kapaun was the son of one of the poorest families in town.[2]

If Kapaun preached in English, the older parishioners sat disgruntled in their wooden pews, their heads down as they read their prayerbooks in the language they preferred. Yet when he addressed the congregation in Bohemian the more Americanized parishioners felt left out.

Bohemian farmers traditionally were cautious individuals. A good harvest did not excite them because they knew it might be followed by a poor one. Many of the Catholics in the community were conservative, too. They mistrusted their own reaction to any new situation, even the appointment of their pastor, turning the subject over and over in their minds.

As a consequence, the residents of Pilsen were consistent in how they lived. If an elderly farmer had contributed a certain sum to the church in the early 1900s, he saw no reason to give differently in the 1940s. Father Sklenar had done things the Bohemian way since he came to Pilsen 39 years earlier. Now their young,

51

new pastor wanted to make changes, and some individuals were unhappy.

Kapaun, even though he was barely 28 years old, understood how his parishioners felt about him. He decided upon "...clearing his conscience..." So he wrote to Bishop Winkelmann in June 1944. The letter was typical of Kapaun's correspondence with Winkelmann and later with Bishop Mark Carroll whenever he encountered a problem.

Those letters combined three principal thoughts. First, the letter usually stated clearly that he would follow orders. Then Kapaun discussed what worried him and indicated what he preferred not to do. Lastly, somewhere in the letter, perhaps in words that were not entirely clear, was the course of action that Kapaun really wanted.

Reviewing barely six months' work as the pastor at St. John Nepomucene parish, Kapaun told Winkelmann:

> I showed no favoritism to anyone. In fact, I treated my relatives and friends coldly (with no special affection). Some people seemed to be scandalized at that, but I am sure all of them realized I was trying to be a good priest to all.

Then Emil struck at the core of the problem:

> I was raised in this parish. There are people here, relatives and friends, who are superior to me (in age, in school, etc.) Some find it difficult to look up to me as their spiritual superior. They do not say anything, but from the way they act and the way they perform their spiritual obligations, I know they find me a great moral obstacle.

> It is in consideration of these people who will not complain or say anything but who really need a 'strange' Bohemian priest that I am writing this letter. My conscience tells me to do it because their souls are at stake. Some of these people feel that I still remember and hold against them things they did in former years. I could tell them a hundred times that all is forgotten—yet they will not be assured but will hold back and be afraid.

> That is the human element and it creates a serious moral obstacle. To remove it, I try to be humble and kind as possible. Your Excellency, I am sure you understand that I am most anxious someone be given them who can be, as St. Paul described it, 'All things to all men.'

> When I was ordained, I was determined to 'spend myself' for God. I was determined to do that cheerfully, no matter in what circumstances I would be placed or how hard a

Front, **Elizabeth ("Bessie") Kapaun and Enos Kapaun.**
Rear, **Emil Kapaun**

Photo property of Eugene Kapaun

life I would be asked to lead. That is why I volunteered for
the army and that is why today I would a thousand times
rather be working, deprived of all ordinary comforts, being a
true 'Father' to all my people, than by living in a nice comfortable place but with my conscience telling me that I am
an obstacle to many.[3]

His message was unmistakable and twofold: Kapaun wanted
to leave Pilsen and the bishop already knew that he wanted to become a military chaplain. This time Bishop Winkelmann agreed. A
few weeks later Father John Vesecky, Kapaun's seminary classmate, replaced him as pastor of St. John Nepomucene church and
Kapaun received permission to join the army.

Surprisingly, his decision pleased Enos and Bessie. They had
reached the conclusion that their son needed more freedom than
the assignment in Pilsen allowed. But before leaving, Kapaun typed
for Father Vesecky a list of the observances which were likely to
please the Bohemian people of the parish.

Kapaun began his military career eagerly in August 1944 among
a class of 145 prospective chaplains. Clergymen of many faiths went
into uniform at the chaplains' training school at Fort Devens, Massachusetts where they prepared for duty in all theaters of wartime
operations.

Government regulations required the fledgling chaplains to be
as healthy as any other soldiers. Kapaun's military records described
a five feet nine inches tall male, weighing 150 pounds, with good
posture. The medical report recommended that one of his upper
and two of his lower front teeth should be restored.

Marches of 15 miles a day, classroom work as varied as lessons in chemical warfare and military sanitation, and rigorous cal-
isthenics invigorated the rookie first lieutenant. German prisoners
of war prepared the chaplains' meals, and Kapaun soon noticed
that their cooking had increased his weight by four pounds.

"In the evening I feel as fresh as a young calf," he wrote to his
parents. "Cannot figure it out, a mile walk is like a short stroll."
However, the infiltration training course worried Kapaun. Crawling
under live machine gun fire did not bother him, but he was concerned about some overweight classmates who were not close enough
to the ground as they wiggled under the bullets streaking overhead.

Despite such hazards Kapaun quickly found that he liked military life. Even before he completed his brief indoctrination in October 1944, he wrote to his friend Gerald Franta, who had been pro-
moted to corporal, "They want to toughen us up in a hurry and I
really enjoy it."[4]

The classroom instruction taught Kapaun rules which he would put to use not only in World War II, but later in combat in Korea and while he was a prisoner of war. He learned that a chaplain must promote the religious life of everyone in his unit; he must travel from outpost to outpost when his troops are scattered; he must comfort the sick and wounded. Above all, Kapaun learned that he must be ready to minister to soldiers of all faiths.[5]

While he was stationed at Fort Devens, Kapaun showed that he still was as generous as the young priest who taught the grade school children in Pilsen. The Chaplain Aid Association from the Diocese of Wichita gave him a kit for saying Mass. Kapaun knew that it was intended to be a gift and that nothing more than a thank-you note was expected of him. Nevertheless, he reciprocated by sending $150 to the surprised donor. Another time Kapaun received a paycheck for $250 and immediately forwarded it to his father as a birthday present.

Upon the completion of his training, the army assigned the new Chaplain Kapaun to the 4th Service Command at Camp Wheeler, Georgia. The scenery there was beautiful, yet the farmer in uniform noticed that this was not wheat country and the soil was poor. Kapaun actually had little time to observe his surroundings. He was happy at Camp Wheeler, but very busy. With 19,000 troops, women soldiers, military families, and civilians living at the post there were enough hospital visits, marriages, and religious services to keep any clergyman constantly on the move.

As he traveled around the base, Kapaun became aware of widespread cursing and indecency among the troops and that angered him. He chose the pages of the Camp Wheeler's newspaper, *Spoke*, to remind his huge congregation of its obligation to God: "If personal opinion is to guide our life, then we might as well throw away our laws, even the laws of God, and proceed to live our life by personal opinion. There is, however, one serious drawback in this procedure: We have a Master who is checking up on us. And this Master is very strict and exacting." Working among soldiers obviously demanded different skills than counseling civilians in a rural parish, and Kapaun told Bishop Winkelmann that he had much to learn.

Kapaun was one of only two Catholic chaplains at Camp Wheeler. Within a couple of months after his arrival, the workload had become so heavy that his monthly report appealed for more priests to be assigned to the base. Still, Kapaun found the soldiers "willing and worthy" and he enjoyed helping them.

By February 1945 the army had transferred Kapaun again. His travels began after a ten-day stopover at Miami Beach, Florida.

Kapaun received cholera and other inoculations there, while awaiting his orders for an overseas assignment. On March 4 he and four
other clergymen took off in a military airplane.

By a quirk of fate one of the other passengers was Chaplain
William S. Bowdern, who later became rector of a high school in
Wichita, Kansas which was named in honor of Kapaun. Ironically,
Chaplains Bowdern and Kapaun never met again after they reached
their destination. However, a few months later Bowdern submitted
a report which praised Kapaun's work in caring for the religious
needs of the American soldiers.

At first the chaplains did not know where they were headed.
Only after the aircraft was over the Atlantic Ocean did they learn
that they were traveling to the China-India-Burma theatre of wartime operations. For someone who had seldom ventured beyond the
borders of Kansas and Missouri, Kapaun's journey was eye-open-
ing; stops at Bermuda, the Azores, Casablanca, Tripoli, Cairo,
Abadan, Karachi and New Delhi.[6] The flight over Bethlehem was
especially poignant. "Imagine the thrill to be up in the clouds where
the angels of the Nativity had sung," he later told Bishop
Winkelmann.

Kapaun's trip ended in New Delhi and he remained there two
weeks, except for an unexpected opportunity to visit the Taj Mahal.
Soon thereafter he received orders instructing him to move on to
Bhamo and Lashio in Burma for his permanent assignments. When
Kapaun reached Bhamo he found a deserted Baptist church and
started work immediately to convert part of the building into a tiny
chapel.

A couple of weeks later the death of President Franklin D.
Roosevelt saddened Americans everywhere. Allied troops conducted
memorial services throughout the world, including a ceremony in
Burma on April 15, 1945. Kapaun delivered the invocation before a
crowd of 9,000 persons, including Chinese and U.S. troops lined up
at attention facing each other. No one imagined on that solemn
occasion that within a few years the armies of the two countries
would be fighting one another.

Most of Kapaun's projects were more routine. Yet he came to
the conclusion that "...the 'insignificant' things are part of our work
and offer a good opportunity for patience and perseverance." Still,
he admitted to Bishop Winkelmann that sometimes his job was
strenuous. In one month, Kapaun noted, he traveled 2,500 miles by
jeep and airplane to visit scattered outposts.[7]

Kapaun celebrated Mass several times on Sundays at whatever locations were available, in Red Cross facilities, army mess
halls and theatres and in native villages where he ministered to

soldiers, refugees, and local civilians alike. Much to his delight, the Burmese children responded in church as readily as the kids back home in Pilsen.

Catholic church rules instructed each chaplain to furnish church officials in the United States with an account of his activities during the previous month. So Kapaun dutifully reported how many Masses he had said and how many miles he had traveled. Sometimes, if the troops were stationed close enough, Kapaun bicycled to pray with them. On other occasions he went by airplane or drove a one-quarter ton truck. The mountainous and tortuous route over General Joseph Stillwell's Burma Road took Kapaun, in his words, "...above the clouds sometimes."

Even the rainy season did not dissuade him. Monsignor George Usher told how every week Kapaun drove to Lashio, a journey of more than 200 miles over nearly impassable roads. Occasionally his trips were dangerous. "Once my pilot and I escaped a very serious accident by about 30 seconds," was how he described one close call to Bishop Winkelmann.[8]

Despite the time-consuming pace Kapaun never lost contact with his friends in Kansas. A priest back home wrote inviting him to go hunting for jack rabbits when he returned. Ever the priest, Kapaun wrote to a young acquaintance in Pilsen and encouraged her to join the church. She accepted his suggestion and became a Catholic.[9]

Other correspondents constantly reminded Kapaun about farming. A friend mentioned that the wheat crop in Kansas was record-breaking. Another letter, written a day earlier, said that it was not. Kapaun's travels gave him opportunities to observe the differences between farming in Kansas and Burma. For instance, one of his letters compared growing wheat at home with rice farming in Asia using plows drawn by water buffaloes.

Kapaun frequently came into contact with Catholic priests and sisters who were serving in Burma and India as missionaries. When he learned that some had been imprisoned by the Japanese and had returned to their work after being released, he openly admired their zeal. "Yes, one cannot help but be impressed that the Catholic Church is one and the same the whole world over; even little children are able to notice that," Kapaun commented to Bishop Winkelmann.[10]

One of the reports which Kapaun sent to church officials proudly announced that American soldiers in Burma had constructed a church and school for the sisters. His GIs also collected $1,700 to help the missionaries. These accomplishments may have been inspired by Kapaun's good example, since he contributed part of his military pay to assist the native children. The local clergy revered this warm-hearted army chaplain not only for his charitable leadership, but also because, in one man's words "...he was a great listener."

The diligent efforts of these missionaries impressed Kapaun so much that they almost changed his career. He told Usher that after he finished his military service he hoped to return home, join the St. Columban's Mission Society and come back to Burma. However, when World War II ended in August 1945, Kapaun did not leave for the United States. Instead, in the middle of September, the army reassigned him from Burma to Ledo, India.

The chaplain surprised his friends when he mentioned that he liked that part of the world. His letter to Winkelmann in November 1945 also left no doubt about his choice of a career. He preferred military duty instead of civilian life in a parish: "I enjoy my work very much, in fact, I have been very happy since the day you told me you were releasing me for the armed forces."[11] Evidently people were equally pleased with the easy-going priest who was known to everyone by his corn cob pipe. "The only thing that he was hard on was matches," said Usher.

His military superiors appreciated Kapaun's work. That was apparent from an endorsement which an officer attached to one of Kapaun's monthly reports:

> The untiring, diligent work of Chaplain Kapaun is indeed commendable. Since he has become a member of the Battalion there has been a definite increase of interest in religious activities by all members of this command. Without regard to his personal comfort he has worked day and night to serve troops from Ledo to Myitkyina.[12]

As soon as World War II ended, thousands of American troops began rapidly to leave Burma and India on their way back to the U.S. Kapaun's Latin class of eight students soon dwindled to two.[13] Even so, there were a few soldiers under his care who remained 170 miles away. He was determined to reach them. "...[t]he few are as precious as the many," Kapaun wrote, "and I believe that a priest who would refuse to go out just for a few would be seriously neglecting his duty."

It became apparent to Kapaun that he would be among the last of the Americans to depart for home. Toward the close of 1945 he wrote to Emil and Vicki Melcher, "Maybe we will make it for next Christmas if God keeps us alive that long. Really by rights I should be a dead fellow now. Had some narrow escapes."[14] His friends were left in suspense, because the letter did not contain any further details.

In addition to the customary socks and cigars Kapaun received a special present at Christmas that year. He was elevated from first lieutenant to captain. The promotion resulted in part from the recommendation of Kapaun's commanding officer, who described the chaplain as "...an untiring, conscientious worker." But Christmas in 1945 proved to be even more heartwarming for Kapaun. He celebrated midnight Mass in New Delhi before a packed congregation of American soldiers and Indian civilians.[15]

Realizing that the end of hostilities would lead to his discharge from military service, Kapaun began to think about his future. Catholic chaplains were being advised to retain reserve commissions in the event that the army needed them again. He still wondered whether he could serve people better as a chaplain instead of returning to work as a parish priest.

Kapaun expressed his dilemma to Bishop Winkelmann early in 1946. The style of his letter was familiar:

> In regard to becoming a Regular Army Chaplain, I would hesitate to assume such a burden, especially since the type of life itself is filled with so many 'unclerical circumstances' and one is so hampered in trying to lead a normal priestly life. However, someone surely has to take up the burden; and if you should decide that I ought to do it, I would accept it as the will of God and try to make the best of it.[16]

A typical 'unclerical circumstance' occurred in Delhi. Kapaun and other soldiers were chosen to conduct an inventory at the Army Post Exchange and he willingly joined in the 'unclerical' assignment. Life in India seemed less frenzied after the war ended. It was so calm sometimes that at the beginning of 1946, Kapaun could write to Monsignor Sklenar, "Nothing new here, only a revolution may shortly arrive."[17] Indeed, the following year India won its freedom from the British Empire in a relatively peaceful transfer of power.

At last, in April 1946, Kapaun received orders to return to the U.S. He turned in his English bicycle at the army supply office, said his good-byes and boarded the U.S.S. *Marine Adder* at Calcutta. The uneventful voyage to San Francisco, including a stop at Shanghai, lasted almost a month.

Chaplain Kapaun became simply Father Kapaun again at Fort Douglas, Utah where he received his final pay of $870.89. The army mustered him out of active service on June 4, 1946. Military life had not been all bad, for Kapaun's discharge papers disclosed that he had gained 20 pounds while in uniform.

As soon as Kapaun become a civilian again he returned to Conception Abbey for a religious retreat. Bishop Winkelmann

Emil Kapaun, *left*, **and Eugene Kapaun**
Photo property of Eugene Kapaun

suggested that he relax until August 1. However, a few days of prayer and rest invigorated Kapaun and he volunteered to supervise the parish at Strong City, Kansas while the pastor there went on vacation.

Kapaun made a quick transition to his pre-war status as a parish priest. He served briefly at Spearville and then at Hutchinson, both in Kansas. But even during those assignments, he looked toward his future. The GI Bill of Rights, which paid for the education of thousands of former servicemen, was available to Kapaun and he intended to use it. The University of Innsbruck in Austria, where Kapaun hoped to study theology, was his first choice.

The GI Bill permitted war veterans to start classes within four years after they were discharged from military service. Bishop Winkelmann saw no reason for a delay. He decided that Kapaun should begin studies immediately at Catholic University of America in Washington, D.C. The master's degree program would qualify him as an accredited teacher for both Catholic and public high schools in Kansas.

For several reasons, Kapaun was hesitant about returning to school so quickly. He urged the bishop to let him wait and listed several arguments: the Diocese of Wichita needed him because a few priests had died; after two years in the army he doubted that he could handle a strenuous course of study; he preferred to work in a parish, and besides, there was no room for him at Catholic University.

The last objection appeared to be valid, but it concerned not whether Kapaun would attend graduate school, but merely where. Bishop Winkelmann reconsidered and decided that Kapaun should go to St. Louis University. He contacted a pastor in that city to make housing arrangements and assured him that Kapaun was an "...'anima candida,' a noble priestly gentleman." Winkelmann's recommendation continued: "He is a studious fellow and I know that night life, shows, etc. does not appeal to him."

Whether Kapaun might have become attracted to the night life in St. Louis never was tested. At the last moment a room, albeit in one of the oldest residence halls, became available at Catholic University and he began work toward his master of education degree in October 1946.[18]

As soon as school started, the new student answered a questionnaire. In what sports did he participate? Softball, basketball, soccer, handball. What were his hobbies or special interests? Landscaping. Could Kapaun actually have learned to enjoy pruning and cutting grass while under the stern supervision of Father Sklenar?

With a headstart of six graduate credits for his military experiences, Kapaun started work on several courses in education along with classes in German and history. At first Kapaun worried whether at age 30 he had been away from textbooks for too long. That might have been the reason why he prepared so thoroughly for his classes. His correspondence and papers relating to his courses eventually filled half a trunk. A notation in Kapaun's graduate school files, "As long as the U.N. offers some hope, we should cooperate....", surprisingly previewed the official U.S. justification for entering the war in Korea.

Once Kapaun resumed the habit of studying regularly he found that he enjoyed it. He was a conscientious student, remaining at his desk sometimes from early morning until 1:30 A.M. But since Kapaun was training to become a teacher, he also arranged to observe classes in the public schools of the District of Columbia.

The university required each student to select a topic and write a dissertation in order to earn a master's degree. The subject which Kapaun chose was "A Study of the Accreditation of Courses of Religion in the Secondary Schools of the U.S." He decided to collect the information that he needed by writing to the superintendents of education in all of the states and territories. Educators who reviewed the final product reached the conclusion that Kapaun's thesis was the first nationwide inquiry into how many American public schools gave credit for courses in religion.

Kapaun had to pay his expenses while he was living in Washington, D.C. Fortunately, he had saved some money during his years in the army. The amount was not sufficient, however, to afford much recreation or the "night life" that Bishop Winkelmann had mentioned. Once in a while Kapaun went bicycling on Sunday afternoons. That was not enough exercise to control his weight, which rose to 175 pounds.

In fact, there was hardly enough time at the university for any activity except classwork. However, the Cana Institute in Washington invited him to lecture about how parents could protect the morals of their children, and he readily accepted the opportunity. Kapaun also offered Mass regularly and sometimes he helped the local clergy at Fort Myers, Virginia and at the nearby Shrine of the Immaculate Conception.

During his first year in Washington Kapaun received the news that Bishop Mark Carroll had succeeded Bishop Winkelmann as head of the Diocese of Wichita. He had heard enough about Carroll's background to tell Emmet A. Blaes, a lawyer whom he knew, that his new superior was "...a very good man..."[19]

Kapaun promptly wrote the first of many letters to Bishop Carroll and congratulated his new superior. Then, wasting little time on pleasantries, he requested that the bishop approve his schedule for the summer of 1947. He sought permission to remain at Catholic University and continue work on his dissertation. Kapaun also was eager to put on his army uniform again. Carlisle Barracks, Pennsylvania had scheduled a one-month training program in June for 60 reserve chaplains. Kapaun asked the bishop if he could attend.

Bishop Carroll approved the plan. However, the chaplains' refresher course influenced Kapaun more than either he or the bishop might have anticipated. Only a couple of weeks after the training ended, another letter from Washington appeared on the bishop's desk.

Kapaun was being pulled between his yearning to return to military service and his obligation to continue as a diocesan priest. The army was winning the mental tug-of-war. Other religions believed that Catholics were neglecting the spiritual needs of soldiers of their own faith, he wrote to Carroll. To alleviate that problem, Father Kapaun wished to become Chaplain Kapaun again after he received his master's degree.

"I do not want to be requesting something that would be contrary to your wishes; but if you can possibly spare me, I surely would love to dedicate myself to this work for a few years," Kapaun told Bishop Carroll.[20] However, his new religious superior did not consent, at least not yet.

While he was awaiting an answer from the bishop's office, Kapaun decided reluctantly that he lacked enough money to spend Christmas with his family in Kansas that year. So instead he remained at the university and helped to celebrate the Christmas services in the parish at Bowie, Maryland.

During the 1947 holiday season Kapaun corresponded with Sister M. Euphrasia, his ninth grade teacher at Pilsen. Even though he had almost completed the curriculum which he needed for a degree in education, Kapaun had made the decision that he was not capable of teaching high school students. He summarized his thoughts for Sister Euphrasia:

> After attending the University I have begun to realize what a tremendous task it is to be a teacher. Surely God must have a very rich reward for those of you who have dedicated your lives to such a work. I hope and pray that God will never inflict upon me such a task, for it would be

calamitous to expect an ungifted person to assume such responsibilities. I am happily convinced that God put me in the class of people who can admire teachers but not hope to imitate them.[21]

When Kapaun's classes ended in February 1948 he notified Carroll that he planned to purchase a car and drive back to Kansas. He explained that it would be cheaper to acquire a car in Washington than in Wichita.

The journey home almost proved fatal. As Kapaun and a couple of passengers were driving through Missouri an oncoming car tried to pass two other vehicles. Suddenly it swerved into Kapaun's lane. He knew instantly that the only way to avoid a head-on collision was to steer toward a ditch alongside the road.

The car reached the ditch safely, but the impact destroyed it. Both Kapaun and his passengers were thrown out of the vehicle, and luckily they were unhurt. No wonder that when Kapaun finally reached Wichita, the bishop told him to take a vacation.

Kapaun received his Master of Education degree in June 1948. By that time he had begun his last assignment as a parish priest.

FIVE

Back into Uniform

Bishop Carroll intended that Kapaun's assignment in April 1948 to take charge of Holy Trinity parish in Timken, Kansas would only be temporary. The bishop planned eventually to transfer him to the diocesan education department in Wichita. Once Kapaun started his duties there, his training in education at Catholic University could be put to use.

The interim decision to send Kapaun to Timken resulted in part from the continual unhappiness in his native parish, St. John Nepomucene. The Bohemians in Pilsen persisted in disagreeing with younger members of the church over whether English should be spoken during religious services. Their repeated complaints to the bishop eventually forced the appointment of a new pastor.

Among other things, the replacement had to speak Bohemian. Only a few priests in the diocese were familiar with that language. Father Aloysius Clupny, the pastor at Timken, was one of them, so Carroll switched him to St. John Nepomucene. That move, however, did not completely solve the problem. The smaller Holy Trinity parish also needed a Bohemian-speaking pastor, and Kapaun's timely return from Washington provided the solution.

Although he remained there barely six months, Kapaun endeared himself to the people of Timken. "He was like a breath of fresh air; young, ambitious and so kind," Virginia Mozouch, a parishioner at Holy Trinity, recalled.[1]

No task was too difficult or beneath his dignity. Kapaun mowed the grass in the church cemetery, something that no priest had done before. The new pastor made other changes, introducing more religious services and delighting the parishioners by performing a double wedding. Kapaun confirmed Anita Pechanic just before she was scheduled to give birth to her second child and she never forgot how solicitous he was about her condition.[2]

Kapaun proved to be as practical as he was spiritual. When Helen Kapaun's mother urged her to hear two Masses on Sunday, he advised Helen to prepare dinner instead of attending church a second time.[3] He also brought smiles to the faces of the local Bohemian congregation by diplomatically preaching in their language as well as English.

The assignment to Timken required considerable energy, but Kapaun was up to the task. He actually tired the parishioners who worked with him. On one occasion he called for volunteers to relocate some gravel on the church grounds. Four men showed up and took turns loading and moving the wheelbarrow. Instead of merely supervising the project their pastor insisted on helping them. Kapaun pushed the men and himself so hard that when he left temporarily to handle some parish business the others immediately sat down for a rest.

"Do I remember him? He used to bowl with me and the boys," remarked Joe Fiala, the proprietor of the bowling alley in Timken. "The Father was a man's man and one of the best sports I have ever known."[4] A person's religion made no difference to Kapaun; he liked everyone.[5]

Another priest recalled the congenial side of Kapaun's personality. He told jokes, but never any which tarnished his clerical dignity or made fun of another person. At time when guests visited he offered them liquor, but rarely drank himself. He enjoyed his cigars and pipe. On occasions when Kapaun chatted with his friends about baseball and other sports, he knew as much as they did.

In Kansas, and later in Korea, Kapaun projected his religion by example instead of speeches. "Never be ashamed to let people know that you pray," he advised Fred Tuzicka. Kapaun never argued to make a point. The quiet priest would not force anyone to talk about Catholicism, but if the subject arose, he discussed it avidly. Indeed, Kapaun found that a humorous approach was more effective at gaining someone's attention.[6] He was, in one observer's words, "a young Levite."

Tuzicka admitted later that Kapaun saved his religious vocation. Discouraged and ready to quit the seminary, he reviewed the problem with his parents. They suggested that he speak to their pastor. So Tuzicka went to the rectory at Holy Trinity church. The door usually was locked, but when the seminarian arrived he saw that it was open.

"There's my seminarian. Come on in," came Kapaun's shouted greeting from inside. Tuzicka found the pastor hard at work making candles for the children of the parish. After the two men talked Tuzicka changed his mind and later became a priest.[7]

Even though everyone liked Kapaun, the members of the parish in Timken had a big problem which indirectly burdened him. The church building had burned several years earlier and the local Catholics had been forced to attend Mass in the basement. The makeshift arrangement failed to satisfy anyone. The roof over the basement leaked and the parishioners wanted badly to rebuild their church.

Kapaun threw his energy into the rehabilitation project. Other religious organizations had donated pews for Holy Trinity's rebuilt church, but they needed sanding and finishing. It was a dusty, sweaty job, especially during the summer, yet the new pastor spent many a hot afternoon doing the work himself.[8]

The congregation in Holy Trinity parish realized that the reconstruction of their church would require a sizeable amount of money. It was apparent to Kapaun that he must lead a fund raising drive among his parishioners. He also knew that the Catholic families in Timken worked hard for their money, and that they were determined to be involved in how their pastor spent what they put into the collection basket. Kapaun worried that some tense meetings lay ahead.[9] The same contentious atmosphere that had bothered him at St. John Nepomucene parish seemed to be brewing again.

Kapaun's assignment in Timken ended after barely six months, before he had to face the financial problems of the parish. However, his career from then on did not proceed according to Bishop Carroll's plan. The former chaplain could not shake off his desire to re-enter military service. "If my Bishop would give me permission, I would volunteer [for extended duty overseas]," he responded to an army survey in April 1948.

Kapaun knew from earlier experiences that the non-clerical aspects of a chaplain's life might slow his spiritual growth. Yet, as hundred of army chaplains transferred to the newly created U.S. Air Force,[10] he felt that the U.S. government needed experienced clergymen, particularly those with his educational and wartime background, to help the thousands of young men and women who were still entering military service.

Despite the never-ending decisions which he faced in Timken, Kapaun had become comfortable there and grew to love the people.[11] He began to question whether he liked it enough to change his plans about re-entering the army. Kapaun's conflicting emotions revealed themselves in another letter to Bishop Carroll in September 1948:

If the choice depended only on personal desires, I would never relinquish my work here in Timken for work in the Army. But in matters such as these, I believe a priest should be desirous of offering himself even though he personally would prefer to remain in the diocese. I have grown to love these people very much; but, in conscience, I believe I should offer myself for work in the Armed Forces, especially in this crisis.[12]

The letter referred to tensions between the United States and the Soviet Union which had flared up in 1948 when the Russians blocked land access into West Berlin. The United States reacted with a round-the-clock airlift which continued to supply the beleaguered former German capital city. As a consequence, America's military might become committed to the Cold War against the Russians, and chaplains were as necessary as ever.

Oddly enough, the aggravating situation at St. John Nepomucene parish at that time helped to solve Kapaun's dilemma. Father Clupny tired of the factions in Pilsen and sought reinstatement as pastor of Holy Trinity parish. When Bishop Carroll agreed to the transfer in September 1948, that created an opportunity for Kapaun to leave Timken and to return to military uniform.[13]

Kapaun really wanted a total change. His application to re-enter the army was clear. It explicitly asked for extended active duty— outside the State of Kansas.

Outwardly Kapaun appeared ambivalent about returning to military duty. He confided to an acquaintance that he preferred the quiet life of a country pastor. Before leaving for the army, Kapaun lunched with Father George N. Schmidt, his seminary classmate. He mentioned to Schmidt that he was uncertain about going back into the military life, but he was accepting the bishop's wishes. Kapaun's writings, however, left little doubt that he really wanted to become a chaplain again.

Leaving Timken was not easy. There was plenty to do before Kapaun departed. The grounds surrounding Holy Trinity church needed a pre-winter clean-up before the incoming pastor arrived. So Kapaun told the men of the parish to bring their grass hooks and rakes and join him in sprucing up the property. The job of refurbishing the pews also had to be completed. But the hardest part was telling the people that he was leaving. Some cried when Kapaun announced the news.

"You know, Fred, there is one thing which a priest must be willing to do, to go anywhere that the Bishop has need of him. Sometimes it is difficult to leave a place, especially after a person has fallen in love with it and the people, but the will of God comes first," he wrote to seminarian Tuzicka.[14]

Before reporting for duty at Fort Bliss, Texas, Kapaun was as busy as ever, visiting his family and attending a religious retreat at Pius X Monastery in Labadie, Missouri. Years earlier, he had taught his students at St. John Nepomucene school that the priesthood was no place for a lazy person.

Even in the few weeks' transition between civilian and military life Kapaun was drawn back to Pilsen. Father Ignatius Strecker had arranged to go deer hunting in Colorado when the mailman delivered a notice which stated that he had been appointed pastor at St. John Nepomucene. As he wondered who might supervise the parish while he was away, the doorbell rang at the rectory. There stood his temporary replacement, a smiling Chaplain Kapaun wearing his army uniform. He was looking for someplace to stay while the government processed his re-enlistment papers.

Strecker welcomed his unexpected guest not only because now he could take his vacation, but also because he needed help learning the ropes in his new parish. Kapaun searched his old desk in the rectory and retrieved the notes about procedures in St. John Nepomucene church which he had prepared years earlier. He even showed Strecker how to start the building's heating system.

The church grounds in Pilsen needed cleaning as much as the property in Timken. While the new pastor was gone on his hunting trip, Father Sklenar's skilled former gardener/assistant pastor recruited a group of parishioners to handle that task. The most important event during that period, and undoubtedly the happiest, occurred just before Kapaun left for Texas: He performed the wedding of his brother, Eugene, and his bride, Helen.

When World War II ended, the army shut down parts of the huge base at Fort Bliss. Kapaun arrived in November 1948 after a three-day drive with his friend, John Maier, to find that the post chapel had been vacant for two years. A layer of dirt and sand had accumulated in the building and Kapaun's first job was another clean-up project. Soon the chapel was tidy enough for religious services.

The office that he was assigned was empty, devoid of chairs, tables, typewriter, or any kind of equipment. In fact, Kapaun was forced to write letters with his typewriter resting on his knees.[15] A bunk was the only piece of furniture that the chaplain could call his own.

The little hut where Kapaun lived was so open to the weather that sandstorms blew in a fresh coating of dust every few minutes. He described his surroundings to a friend from Kansas, "I am happy to be back with the 'boys' again, but this is really a rough place. The wind just now nearly took the roof off my shack."

Hundreds of ants made living uncomfortable, but Kapaun did not complain. He simply reported events as he saw them; dust storms thick enough to prevent a driver from seeing two feet in front of his vehicle, and cold weather that "...goes right through a fellow and makes him shiver like a jitter bug."[16]

In that case, wasn't Fort Bliss a misnomer? Tuzicka inquired. Army life was strenuous, Kapaun conceded, but he liked it anyway.[17] Besides, Christmas was just around the corner and there was work to be done. Disregarding the inconveniences of his new home, Kapaun quickly organized a choir and arranged for two decorated Christmas trees inside the chapel and another outside.[18]

Conditions at Fort Bliss were about to change dramatically. Some 35,000 soldiers were being shipped there to begin training in January 1949. Between 40 and 60 percent of the newcomers to the 35th Anti-Aircraft Brigade were thought to be Catholics. Yet Kapaun was one of only two Catholic chaplains on the post.[19] As was the case at Camp Wheeler, there were not enough priests to serve everyone.

Kapaun almost started his career at Fort Bliss on the wrong foot. Arriving tired and dirty after a long drive, he immediately went into the shower room where he found that another occupant was washing himself. Kapaun introduced himself as one of the chaplains. The other man replied that he was the commanding general of the base.

Somehow this casual meeting made the wrong impression on the general. He decided that the new chaplain was not performing his duties quickly enough and several days later he admonished him. Kapaun disagreed and defended his conduct in no uncertain terms. Once they cleared the air the two men got along well. Kapaun discovered later that the commanding officer merely wanted to be sure that his chaplains were doing a good job.

Kapaun, too, was keenly interested in performing well. He was constantly dealing with everyone around him, baptizing the soldiers' children, visiting the sick, and instructing converts to Catholicism. His daily schedule was as diverse as joining the troops on the firing range and leading the Catholic troops in the Stations of the Cross. In between these duties, Kapaun also found time to serve as interim custodian of the St. Michael's Catholic Fund. When he added up his activities he found that he had worked continuously for six months before taking a day off.[20]

In his own descriptive words, Kapaun was "...as busy as a bee in a clover patch." Consequently, he did not have much opportunity

Emil Kapaun

Photo by Les Broadstreet, Wichita

for recreation. According to Walter J. Mullen, Jr., an officer who shared a two-man hut with Kapaun, usually the best that the chaplain could manage was an evening sitting on his bunk reading.[21]

The chaplains at Fort Bliss had to handle a variety of problems among the young soldiers. Some had marital disagreements. Others could not pay the money they owed. Kapaun and Chaplain Clifton Bell guaranteed the debt of one soldier, and later they learned the consequences firsthand. When the soldier defaulted, they each paid $148.50 in installments to satisfy the obligation.

The education courses which Kapaun had studied at Catholic University proved their value over and over again when he was instructing the soldiers. In one month, December 1948, he lectured about morality to more than 2,000 men. Kapaun worked especially hard to set a good example because he noticed how closely the troops watched him. Just his presence at Fort Bliss and his talks with the soldiers produced results. Four men confided that they intended to study for the priesthood.

Most soldiers look forward to receiving mail, and Kapaun was no exception. When his friends from Pilsen neglected him he teased them that their correspondence was so rare that it had become precious. While Kapaun also sent letters frequently, he often criticized himself for not writing often enough. However, he decided to contact each soldier's parents to assure them how much he wanted to help their son and ultimately sent dozens of letters to the families.

Although his duties were different, the chaplain shared the same discomforts as any rifle-toting GI. The nights were getting colder in mid-November, but the hut where he slept still was unheated.[22] He liked to do the things that the other men did. When Kapaun was given the opportunity to fire the first shot from one of the army's most powerful anti-aircraft guns, he jumped at the chance. "My, that is a thrill," he exclaimed. "We shot at targets about 5 miles away pulled by an airplane."[23] The chaplain was a familiar figure in the field during training exercises, driving his jeep to visit the troops and wearing a pistol belt which carried his canteen and first aid kit, but no weapon.[24] Yet he seldom passed up an opportunity to practice on the rifle range.

One time Kapaun and another soldier were driving through the camp. As they passed by, a group of GIs standing alongside the road shouted, "Hi, Father!", but he failed to acknowledge them. His companion finally turned and said, "Hey, Father, can't you hear those guys saying hello to you?" Kapaun suddenly realized that he had been daydreaming and had unwittingly ignored the soldiers. Uttering an "Oh! Shit!", he spun the jeep around and headed back to greet the men.

Kapaun usually was more aware of what was happening around him. For example, on St. Patrick's Day in 1949, he arranged a special service at Fort Bliss for some Irish immigrants who had joined the army. Later, the parents of one man thanked him by sending a fresh shamrock.

The busy pace of Kapaun's daily activities came to an abrupt halt in the spring of 1949. He became ill from blood poisoning and was forced into bed for two days, followed by a short period on crutches. He had to rearrange his schedule again that year when his car broke down. Something was obviously wrong because the only way that he could start it was to park at the top of an incline and then give it a push.[25] Like it or not, Kapaun had to repair the vehicle because he intended to give it to Eugene and Helen instead of taking it along if he were assigned overseas.

The soldiers were finishing their training at Fort Bliss late in 1949. They would be sent overseas, but Kapaun did not expect to accompany them.[26] There still was a shortage of priests in the army, and the chaplain believed that he would be kept at the base in Texas. Therefore, he was surprised to receive news in December that he was being reassigned.

The orders notified Kapaun to report to Seattle, Washington by January 2, 1950. That left plenty of time for an 18-day leave, including his first Christmas at home in several years. But it was scarcely long enough for everything that Kapaun scheduled for himself: a week-long spiritual retreat at Conception Abbey; a visit to friends in Timken with a hasty return to Pilsen ahead of a snowstorm;[27] lunch with a seminary classmate during which Kapaun noted that army service would deprive him of opportunities to work in the field of education; a two-hour visit to boost the spirits of an acquaintance who was recovering from a spinal operation.

Aware of the uncertainties of military life, especially in a foreign country, Kapaun also arranged to sign his will during the vacation. It left most of his small estate in equal shares to his parents and whoever was the bishop of Wichita at the time of his death. However, the document included one unusual provision. Kapaun decided that money which he had received to say Masses must be held in trust. Therefore, the will stated that if he died the unused balance of that fund must be delivered to another priest to celebrate the Masses.

Kapaun returned to the rectory of St. John Nepomucene church once again and lived there during the Christmas season of 1949. He made sure to be present for all of the holiday activities in his home town. Kapaun remembered the fun at the Christmas parties when he was a pupil in the parish school, so that year he agreed to play Santa Claus.[28]

The women in the parish Altar Society invited Kapaun to speak at their meeting. He used the occasion to reassure them that their sons in military service were well cared for, both physically and spiritually. There was even time during the holidays for Kapaun to give driving lessons. The pastor at St. John Nepomucene had just bought a car and needed instructions about how to handle it.

The religious aspects of Christmas were the most meaningful. Kapaun celebrated Midnight Mass on Christmas Eve and said three Masses the next morning, yet he still managed to spend part of the day with his family.

Enos and Bessie enjoyed their son's short visit in Pilsen more than anyone. If he could not come home for his mother's duck and chicken dinners, she sent the meals to the rectory. The festive mood unfortunately ended on December 26. Although he did not know where the army was sending him or how long he would remain there, Kapaun reminded his family how badly the young soldiers overseas required the guidance of a chaplain. His plans to give his almost new 1949 Plymouth car to Eugene and Helen had to be changed. Kapaun and a friend, Joseph Meysing, needed it to drive to California en route to Seattle.

The first stop was Eugene and Helen's home. Kapaun brought a Christmas gift, a toy dog, for their four-month old daughter, Angela. As his brother departed, Eugene had a feeling that he might never see him again.[29] A friend whom Kapaun met on the way to the west coast also had a premonition that he would not return. Kapaun suspected the same thing; he told another priest that he might not come back. Unfortunately, all of their fears were correct.

Another near-fatal incident marred an otherwise pleasant trip to California. Kapaun and Meysing were driving through Oklahoma one night when headlights loomed up directly in front of them. The accident almost two years ago on Kapaun's way home from Washington, D.C. was being repeated. He spun the wheel and headed off the highway toward the side of the road. But it was too late. The other vehicle smacked the side of his car and raced away into the darkness without stopping.[30]

No one was hurt and Kapaun's car was not disabled. The mishap was almost forgotten by the time the two men reached San Francisco. Kapaun went shopping and purchased a furlined jacket and gloves which the new pastor at Pilsen could wear on his hunting trips. Parting company with Meysing ended with a question, "Well, Joe, when are we going to meet again?"

Kapaun continued driving alone toward Seattle. Growing up in Kansas had accustomed him to hazardous wintertime weather, but the hair-raising drive up the west coast was even more than he expected. He crossed the Golden Gate Bridge in fog so thick that he could barely see the outline of the span. Oregon was colder than California, and Kapaun wondered why so little traffic was going through Grant's Pass. Only when he was headed up the mountain road did Kapaun realize that the surface was covered with ice.

Turning back was impossible, and slowing down might have caused his car either to slide off the precipice which abutted the highway or to smash into wrecked vehicles alongside the roadway.[31] By the time Kapaun reached Fort Lawton in Seattle the man who within a few months would be dodging Communist bullets on the battlefield admitted that the episode "really scared" him.

By mid-January 1950 Kapaun was aboard the troopship U.S.S. *General H. M. Patrick* en route from the United States to Japan. The northern Pacific Ocean was stormy, and at the beginning of the voyage the chaplain and the other soldiers were, in his words, "as sick as dogs."[32] After three days he regained enough strength to celebrate Mass. Kapaun had only limited responsibilities for the rest of the trip. He helped to run the shipboard bingo games and joined in the celebration when the vessel crossed the international dateline.

Kapaun was on deck one day enjoying some fresh air and exercise when another soldier, Anthony Pecoraro, joined him. Their friendly conversation and walks around the deck of the troopship became a daily routine. By the time the *General Patrick* docked at Yokohama early in February the two men knew each other well enough that Pecoraro would remember his shipboard companion as an extraordinary person.

Each man went his separate way when the ship reached Japan. Several months later, Kapaun and Pecoraro met again, this time in a Communist prison camp in North Korea.[33]

SIX

Going to War

Approximately 83,000 American troops under the command of General Douglas MacArthur occupied the defeated nation of Japan in 1950. Their most important assignments were to maintain order and to help a beaten foe. However, a large number of the enlisted personnel were poorly qualified teenagers who were ill-equipped for their job. In fact, approximately 43 percent of them ranked in the army's two lowest aptitude classifications.[1]

Except for many older noncommissioned officers, the enlisted men who served with Kapaun in peacetime Japan often also were immature and lackadaisical. They differed from the GIs whom he had known in India and Burma. The patriotic fervor of World War II no longer inspired some American youths.

Kapaun saw that too many of the troops in Japan were hardly interested in being in the army. They never realized that the military's principal business was, if necessary, to go to war. But the recruiting posters were enticing, and for some young men army duty in a foreign country appeared glamorous.

When they arrived in Japan, however, the soldiers found that peacetime army service was dull. Their routine was far different from a normal family life back in the U.S. It was commonplace to live off base with a Japanese girl friend who, in exchange for cigarettes and food, willingly pressed the soldier's uniforms and shined his shoes. Liquor was plentiful and girls were always available. These conditions led to a languorous attitude which produced many troops who were physically soft and mentally unmotivated.[2]

Kapaun had not been in Japan very long before he reached the conclusion that many GIs needed serious guidance. "I was really surprised that most of our soldiers are below normal in education and knowledge. Many come from the unemployed—and quite a number joined the Army just to get away from home. These lads need a priest very badly," Kapaun lamented to Bishop Carroll.[3]

After training during the week the troops preferred to leave camp on Sunday mornings instead of attending church. Even though Kapaun needed no reminders, Bishop Carroll wrote and repeated why he had allowed him to re-enter the army: the Catholic soldiers would begin to lose their faith if priests were not working constantly to keep them on the right track.

Some of the men practiced their religion, but overall Kapaun was not pleased with the statistics. "This situation, on the surface, looks discouraging, yet we Catholic chaplains have a large field to work in to bring back these 'straying sheep'," Kapaun wrote. Then he added, "My soldiers are not the very best a man can find, but some of them are good boys."

The army assigned Kapaun to the 8th Cavalry Regiment of the 1st Cavalry Division on February 7, 1950. The name suggested horses, Kapaun wrote to Eugene and Helen, but he added, "In fact, we are just plain infantry. You know—walking and marching!! I love it."[4] He even bragged to his brother that his boots were his most comfortable footwear.

Although units of the 1st Cavalry were dispersed around the Kanto Plain on the main Japanese island of Honshu, the division maintained its headquarters at Camp Drake outside Tokyo. One of its officers remarked critically that an assignment there "...served as a place to give senior officers a 'going away present' before they went home and retired." In that respect the 1st Cavalry was similar to other American units in Japan at that time.

Living near the big and bustling capital of Japan was an exciting experience for someone who had grown up on a quiet farm in Kansas. Within a month after his arrival Kapaun survived three earthquakes, one lasting 20 minutes, which frightened Americans and Japanese alike.

The streets of Tokyo were unmarked, Kapaun told his parents, and ran off in every direction. Bicycles and individuals pulling carts crowded the roads. The cars, however, were the most intriguing. Some operated from the heat of a wood-burning stove. If the fuel supply was exhausted, Kapaun explained in a letter to Joseph Meysing, the driver simply burned some twigs which he had gathered along the roadside.[5]

One day as Kapaun walked along the pavement, an old Japanese man approached him. The man stepped into the gutter and bowed. The chaplain returned the greeting and continued on his way. Although that simple gesture expressed Kapaun's unspoken friendship, it failed to satisfy him. He decided that he should study Japanese in order to become acquainted with the local residents.

The least that an American should be able to do, Kapaun told Bishop Carroll, was "to exchange the ordinary pleasantries," with the Japanese citizens. Talking with them was difficult, but, as he observed to Eugene and Helen, "The Japanese babies learn the language—surely we should be able to learn it, too."[6]

At the same time Kapaun continued studying the Czech language. He hoped that he might use it if the army ever transferred him to Europe. A few months later Kapaun happily informed Monsignor Sklenar that he scored higher than he had expected in the army examination in the Czech language.[7]

The 8th Cavalry's new chaplain made friends easily, occasionally joining some of the men for a beer at the officers' club. He also headed into Tokyo once in a while, after shouting to his friend, Phil Moore, "Hey, I'm going to town tonight. Does anyone want anything?"[8]

Kapaun's car, the one which survived the harrowing drive from San Francisco to Seattle, reached Japan during February 1950. He planned to drive from Tokyo to nearby Mount Fuji. In some ways Kapaun was the same as any other tourist, and he intended to photograph the famous mountain scenery.

Since Kapaun's army pay was considerably more than an assistant pastor's salary at St. John Nepomucene parish he bought a new camera and began to settle some debts. He paid off a car loan and also returned money which he had borrowed from his parents. When he heard that Eugene and Helen wanted to buy a house, Kapaun wrote and offered to help them make monthly payments on a mortgage.[9]

Many foreigners in Tokyo made sure to visit the high-walled, closely guarded home of the Japanese emperor. The chaplain was no different from any sightseer. After he had looked at the imperial palace, his observations described his future much better than he understood: "If I had been here 5 years earlier I probably would be in some prison or have to work real hard as a prisoner."[10]

The ordinary citizens of Tokyo were more impressive to the former farmer from Pilsen. His correspondence pictured them as neat, courteous, and unafraid of hard work. The children delighted Kapaun; he called them as plump as balls. Yet some of his other comments about Japan must have shocked his family. He informed Eugene and Helen that for the time being living there was nicer than remaining in Kansas.

Writing continued to be a time-consuming chore. In fact, one day Kapaun sent seven letters. Occasionally he was woefully late in replying to correspondence, but he always caught up and acknowledged every present and letter. Indeed, when the pastor at St. John Nepomucene church mailed Kapaun a gift from Rome, he dispatched a thank-you note before the priest returned to Pilsen.

Kapaun's writing often was long and tailored to his perception of the addressee. Sometimes a letter excluded information that he included in other correspondence because he knew that it would disturb the recipient. Everything that he sent to Bishop Carroll remained friendly, but formal.

What Kapaun wrote to Eugene and Helen was more folksy, but nevertheless even with his own family he still signed, "As ever in Christ, Fr. E. K." While he never lost sight of his status as a priest, it did not stop him from kidding a friend in Kansas, "I think you worry too much, Leonard. Do as I did, join the Army, see the world and put all cares aside."

Enos and Bessie's son was well aware of what information might upset his parents and what news would not alarm them. Kapaun was sure that writing about farming would not disturb them, so his letters usually turned to that subject. For example, the biggest wheat field that he had seen in Japan was the size of the Kapaun garden in Pilsen. Unlike their role in Kansas, women normally participated in cultivating and harvesting the crop.

The local method of farming was different, and Kapaun wanted to let his parents know as delicately as possible how Asians fertilize their crops with human waste. "Some of these rice fields smell as if they were sour," was his awkward analogy.

A regimental chaplain's job, of course, involved more than writing letters. According to army manuals, one of his duties was to guide the molding of the mature character of his men over long periods of purposeful training. Kapaun quickly set out to do exactly what was expected. He and Chaplain Donald Carter took charge of the character guidance program for their battalion.

Corporal Ferguson, Kapaun's assistant, supplied him with a list of 400 Catholic soldiers, almost a quarter of the men in the 8th Cavalry. Next to one soldier's name was the corporal's notation, "I have talked to this man and he wants to see you as soon as he can."

Kapaun's periodic reports to the Catholic Military Ordinate in New York City were thorough accounts of his work. His March 1950 statement summed up a busy month: Masses at Camp King, the Camp Palmer firing range and the regimental chapel on Sundays, Masses at two locations during weekdays, a wedding and several marriage instructions for cavalrymen who were planning nuptials.[11]

The combined efforts of many military chaplains, including Kapaun's column which was published in the 8th Cavalry's newspaper, proved unusually successful in persuading soldiers to attend religious services. The 1949–50 attendance records at the Tokyo Chapel Center revealed a seven-fold increase over a few years earlier. Surprisingly, the chaplains achieved the spiritual growth without using much money. For instance, the Catholic Chaplains' Fund received only $92.84 in the first four months of 1950 and spent about half that much.[12]

Nevertheless, it was disappointing for Kapaun that so few of the Catholic troops in Japan received the sacraments of the Church. Yet, he also was hopeful. "It seems that the soldier that we have today comes from families who had been neglectful. It is a great joy for me to be instrumental in bringing at least a few of them back into the fold," his monthly report commented.[13]

Kapaun reached out to his military flock, physically as well as spiritually. He traveled constantly to visit 8th Cavalry units which were training in the mountains, often enough that during one week his jeep had four flat tires. Once a month during the spring of 1950 he enjoyed a spiritual respite. All of the Catholic chaplains attended a day-long retreat in Tokyo. These gatherings were especially meaningful to Kapaun and he called them "...an oasis in a desert to a weary traveler."

Easter 1950 was a calm and sunny day in Tokyo. Writing to Eugene and Helen about the holy day, Kapaun also described the beauty of the Japanese cherry trees which were in bloom at that time. Celebrating Holy Week in Japan was especially poignant. Perhaps he had forgotten his earlier aspirations when he told Tuzicka, "I never dreamed of being a Missionary, yet here I am in a Mission Land, a pagan land, but one which has received exceptional blessings from God and the way it looks (if Russia does not get in here) many of the Japanese are going to receive the true faith."[14]

Bessie's Easter package to her son arrived in Tokyo several weeks late. According to Kapaun's letter to his brother and sister-in-law, it was damaged "...just like a broken accordion. Mother had put some Easter eggs (candy ones) in it, and they looked like pieces of inner tubes which had torn off after the tire blew out. I laughed until I nearly split. But anyway I still ate them and they were good."[15]

In mid-April it was Kapaun's turn to deliver a week-long series of 15-minute "Morning Meditations" over the U.S. Far East Radio Network.[16] Those daily religious programs had begun shortly after the end of World War II. By 1950, chaplains for the U.S. armed forces were broadcasting to Okinawa and parts of China as well as the main Japanese islands.

Kapaun chose the Beatitudes from Matthew's Gospel[17] as the theme for his five talks. Events that happened to Kapaun during the next year proved that those broadcasts were almost a series of predictions about his own life.

In one of his radio sermons, using the thought "Blest are those persecuted for holiness' sake; the reign of God is theirs," Kapaun spoke about the persecutions of the early Christians. However, what he said actually previewed his own ordeal as a prisoner of the Chinese Communists:

> We can surely expect that in our own lives there will come a time when we must make a choice between being loyal to our faith or of giving allegiance to something else which is either opposed to or not in alliance with our faith. O God, we ask of Thee to give us the courage to be ever faithful to Thee.

Kapaun's remarks about another Beatitude, "Blest too the peacemakers; they shall be called sons of God," may be read now as a description of his own performance on the battlefield a few months later:

> The peace which God gives is a gift which exists even in suffering, in want, and even in time of war. People who try to promote peace and love among their fellow men are peacemakers in the true sense of the word. And the people who try to bring the peace of God to souls are peacemakers of a higher order.

On his 34th birthday, April 20, 1950, the chaplain's talk reminded his listeners to forgive those who offended them. Before his next birthday Kapaun would face the same question: Could he pardon his Chinese captors?[18]

Although the U.S. soldiers in Japan were principally an occupying force, the possibility of a clash between American and Communist armies existed elsewhere in Asia. Those concerns became more serious after June 1949. Secretary of State Dean Acheson announced that South Korea was outside of the U.S. defensive orbit, and American units withdrew from that small Asian country.

By early 1950, government leaders in Washington were becoming more uneasy about Asia. They worried that Communist-dominated North Korea would try to take advantage of the absence of U.S. forces in South Korea and seize control of the entire Korean peninsula. Kapaun nevertheless continued to reassure his parents, "As long as Russia does not drop a bomb on Japan we will be getting along pretty well."

In light of the military tensions in Asia the army instituted a different policy toward its troops in Japan. Early in 1950 the 8th Cavalry Regiment began to change from a peace-keeping force to a battle-ready unit. The government was mindful of General J. Lawton Collins' warning that peacetime duty in a foreign land was the worst possible precondition for combat. With an annual turnover rate of 43 percent among American soldiers it was difficult to develop cohesion and unit pride among the troops. To make matters worse, the 8th Cavalry was seriously understrength.

The army began to tighten up the way that it operated. Local commanders found Japanese workers playing checkers in the army motor pool and fired them. The American soldiers "...were pretty well looked after by the local folks and had a lot of people clean barracks for them and one thing and another. We stopped that," the commander of the 8th Cavalry reported.

The training became more intensive. The troopers maneuvered for several weeks near the snow line on Mount Fuji. Kapaun traveled with them. In May 1950 the chaplain drove 800 miles over narrow mountain roads that lacked guard rails in order to conduct services for the soldiers.[19]

He was proud that his regiment would be ready in case of trouble. "Ours is a combat unit, and if we get into war I guess we will be seeing the real thing again. I sure hope not. The soldiers need a priest as badly as anyone, and I guess I am it," Kapaun wrote to Eugene and Helen. If fighting broke out, he told friends in Timken, the 8th Cavalry would be among the first to go into combat. If that happened, the chaplain expected to be in the thick of battle.

Maneuvers were rugged work, even in springtime. When friends asked Kapaun how he put up with riding a jeep for hundreds of miles, he replied that it was a necessary hardship which was part of his job. "Making 1,100 miles in a jeep on these bumpy mountain roads puts color in a person's cheeks and calluses on the extremity which has to bear the bumps and bruises," Kapaun explained in a report to Bishop Carroll. He continued, "I love this kind of work, even though the figures are not a true scale of one's efforts."[20] The active outdoor life must have improved Kapaun's appetite, because he complained that his uniform was getting tight.

Communism, which so repulsed Kapaun, was visibly active in Japan. The red emblem with its hammer and sickle flew above party headquarters in Tokyo. American military officials expected confrontations with Communist civilians in the capital on May Day, Kapaun told the bishop. Meanwhile, the 8th Cavalry continued its combat training in the countryside until May when the regiment transferred to Camp Zama and Camp King outside Tokyo.

There were no signs of trouble on the last Sunday in June. Humidity and 90 degree temperature gripped the city of Tokyo. Everyone enjoyed sunshine for the first time in several days. Yet, at 11 A.M. that day, word flashed from Seoul, South Korea, some 600 miles away across the Sea of Japan, that before dawn the Communist armies of North Korea had smashed across the 38th parallel and were advancing rapidly toward the capital of South Korea.

In less than a week the U.S. had decided to intervene militarily on behalf of the South Koreans. American diplomats first hastily mustered support for the U.N. and agreed that U.S. troops would head a U.N. contingent. Although the 8th Cavalry and the other two regiments of the 1st Cavalry Division were rated the most combat-ready of the American units in Japan, they were not the first to go into action.

Instead, the army reassigned approximately 750 of the division's officers and most experienced noncommissioned officers to other units and dispatched them to Korea as the advance guard of a U.N. force. Now, the nervous young men of the 8th Cavalry who remained in Japan awaiting shipping orders required the reassuring presence of their chaplain more than ever.

General MacArthur had always favored the 1st Cavalry, which had been under his command in World War II. Therefore, MacArthur's headquarters in Tokyo did not surprise anyone when by July 1 it alerted the division for a possible amphibious attack in Korea. Code-named Operation Bluehearts, the plan was to put the 1st Cavalry ashore behind enemy lines near Inchon.

Normal army procedures allowed a division up to three months to plan and carry out such a operation.[21] This time MacArthur beefed up the 1st Cavalry with men from other units and issued orders for the troopers to embark by the middle of July.[22]

From then on everything was hurry-up for Kapaun. He arranged for another priest to take custody of his car after he left for Korea. Kapaun knew that his parents worried about him, so even as preparations for war intensified he assured them that everything was peaceful. However, his letter to Eugene and Helen early in July was more candid: "One nice thing, this time we are not caught unprepared. None of us likes war. And we do not like the way the Russians are doing either. We will have to stop them some way."

In Kapaun's mind the war in Korea clearly was a clash between Soviet Communism and the United States. "This time Russia is going to get it in the neck," he boasted to his family. His first opportunity to face the Communists, however, did not occur as quickly as Kapaun had expected. The North Korean armies advanced so rapidly that the 1st Cavalry's scheduled amphibious assault at Inchon had to be cancelled.

U.S. headquarters prepared new plans to land the division within allied lines at the village of Pohangdong on the eastern coast of Korea. By July 14, Kapaun and thousands of other cavalrymen had been transported to the Japanese port city of Yokohama for embarkation to the battle zone.[23]

Each man carried rations, two sets of fatigue uniforms and two pair of combat boots. Kapaun wore the same clothing as the other troopers, but his pack also included a crucifix, holy oils and other religious items that he would use for his distressing task of ministering to dead and wounded soldiers.

Moving that many troops and their equipment to Korea was a massive effort which required both American and Japanese ships. Loading the vessels and organizing the convoys to the Korean coast required several days, time enough for Kapaun to send letters to friends and relatives about the fearful events that lay ahead.

Kapaun never deviated from his conviction that the Soviet Union was participating in the war. "We are expecting plenty of resistance from the Russians," he wrote to Aunt Tena on July 11 from one of the ships which carried the 1st Cavalry to Korea. "It hardly seems possible that we are actually going to war. I hope we will be strong enough to put the Russians in their place."[24]

Rumors ran wild among the troops at sea. Some speculated that Chinese Communist forces which had been preparing to invade Taiwan (then called Formosa) were being diverted to fight alongside their North Korean allies. Everyone expected that the enemy would vigorously oppose the American landing.

Kapaun finished his last pre-invasion letter to Bishop Carroll. It revealed how the as-yet untested soldiers of the 1st Cavalry were uppermost in his thoughts: "The way the Catholic soldiers are rallying around the priest is edifying."

He was fully aware of the risks that loomed over the horizon. "Tomorrow we are going into combat," Kapaun told the bishop. "I have everything in order, all Mass stipends, my will, etc."[25]

SEVEN

The Struggle in Korea

July 18, 1950. Dawn stretched across the Sea of Japan as American landing ships and support vessels quietly approached the Korean fishing town of Pohangdong. Aboard were Kapaun and members of the 1st Cavalry Division preparing for an amphibious landing. He could not help thinking about what harrowing events awaited them on the beach.

Kapaun was as nervous as the soldiers around him. His worries were apparent in a letter which he wrote to his parents while at sea a few days earlier, "We just wonder what will happen once we reach our destination." As usual, Kapaun asked for prayers for the troops who would go ashore with him.

Another letter, to Eugene and Helen, was more reassuring. "I am just fine and so are my soldiers," Kapaun declared. "We are on an LST now, just one of a large invasion force. It sure looks impressive to see so many ships loaded with soldiers & equipment. The Marines, Navy, Air Corps, submarines & our soldiers are in this."[1]

Their objective was a peaceful village of about 15,000 persons, some 25 miles from the closest enemy forces. Yongil Bay curved around Pohangdong, and the beach was shallow enough to allow the landing craft to unload the troops in hip-deep water within 100 feet of shore. A coastal road just beyond the water's edge pointed north out of the town toward the front lines.

At that point the North Korean invaders possessed vastly superior manpower, and the few U.N. forces which were already defending South Korea desperately needed reinforcements from the 1st Cavalry. But first the fresh troops had to reach shore safely.

85

Undoubtedly Kapaun and many others in the U.S. armada were unaware that the navy's sonar devices had detected submarines, presumed to be Russian, shadowing the invasion convoy on its voyage from Yokohama.[2] Once the GIs landed, the situation would become clearer because U.S. intelligence specialists had cracked the North Korean radio code and knew the location of the enemy forces.

Although Communist guerilla activity had been reported near Pohangdong, the landing began without any resistance from the North Koreans. The most severe problem turned out to be the weather. Shortly after the first contingent of the 8th Cavalry reached the beaches about 7 A.M., Typhoon Helene came roaring across the Sea of Japan and struck the coast of South Korea.

Kapaun and most of the regiment managed to land that day, but the storm interrupted the remainder of the army's schedule.[3] A few days passed before the sea calmed and all 10,027 men and 2,022 vehicles of the division were on Korean soil.

The first night ashore was a hectic time for the inexperienced American soldiers. Although they had not yet encountered any enemy forces, the GI sentries fired hundreds of rifle rounds wildly at every flickering shadow before calm was restored. "I thought their enthusiasm, morale was really good when they went in there," said Colonel Raymond D. Palmer, commanding officer of the 8th Cavalry, "but we just didn't have the time to build them up to the point where they knew more about what to do and how to react." A couple of days later trains and trucks began hauling Kapaun and other 8th Cavalry soldiers toward the oncoming North Korean armies in the vicinity of Yongdong.

Morale was high even though the troops knew that the first American units fighting in Korea had been overwhelmed and forced into continual retreat. By July 22 some detachments of the 8th Cavalry had taken positions in the front lines. At that point Kapaun's work as a battlefield chaplain began in earnest.

Within hours the horrors of war descended on the 8th Cavalry. The 3rd North Korean Division started an attack along the main highway west of Yongdong and infiltrated among the Americans. On the same day the 1st Cavalry Division opened its first cemetery,[4] and interments of casualties took place almost immediately.

The 8th Cavalry's entry into combat was unsuccessful and the men soon joined all of the U.S. forces in retreat. The brutality of the enemy soldiers shocked everyone, for as the North Korean troops attacked they shielded themselves by pushing hundreds of South Korean civilians into the American mine fields.

From the opening onslaught Kapaun established a reputation for courage and concern for the wellbeing of his men. He showed up wherever the soldiers needed reassurance or religious services. If a lull on the battlefield allowed time for a Mass he said one on a makeshift altar, sometimes just a litter placed atop a pair of ammunition boxes.[5]

When Kapaun heard that a Protestant chaplain was wounded he walked several miles to come to his aid. For a while Kapaun was the only able-bodied chaplain with the entire regiment. He asked no questions, he just helped. Jack Stegall told how Kapaun scrambled to jump into a foxhole with Stegall and said, "I don't know what religion you are, but let's have a prayer together."[6]

Despite the constant fighting, Kapaun still managed to see the lighter side of some situations. Eugene and Helen wrote that he appeared "good-looking" in a photograph which he had sent home. Their letter pleased him so much that he jokingly called the picture "a great treasure of art." In another letter Kapaun chuckled when he revealed that his assistant had received a paper from his draft board back home. The notice ordered the soldier to undergo a physical examination before being called into the army.[7]

A few paragraphs from the battlefield congratulated Eugene and Helen on the house which they had purchased after he left for Japan. Then Kapaun added, "Some day with God's help I may see your happy home. Right now my home is a fox hole with heavy artillery shells bursting all around." After three narrow escapes, including one when he cut his hand, and two weeks of facing North Korean tanks and machine guns the chaplain confessed to a friend in Kansas that his handwriting had become unsteady.

Several other letters that Kapaun wrote shortly after he arrived in Korea showed how he was distressed at the maelstrom around him. A single-page summary on Red Cross stationery notified his parents that he was fine, but he added cautiously "...we are not getting ahead the way we would like."[8]

The destruction and death that Kapaun witnessed every day made him wonder if he would survive the war. "This fighting is nerve-wracking. Many of my soldiers crack up—they go insane and scream like mad men. It seems like a dream. I don't know if I will live through the day or night. We are close to heaven, but really we are more like in hell," he told a friend. A fundamentally peaceful man, Kapaun found it hard to accept that deaths and injuries were a natural result of battle. "This war!! What a hard thing to understand," the chaplain wrote.[9]

Combat was more than a misunderstood occurrence. Although Kapaun claimed that the Catholic men were prepared spiritually, many soldiers were not ready psychologically for war. Some historians asserted that the army had not adequately trained its soldiers.

The belief that American-made products were superior to anything else quickly vanished in Korea. Radios could not communicate because their batteries failed. Maps proved incorrect. Equipment left over from World War II would not function.[10]

The abysmal conditions on the battlefield made matters worse. The troops endured torrential rainfalls during the summer monsoon season, temperatures in excess of 100 degrees, flies, mildew, rusty weapons and sporadic meals of canned foods while combat raged. The U.S. units were continually retreating and the exhausted men slept on the ground for two or three hours whenever they could.

There were so many mosquitoes and they were so tenacious that Kapaun quipped in a letter home, "We make a lot of jokes about them being so big that they try to carry a fellow away."[11] Another observer's account recalled, "When under fire, the soldier who slipped into the stagnant, sickening waters of a rice paddy might find that only by pulling his feet out of his boots could he escape from the slime and crawl to safety."[12]

The enemy frequently poisoned the streams in South Korea, Kapaun told Eugene and Helen, so just a drink of pure water was a genuine treat. If thirst drove a sweating GI to slurp a mouthful of liquid from a roadside pond he invariably contracted dysentery from the human excrement that polluted almost all bodies of water.

Kapaun eventually fell victim to a similar ailment. He traveled constantly to visit scattered groups of troops and therefore sometimes he lost contact with the 8th Cavalry unit which was supposed to feed him. "I haven't had a decent meal in days," Kapaun complained to Elmer Palmer. For a short time he resorted to picking fruit off trees, but then the chaplain suffered the consequences, an attack of diarrhea.[13]

The U.S. soldiers had grown accustomed to moving in trucks. In Korea, however, sometimes that was impossible. Even many of the better roads were unpaved pathways intended for ox carts. The landscape was hilly and more and more the American troops had to proceed on foot. Climbing over the ridges in the relentless heat wore out many of them, so many that a majority of the American casualties were the result of exhaustion or sickness.

Even though Kapaun was a dozen years older than most of the soldiers, he was so hardy that an army doctor called him a "mountain goat" because of the speed at which he scrambled up the slopes. Climbing up and down the rocky hills could tear up an infantryman's boots within two weeks. It was no wonder that Kapaun soon suffered from sore feet.

Front lines often did not exist in the hilly areas of South Korea. The fighting was everywhere, in the sunshine and in darkness, ahead of and behind far too few U.S. troops. Not knowing where the Communists might be lurking, Kapaun forced himself to remain awake at night. He was taking no chances, having learned that the pre-dawn hours were the time when the North Koreans sneaked up on unsuspecting sentries. Indeed, an enemy soldier had slit the throat of another chaplain's assistant. Equally appalling was the news that when the Communists captured GIs, they sometimes tied them up, shot them, and left their corpses side by side on the battlefield.

At night the enemy frequently clambered over the ridges and moved into the valleys, cutting off unsuspecting American units. "They outnumber us about 15-1, coming at us from all sides. But we will win this thing yet," Kapaun predicted to John and Tena Maier.[14]

Everyone, crowds of civilians as well as U.S. and South Korean military forces, continued retreating south, away from the advancing Communists. Hundreds of North Korean soldiers died in battle, but the enemy kept attacking. "They seem to have no sense," Emil lamented to his father and mother.[15] The troopers who landed in Korea so optimistically less than two weeks earlier were not strong enough to stem the tide. By July 29 the Communists had forced the 1st Cavalry backward some 30 miles from Yongdong to Kumchon.

Throngs of refugees jammed the sometimes dusty, sometimes muddy trails where the U.S. soldiers also traveled. By one estimate another 25,000 civilians joined the trek every day. They included worried mothers with unclad children, farm animals, bewhiskered elders in stovepipe hats carrying whatever belongings they could salvage.

The noncombatants included enemy infiltrators wearing civilian clothes and ready to ambush the Americans. Kapaun sympathized with all the victims of the war but especially with the fleeing South Korean peasants and their families. The former farmer from Kansas wondered if the tide of the fighting would reverse in time to allow them to harvest their rice crops that year.

Other soldiers quickly became acquainted with the strength of Kapaun's character. In one instance, artillery shells were exploding everywhere and his unit was threatened with imminent capture. Nevertheless, the chaplain informed Captain Joseph O'Connor that he wanted to say Mass at a front-line position.

"Father, things are pretty hot here at present and I don't think you should be up here," O'Connor replied. Kapaun persisted, "Then I think we need a Mass, Captain, and if you can spare the men for a few minutes, I'll say it."

Kapaun chose a spot in the yard of a Korean house. The Catholic soldiers who could be released from duty assembled there. As the

Emil Kapaun in Korea preparing to write a letter
U.S. Army photo

Mass progressed, shells began falling on a hill 150 yards away. The men were ready to run for cover, but Kapaun ignored the danger and continued praying.

When they saw how engrossed their chaplain was in completing the Mass, no one moved until the services ended. Later, O'Connor concluded that Kapaun and those with him were the intended targets of a heavy barrage which had missed them by only a few hundred yards.[16]

On another occasion a few GIs wandered into an adjacent field while Kapaun was celebrating Mass. They mistakenly detonated some mines about 30 yards away, but Kapaun did not interrupt the prayers and neither he nor those with him were hurt.[17] Soldiers remembered times when they had to move the corpses of North Korean soldiers to clear the space for an altar and other occasions when Kapaun said Mass within 500 yards of the forward U.S. positions.

Kapaun eventually earned a reputation for holding religious services no matter how close he was to the enemy.[18] Yet, despite the strife all around him, he never preached about the war. Instead, the chaplain limited his brief sermons to explaining the Gospel message for that particular day.[19]

Word of Kapaun's affection for his troops spread throughout the 8th Cavalry. "Father Kapaun was a man who seemed to sense when others were in trouble," an officer said. The GIs revered him as tireless and fearless. To one of his comrades the chaplain's cheerfulness reflected his inner piety.

The amount of work never disturbed him, nor did the distance that he had to travel. Chaplain Donald Carter recollected that Kapaun "...covered our units as few other chaplains I knew."[20] Some cavalrymen knew that Kapaun had served in India and Burma and they relied on him to advise them what native produce was safe to eat.[21] Working together, Chaplains Kapaun and Carter were so persuasive that almost every member of each unit which they visited, Catholics and men of other faiths, attended religious services.

Lieutenant Walter L. Mayo, Jr., who became a prisoner with Kapaun, was impressed from the time they met. Mayo was in a forward position observing the results of American artillery fire. He turned around and saw that the chaplain was sitting directly behind him. The surprised Mayo demanded to know what he was doing there. Kapaun calmly explained that he was searching for wounded GIs.

Only when Mayo warned that Kapaun was exposed to enemy gunfire did he agree to move into the protection of a gully.[22] Kapaun made the same impression on another Catholic chaplain who remembered how serene he appeared during combat.

Lieutenant William A. McClain, another cavalryman who became a POW with Kapaun, told how the chaplain conducted himself during battle:

> He seemed to appear from nowhere during a combat operation and stay long enough to perform his duties and then disappear. He was never bothered by enemy mortar and small arms fire coming into the vicinity of where he was helping others. He would conduct religious services whenever possible.
>
> He expressed no fear of the enemy and stories of his brave deeds of dragging soldiers to safety, tending to their wounds and suffering circulated among the officers and men. How many lives were saved because of him? Only God knows for sure. His exposure to the terrible combat operations was for him, I believe, a dress rehearsal for what followed.[23]

Kapaun's deeds proved to be more significant than his words. To an army doctor who was attached to the 8th Cavalry, "He was my best litter-bearer and the more risk any wounded soldier was in (ours or theirs) the more he would risk his life to save them." It made no difference whether dead soldiers were American or North Korean. He always assisted in burying them.

Perhaps Kapaun failed to show it during battle, but he admitted to his family that sometimes he was scared. There were valid reasons for being nervous. Protestant Chaplain Arthur Mills, who frequently accompanied Kapaun on trips to the front lines, lost part of his leg to a North Korean mortar shell.[24] Although Kapaun had begun his ministry in Korea with a full-time assistant, plus a jeep and a trailer for his equipment, by the end of July the enemy already had disabled the jeep. North Korean gunfire wounded his helper five times[25] and the army transferred him to a hospital in Japan.

The destruction of Kapaun's kit for saying Mass and the loss of his records did not dishearten him. He arranged for the army to ship replacements from Japan.[26] After shrapnel hit the second Mass kit and Kapaun decided that it could not be salvaged, Korean priests furnished still another set.

This time he decided to protect his equipment by carrying it in a typewriter case. Kapaun came to the conclusion, however, that was not a satisfactory idea. He realized that he might have to leave his possessions unprotected in a jeep if he were forced to flee from artillery fire. The chaplain finally hit upon a solution to the problem. He would wear his field jacket and inside it he would keep all of the articles that he needed to celebrate Mass.[27]

When Kapaun could not obtain another jeep he found a bro-ken-down Korean bicycle to carry him around the battlefield.[28] "I have a lot of fun with the bicycle for it is so shaky and one wheel goes in one direction and the other goes in a different direction," Kapaun told his parents.[29] The two-wheeler quickly became his iden-tification piece. With peaches and other fruits from nearby orchards jammed into his pockets[30] and a pistol belt that held canteens of water for the thirsty troopers, the cycling chaplain became a famil-iar figure among the frontline troopers of the 8th Cavalry.

Even after the rear tire of his two-wheeler went flat Kapaun still pushed it along a dusty road.[31] "He was looking for a pump and grape jelly," McClain remembered. "He wanted the jelly to put in the tire to stop the leak."[32] Major Filmore A. McAbee later told how the enterprising chaplain also tried to confiscate a motorcycle which the Americans had captured from the North Koreans.[33]

Kapaun's correspondence seldom revealed what he did to help others. However, official documents and accounts from his com-rades told the story. Army records reported the heroic way in which he saved the life of one soldier at Kumchon. That act on August 2 earned Kapaun the Bronze Star. The U.S. government citation read:

> Chaplain Kapaun received information that there was a wounded man in an exposed position on the left flank of the First Battalion who could not be removed as there were no litter bearers available. Chaplain Kapaun, together with another officer, immediately proceeded to the front lines where he contacted the Battalion Commander in order to obtain the approximate location of the wounded man. With total disregard for personal safety Chaplain Kapaun and his companion went after the wounded man. The entire route to the wounded soldier was under intense enemy machine gun and small arms fire. However, Chaplain Kapaun success-fully evacuated the soldier, thereby saving his life.[34]

Private Tibor Rubin recounted an incident which illustrated how Kapaun cared for the young GIs. Rubin had been wounded when a mortar shell exploded nearby. Only 21 years old, the infan-tryman was certain that he was dying. Rubin explained that he was Jewish and asked Kapaun to pray with him. The chaplain reluc-tantly said that he did not know any Jewish prayers.

However, Kapaun found another way to help Rubin. He stayed with the stricken soldier and assured him that he was not going to die. Then he removed his own poncho, used it to cover Rubin and hurried off to find a medic. The soldier recovered and when they met again on the Jewish holyday of Yom Kippur, Kapaun welcomed him warmly.[35]

Somehow Kapaun seemed to show up wherever and whenever he was needed. The Catholic chaplain for the 8th Cavalry knew the face of every man in his regiment. He greeted them by first name and chatted with everyone.[36] One cavalryman recalled that Kapaun brought some oranges to his foxhole and then stayed while they spoke about food, a constant subject of conversation among the men.[37] If any of them needed cigarettes or if they were not receiving mail from home, Kapaun tried to solve the problem.

Most importantly, his actions made it clear that he was interested in the well-being of each soldier. One time when Kapaun was saying Mass the military police brought in a soldier who was confined to the stockade. As the man approached the altar to receive Holy Communion, Kapaun noticed that he was handcuffed. He angrily ordered the MPs to remove the manacles for as long as the soldier was attending church services.

Being so close to the front lines was as perilous for chaplains as anyone else. In the first few months of fighting the locations of the opposing units changed so rapidly that any soldier suddenly might come face to face with the enemy. Kapaun understood the risks and accepted them. To a priest-friend in Kansas he admitted, "Incidentally in this war we have to be armed. The Reds are not taking prisoners. So we resolved to fight them to the finish because we would not have a chance if we chose to surrender in any particular hopeless situation."[38]

Kapaun was in a forward position when he met Lieutenant Ernest Terrell, Jr. for the first time. Terrell had been trapped behind the enemy lines and saw Kapaun as he returned to friendly territory. Kapaun held a rifle while he sat in his jeep and greeted the lieutenant. When Terrell asked him why he was carrying a weapon, Kapaun replied, "The Lord helps those who help themselves."[39] The chaplain clearly had made up his mind to defend himself if necessary.[40] "If it's a question of a North Korean sending me to heaven or me sending him someplace, I'm not prepared to go to heaven right now," he told Mayo.[41]

Because Kapaun frequently was alone as he roved the front lines he decided to carry a rusty old carbine. Yet no one ever saw him fire a gun at the North Koreans. He only appeared to be armed. The gun actually was not loaded.

The empty weapon served its purpose when Kapaun was out in front of the American outposts. He was searching for any wounded men who might need the last rites of the Church. Kapaun was alone and to his surprise an enemy soldier approached him. The chaplain was wary, but the man made signs which indicated that he wanted to surrender. Since Kapaun could not speak Korean he pointed his unloaded gun at the unsuspecting North Korean and took him into custody. Then he marched the soldier back to the American positions.[42]

Indeed, Kapaun was as humane to the Communists as to the Americans. When the 8th Cavalry captured a particular hill the men found that it was littered with the bodies of friends and foes alike, victims of an earlier battle. The remains were decomposing fast in the summer heat and the stench was overwhelming. The bodies obviously had to be buried as soon as possible.

Kapaun gave gas masks to a detail of South Korean troops and led them up the slope to where the corpses lay. He ordered them to load the dead Americans into body bags. A few of the South Koreans balked at their unpleasant assignment, but Kapaun threatened them until they completed the task.[43]

After another battle ended, Kapaun asked Carl T. Wohlbier to accompany him down the slope of a hill to reach a dead North Korean. When they reached the body, Kapaun suggested that they dig a shallow grave to protect the remains from vermin and flies. The next day he asked Wohlbier and his buddy to bury several North Koreans who had been killed in front of the American positions.

Years later Wohlbier wrote, "...I think it would make the families, especially the mothers, happy to know that one man had the decency to protect the remains of the fallen enemy soldiers....I now feel at peace with myself knowing that Pfc. Stapleton and I gave a decent burial to some of the enemy because of an uncommon, decent and forgiving soldier (of God) known as Captain Emil Kapaun, Chaplain, United States Army."[44]

After working side by side with the men of the 8th Cavalry, Kapaun did not have much time available to devote to the North Koreans. "He was always right up in the front lines with the troops," a former soldier recalled. "We were always telling him to keep his damn head down." The chaplain would move from one soldier to another, Douglass Hall wrote later, reminding each man, "It's tough, but remember one thing: that if something happens you are in God's hands."[45]

Hall described how a group of GIs was cut off and surrounded for several days. A rescue force finally broke through and among the first to reach the beleaguered men was their chaplain. At another time the 8th Cavalry and the Communists fought desperately near the South Korean town of Taegu. Kapaun appeared suddenly and came strolling down the road toward his unit, seemingly oblivious to the gunfire around him. He appeared to Hall to be sheathed in armor. "God has his hand on me," was Kapaun's only explanation.[46]

Wohlbier remembered the first time that he saw Kapaun. The soldier was watching a heartbroken American machine gunner who had just witnessed two of his buddies die on the battlefield. An officer, whom Wohlbier later identified as Kapaun, had his arm around the crestfallen soldier and was trying to console him. Wohlbier later summed up his feelings toward Kapaun: "I was so impressed by his actions that if he had been a line officer I think I would have followed him anywhere."[47]

The unselfish way in which Kapaun acted influenced the other men greatly. In fact, one of them boasted that he became a Catholic because of the chaplain's example. Another trooper wrote this description of Kapaun:

His demeanor and appearance is most representative by the statement that he completely blended with the human environment. His interest in the soldiers' welfare completely transcended his own religious preference (RC).

Fr. Kapaun in my opinion had that quality that permits one to raise the morale and spirit of troops in his presence. Under no circumstances would the Fr. Kapaun I knew pass an inspection in ranks. He inspired people by truly accepting and undergoing their hardships and trials, which to say the least were very, very trying at this time.

Kapaun made other vivid, yet different impressions on the troopers of the 8th Cavalry. They remembered him as extremely humble, a superior soldier, friendly, a motivator, always talking about sports.[48] Neither Kapaun nor any GI enjoyed digging foxholes, but he did his share and more. He understood the importance of making the right impression. Indeed, several years earlier he had handwritten a sermon about how young soldiers imitate others who are brave and love their country.

Another man reached the conclusion that Kapaun "...inspired soldiers by his down to earth caring that he had for his fellow man." He fit in so well that a certain GI regarded the chaplain as just "one of the guys."

Lieutenant Robert Mack drew a detailed word picture of how the chaplain looked:

To the best of my recollection, Fr. Kapaun's normal appearance was that of a gaunt man, nearly 6 feet tall, wearing rumpled fatigues, with his chalice securely held in a canteen cover attached to his belt, with other accoutrements for saying mass slung over his shoulder. He was indeed saintly and manly in his appearance.[49]

Emil Kapaun, *right front,* **assisting soldier off the battlefield in Korea**
U.S. Army photo

Kapaun was a spiritual person, but according to Lieutenant Raymond M. Dowe, Jr. it was not apparent to the casual observer. "He wore his piety in his heart. Outwardly he was all GI, tough of body, rough of speech sometimes, full of the wry humor of the combat soldier," Dowe recalled.[50]

From his first day in Korea, Kapaun's hectic daily life left him without time to reply to the mail which he had received in Japan just before he left for the war. It went unanswered until mid-August when he finally wrote several letters while on the battlefield. The correspondence followed the style of his boyhood diary and revealed how tactfully he expressed himself to various persons back in Kansas. Most telling were his descriptions of the way in which he obtained his stationery.

His letter to the Grafton family in Kansas contained a brief but graphic account: "I ransacked a Korean house and found this paper and ink."[51] The description which he gave to his mentor, Monsignor Sklenar, sounded less like thievery: "I had no paper, but yesterday I found this piece of paper and some ink in a house...."

The stationery was a coarse variety with Oriental markings, leading Kapaun to take an apologetic tack with Bishop Carroll. "Please excuse the crudeness of this letter," he wrote. Then he changed the subject, "Yesterday I found this paper and ink in one of the abandoned houses of the Koreans."[52] It was a tactful way of informing his religious superior that he had intruded into some strangers' empty home and helped himself to their writing material.

His letter to Enos and Bessie in the middle of August simply reported that he had found some paper in an unoccupied Korean house. Kapaun rarely told them about the bloody details of combat. His letters to his mother and father still concentrated on facts that an elderly farm couple could understand. "The villages are built of mud houses & grass roofs," the chaplain said. "When 1 house catches fire the whole village burns with everything. The people had rice and barley stored away. That burns too."

Although Kapaun had little opportunity to help the civilian victims of the war, he was sympathetic to their plight. "It is a pity how the poor people here have to suffer. They don't own very much and they even had to run away from their homes. Here they will have nothing to eat. Some of the town have already been set on fire and burned. These people will never have a home to go back to," he told Monsignor Sklenar in August 1950.[53]

The continual stress under which Kapaun lived was apparent from his writings. A note to friends in Timken disclosed, "God has been good to me. Others have not been so fortunate. There are many horrors in war. A fellow can stand only so much." He assured other

Emil Kapaun showing pipe which was hit by enemy gunfire
U.S. Army photo

friends in Kansas, "The prayers of loved ones helped me escape. I have seen soldiers with both legs blown off; one had the top of his head completely blown off. He did not know what hit him."[54]

Kapaun survived several close calls during his daily efforts to retrieve dead and injured soldiers. He admitted that he was surprised that he had escaped being badly wounded. "I had a freak accident—got hit in the elbow with a .50 calibre slug," Kapaun informed Eugene, Helen, and their daughter, Angela.

"I was rescuing the body of a pilot who crashed his F51 fighter plane on the side of a mountain. He was thrown clear of the wreckage which was burning, so we rescued the body," the letter continued. "The ammunition was going off in the fire and one of the slugs hit me. It must not have had much momentum for I still have my elbow without injury."[55]

An even closer call almost killed him. A North Korean sniper's bullet missed Kapaun's head by inches and instead shattered the stem of his pipe.[56] Typically, he had been in an exposed position, crawling along the battlefield to help a wounded soldier. Undeterred, Kapaun picked up the stub of the pipe and continued puffing. "You know, Father Emil must have a very good guardian angel," his mother reacted when she heard about that incident. Another battle was equally hair-raising; an artillery shell whizzed by so close that it blew off the chaplain's helmet.

Writing one summer day while seated amid rows of sugar cane plants standing ten feet high and besieged by hordes of mosquitoes and flies, Kapaun casually informed a priest in Kansas about another precarious circumstance. "I used to get sick at the sight of blood & wounds. Recently I was messed up with blood myself. I grabbed a towel to stop my hand from bleeding. That was the only thing I saved as the Reds nearly got us that time."[57]

At the beginning of August, the military situation of the U.N. forces was still perilous. The superior manpower of the enemy had pushed them back into an enclave called the Pusan perimeter, named after the port city at the southern end of the Korean peninsula which juts out from the mainland of Asia.

Kim Il Sung, the Communist premier of North Korea, boasted at that time that the Americans and their U.N. allies clung to only about ten percent of the land area of South Korea.[58] That small section was mostly mountainous terrain. Unless the Communists could be stopped quickly, U.S. military leaders worried that their armies might even be forced into the Sea of Japan.

Only 50 miles wide and about 100 miles from north to south the Pusan perimeter was intersected at its northwest corner by the Naktong River. The weary and still-outnumbered men of the 8th

Cavalry retreated across the broad Naktong early in August to dig in at new defensive positions. Almost in their shadow came hordes of white-robed refugees fleeing the oncoming North Korean troops.

Those civilians were intent on reaching safety with the U.S. soldiers. They were so determined that as the Americans were blowing up the last bridge across the river hundreds of South Korean refugees, oblivious to warnings to remain on the far side, were dashing across the span trying to catch up with the rear guard of U.S. infantrymen.

Once across the Naktong, the 8th Cavalry, together with other American and South Korean units, established a coordinated front to face the Communists.[59] As the frantic retreats slowed, the conditions under which Kapaun lived started to improve. Even though the chaplain still had to sleep on the ground, for the first time in more than two weeks at least he rested with a roof above his head. "It is surprising how long a fellow can go without sleep," he wrote to his parents.[60]

Kapaun was where he wanted to be—with, in his words, "my boys." During a lull in the fighting he could be seen hearing confessions on the bank of the Naktong. Another time Kapaun sweltered as he said Mass in his heavy vestments while behind him naked GIs bathed in the river.

"I am glad to be with the soldiers in time of need," he commented in a monthly report to Bishop Carroll. "So far, I have been right in the front lines giving absolution and Extreme Unction to the dying." Then, without further clarification, Kapaun added, "I had no chance to change clothes and my uniform got all bloody."[61]

Besides saying Mass as often as he could, Kapaun gave the necessary instructions to Catholic soldiers who never had received their first Holy Communion. Summarizing his experiences for his friend, Father Joseph, in Kansas, Kapaun wrote, "If the boys ever needed a Catholic priest they sure need one in battle."[62]

At that point, early August 1950, the 8th Cavalry and the two other regiments of the 1st Cavalry Division were defending the approaches to Taegu, a mid-sized city in South Korea. Although the North Korean 1st and 13th Divisions managed to cross the Naktong, the 1st Cavalry stopped the Communists temporarily at Waegwan.[63]

American losses were severe, especially noncombat casualties from the heat. The summer weather soaked Kapaun's uniform every day, either from the monsoon downpours or his own sweating in the mid-day humidity. Salt tablets became so necessary that U.S. planes dropped them to the front line detachments.

The army tried in other ways to make life more bearable. Fresh vegetables, grown on hydroponic farms in Japan, lifted the soldiers' morale. Portable showers and equipment for making ice cream arrived at units in Korea. Unfortunately, moving refrigeration units required a pair of two and one-half ton trucks, and using so much equipment proved impractical.[64]

The 1st Cavalry had a stroke of better luck with a huge quantity of beef. Someone made a mistake and switched a freight car to the division's railroad siding. It contained unrefrigerated meat which had to be consumed immediately. None of the cavalrymen objected.

Later during August, after U.N. ground forces and airplanes repulsed the North Koreans outside Taegu,[65] the army established radio stations there and at two other locations. Their purpose was not only to counteract Communist propaganda being broadcast by "Seoul City Sue," but also to provide country and pop music and news to the U.S. troops. The soldiers even persuaded Korean civilians to hand-wash their uniforms, reminiscent of one of the services that many of them had enjoyed in Japan.

Those extra comforts admittedly were unusual in wartime. One of Kapaun's letters reported what the men were more accustomed to in Korea: "It is quite comical & we have a lot of fun kidding each other about steak dinners, ice cream and beer. A slice of bread is a treat. Warm coffee is a delicacy."[66]

Despite the deaths, savage wounds, and physical exhaustion that he witnessed, Kapaun remained hopeful about the progress of the war. A little optimism was justified because, as the fighting proceeded from August into September 1950, both the American and U.N. forces were becoming stronger. The tonnage of supplies being delivered by rail and water tripled. Troop strength increased significantly.

At that point the 3rd Battalion, which Kapaun joined later just before its annihilation at Unsan, arrived from its training in Massachusetts. The men increased the strength of the 8th Cavalry to its authorized number. At the outset, however, in the words of its commanding officer, the 3rd Battalion was a "thrown-together outfit" with little combat effectiveness.

The 8th Cavalry held positions north of Taegu near a hilly area known as the Bowling Alley. It was a narrow two and one-half mile long valley filled with rice paddies and a line of poplar trees down the middle. For days the battle centered around the heights of the ancient city of Ka-san. With the remnants of a 30-foot high stone wall around the crest and the Buddhist Poguk Temple at one end, Ka-san was revered by Koreans as their Sacred Mountain.

In steaming heat, fog, and heavy rainfalls, the surrounding hills changed hands several times. Finally, the North Korean 13th Division blunted the 8th Cavalry's move in the direction of Tabu-Dong.[67]

Superior numbers overcame the Americans and pushed them back to within seven miles of Taegu. Its refugee-swollen population had ballooned up to 700,000 persons, and now they were within range of the North Korean artillery.

By mid-September the 8th Cavalry and the other units of the 1st Cavalry had become short of riflemen and low on ammunition. They barely held the hills around the city. The price of just hanging on was stupendous; the 3rd Battalion had already suffered staggering casualties. The army hastily organized its only remaining group of reserves—the division band, cooks, quartermaster troops, clerks—for a last-ditch effort to stem the North Korean thrust toward Taegu.[68]

Kapaun struggled to sustain the spirits of the weary troopers. But the U S. forces needed something dramatic to shift the fortunes of war before the onset of winter.

EIGHT

A Reversal of Fortune

From the morning when the army's 7th Division and the 1st Marine Division stormed ashore at Inchon on September 15 a dramatic change of direction occurred in the course of the war. The armies began to move northward instead of south. Almost instantly word of the invasion spread to the Pusan perimeter where the beleaguered U.S. soldiers still held off the North Korean invaders.

When Kapaun learned that U.S. units had landed behind enemy lines, the news answered his prayers. The 8th Cavalry sensed that this time it was the Communists who were trapped. The North Koreans would soon be on the run. The fighting would end. The GIs would be going home—or so they thought.

Unfortunately, the Americans were unaware that almost simultaneously, a massive force of Chinese Communist soldiers was assembling in Manchuria a few hundred miles away. Hurried preparations were under way to move the Chinese into North Korea to oppose the U.S. and its allies.

At first the North Korean troops who faced the 8th Cavalry lacked information about the Inchon landing and did not react. However, within three or four days the North Korean 1st and 13th Divisions virtually evaporated, suddenly abandoning the hilltops near the Naktong River and fading away from the Pusan perimeter.[1]

The Americans followed in close pursuit, driving rapidly up the wreckage-strewn Bowling Alley. They crossed the Naktong by ferry and over an underwater bridge which was built out of sand bags placed a few feet below water level. Within a week the North

104

Korean army was disintegrating. Its soldiers, disguised as farmers and refugees, were scurrying out of South Korea.[2]

The 1st Cavalry advanced so fast and so far north that by late in the evening of September 26 it linked up with the 31st Infantry Regiment which had landed at Inchon. So many North Koreans were being surrounded and taken prisoner that the U.S. troops could hardly process them. A Communist colonel even awakened two 8th Cavalry sentries so that they could capture him. What the Americans did not know was that the enemy officer had been instructed to surrender in order to foment a revolt among the Communist prisoners of war.[3]

The sight of hundreds of North Korean corpses littering the fields and roadsides troubled Kapaun. "He was always burying the dead enemy soldiers and helping graves registration with ours when things got quiet," a cavalryman recalled. The onrushing Americans also witnessed the opposite end of the spectrum of life. One morning they learned that during the previous night five babies were born among 2,000 refugees encamped at Sariwon.

After the 1st Cavalry and other U.S. units reached the South Korean capital and drove out the North Koreans, some of the Americans went to the Catholic church. What they saw horrified them. The Communists had removed the crucifix over the altar and in its place they had installed a picture of Stalin.[4]

While the fortunes of war shifted from better to worse and back again, Kapaun's reputation only became stronger. "He was sort of a tradition among the men," an American officer stated. "It is a tough job being a chaplain, but I never knew him to be anything but a gentle, nice guy. I believe he was divinely inspired." Yet the exhausting pace exacted the same toll on Kapaun as it did on other foot soldiers. Mentally, he remained on an even keel, but he lost considerable weight and some of his hair.

Captured enemy officers informed Kapaun that their North Korean leaders had treated them as poorly as their South Korean foes. "They said that the Communists did not care how many Koreans got killed or how hopeless a drive would be & they would order the soldiers to drive on even though all of them got killed," the dismayed chaplain wrote to Eugene and Helen.[5]

Kapaun escaped injury again in September. "The Reds started shelling us with mortar and artillery," he reported in one of his letters. "I was caught up on a ridge & had no fox hole. Boy, that seemed to be the last for I know what those shells can do to a fellow."

The folks back at St. John Nepomucene church obviously had reason to worry about their former pastor. Many attended a special High Mass and prayed that he would return safely. Kapaun told his parents how much he appreciated that his friends were thinking about him.

The chaplain survived other close calls in addition to the artillery barrage. North Korean troops continued to resist, mining roads and destroying bridges as they pulled back into their homeland. Kapaun summarized the situation for Albert and Pauline Klenda in Kansas:

> I thank you for all the prayers, etc. My boys need them worse than I do, for some way or another I have not been hit, although we were in some tough spots with bullets whistling past our heads. A fellow's nerves take an awful strain and a fellow surely can pray when these big shells explode around the area. It is no fun.[6]

By early October the 1st Cavalry, by Kapaun's calculations, had advanced 150 miles to the 38th parallel. As the troopers prepared to march into North Korea, he found an old map which he used for writing paper. The chaplain scribbled a hopeful note to Eugene and Helen, observing "It looks like the war will end soon."

Communist China, however, had other plans and had decided to intervene in the conflict. The reason, an official Chinese magazine declared ominously, was that "North Korea's defense is our defense." A major confrontation with the American forces was brewing. Meanwhile, the 1st Cavalry proceeded across the border into North Korea, and Kapaun probably enjoyed the distinction of being the first U.S. Army priest to enter that country.

As usual, Kapaun forwarded his monthly report to Bishop Carroll. It revealed that he still worried about the GIs whom he served: "During this awful conflict I was impressed with the way most of the soldiers were prepared spiritually. I hope that all of them who lost their lives have found a merciful Judge."[7] The optimistic attitude which continued to prevail among the U.S. troops appeared in his correspondence. "The situation looks much better for us now..." the chaplain wrote.

A light frost formed in those early October evenings, a prelude to the harsh Korean winter, as the 1st Cavalry occupied the largely abandoned city of Pyongyang. Kapaun and many others had been fighting continually since July and undoubtedly they were glad when the army flew reinforcements into Pyongyang. Now that the division had halted its rapid advance, more food, clothing, and other supplies began to catch up with the troops.

The army even began to enforce some of the regulations of peacetime military life. It ordered the grimy men who had become accustomed to living in muddy foxholes to clean themselves and their quarters around the North Korean capital.[8] Final victory and a return to normality seemed imminent.

For a few days life around Pyongyang was relatively relaxed. The Americans were pretty much alone after South Korean units departed to chase the remnants of the North Korean army toward the border with Manchuria. Kapaun continued to say daily Mass on the hood of a jeep. Sergeant Major Leo F. McNamee met Kapaun while they were in the North Korean capital and gave him six miniature bottles of whiskey. Perhaps anticipating that he should wait before celebrating the end of the fighting, Kapaun promised to save the liquor for a cold night.[9]

The 1st Cavalry's rest period ended hastily. Unexpected enemy resistance developed without warning in the mountains below the Yalu River. General Walton H. Walker, commander of the U.S. 8th Army, dispatched all three regiments of the division north toward Unsan to assist the South Korean units.

Hope still existed for a quick end to the war when the 3rd Battalion of the 8th Cavalry settled into a reserve position south of Unsan. It was quiet on the night of October 30 and Kapaun and many of the troopers slept easily. The rest of the regiment, however, had locked horns with a ferocious and unorthodox new foe, the Chinese Communists. And, suddenly in the chilly darkness, hordes of enemy infantrymen surrounded Kapaun and the 3rd Battalion.

There were no more letters home to Eugene and Helen or to Kapaun's parents. Within a couple of days several hundred soldiers of the 3rd Battalion and their Catholic chaplain were decimated by overwhelming Chinese forces. Several weeks earlier Kapaun had been determined never to surrender. Now, surrounded by wounded Americans, Kapaun implored his captors not to hurt the helpless men whom he had sheltered in a crowded dugout. Eugene Kapaun knew that his brother allowed himself to be taken prisoner because he "...wouldn't have felt right..." if he abandoned the other Americans.[10]

A high-ranking officer of the 1st Cavalry became upset when he learned later that Kapaun had become a captive of the Chinese. He asked Chaplain Aloysius M. Knier of the 5th Cavalry Regiment why Kapaun had surrendered. Was Kapaun sympathetic toward the Communists? No, Knier assured the officer. Kapaun was under lots of pressure and did what he thought was best for the wounded men in the dugout at Unsan.[11]

Most of the 8th Cavalry soldiers who fought at Unsan were killed, wounded, or herded toward captivity in North Korea. Any troopers who were unable to walk off the battlefield or who could not be carried had to be left behind. Several days later the Chinese released a handful of the wounded on stretchers reportedly marked "Donated by American Red Cross."

Emil Kapaun saying Mass in Korea

A few men who avoided being taken prisoner returned to the American lines during the next three weeks with bits of news which confirmed that Kapaun had been captured. One soldier whom the Chinese released reported that the chaplain had lost weight, but otherwise he was in good condition.[12] All that Kapaun could manage was a note back to Father Francis McCullogh, "Dear Mac, I am a prisoner, I am saying Mass."

Within three days all of the home-by-Christmas predictions had flickered out. The enemy blunted an attempt to rescue the 3rd Battalion and later the army cancelled the effort. Most of the U.S. forces joined the South Koreans in retreat.

The Chinese commanders gave special instructions to their infantrymen who fought at Unsan: capture as many Americans as possible.[13] When the U.S. prisoners discovered that their captors were Chinese, the news stunned them. One American blurted out, "For God's sake! This isn't your war." But it was, and an enemy officer, trying out his mission-school English, affirmed, "It is now."[14]

The Chinese viewed the war as a clash between Communism and the western world. They assembled the survivors of the 3rd Battalion and announced that Wall Street imperialists were responsible for ordering American soldiers to fight in Korea.

The unexpected Chinese offensive netted hundreds of U.S. captives at several locations in North Korea. The Communists detained a number of the Americans, including Joe Ascue and Kapaun, for several days in a school house.[15] On November 5, the men moved about 20 miles away from the battlefield. Five days later they started a march northward toward the border with China.[16] The men who were captured at Unsan and elsewhere in North Korea quickly realized what it meant to become prisoners of war. The enemy soldiers examined their watches and wallets and confiscated whatever they wanted.[17]

The GIs had been scheduled to start receiving winter clothing on September 15. Although some heavy jackets had arrived, too few caught up with the fast-moving troops.[18] Consequently, most of them still had only lightweight summer uniforms when they surrendered. Anyone wearing heavy clothing had to hand it over to their captors.[19] The enemy guards even seized the boots that some of the POWs were wearing, forcing them to wrap their feet in gloves or any covering that was available.[20]

Early one chilly day in November, the Communists assembled the POWs to continue their trek northward. Warrant Officer Felix McCool asked if there were a chaplain among the Americans. Yes, he was told, there was. He could be identified by a patch covering one eye and a stocking cap over his ears.

McCool found Kapaun rummaging through the debris of a burned-out building. According to McCool, the chaplain was "...down in a hole digging out a jar so the troops would have something to get water in. We needed one. He was one of the most unselfish men I've ever known—he was always doing something for someone."

"Look here in this cellar. There is a water crock," Kapaun informed McCool. "We can keep water in it and have it boiled and sanitary. Maybe so many men won't die from drinking filthy water."

The crock was jammed into a hole in the damaged building. A rat had crawled into the crock and died there. Nevertheless, Kapaun was intent on retrieving the vessel. McCool lowered himself into the hole, but at first he could not loosen the crock. Kapaun helped by clearing away some of the broken boards. But then the trouble happened. Dirt started to fall into the opening on top of McCool and a large rock began to slip toward the hole.

Kapaun immediately stuck his foot in the path of the sliding rock in an effort to stop it. However, that did not work and he succeeded only in bruising himself severely. McCool came to the conclusion later that this mishap ultimately caused a blood clot to develop in Kapaun's leg.

The rock continued crashing downward, cracking off part of the rim of the crock and momentarily trapping McCool. In a short while, with help from Lieutenant Henry Pedicone, Kapaun freed McCool. They spent the remainder of the afternoon carefully separating the debris in order to lift out the damaged container. The crock was still serviceable, sound enough for Kapaun to distribute boiling water among the prisoners.[21]

Thirsty, frightened, freezing, their dreams of a quick end to the war having ended abruptly, the demoralized young GIs who were captured with Kapaun began trudging through the hills toward an unknown destination. As the men passed through the North Korean villages, they soon became accustomed to being spit upon and bullied. "Bali...bali!," the guards shouted to quicken the pace of the prisoners.[22]

The Communists' chilling words soon after they captured the American outlined what lay ahead, "We are your friends. Your conditions of living are bad now, but we will work together to improve them. We will correct the errors in your thinking. Once you have learned the truth we will send you back to your families."[23] The guards issued a frightening warning: Unless the prisoners accepted the validity of Communism they would remain in North Korea for the rest of their lives.[24]

Night after frigid night for more than two weeks the POWs struggled onward through freezing streams and over the snow-covered crests of North Korea.[25] Children along the roadside threw stones at the Americans. Even though many, including Kapaun, suffered from trenchfoot and frostbite, the guards forced their prisoners forward. Somehow they covered up to 20 miles each night.[26] The silent journey was interrupted only by the moans of the wounded and occasional cries for water.

From the outset the Chinese intended to break down the will of their captives. The first step was a near-starvation diet.[27] The guards forced local inhabitants along the route to prepare the prisoners' food. But the meals usually consisted of only one ball of cracked corn and soybean paste early in the morning after the overnight march ended and another before it resumed at dusk.[28]

Sometimes no one fed the prisoners for two or three days.[29] Kapaun understood what was happening. He remained calm, but acted decisively. He simply walked over to the kettles and took whatever amount of boiled corn or sorghum he thought was necessary to feed the wounded.[30]

An inadequate diet which lacked sufficient salt and vitamins led to severe physical problems among those and other American POWs. Night blindness was one of them. Unable to see the trail ahead, the only hope for some prisoners was to grab on to the shoulder of the man staggering along in front of them.[31] Others began to show signs of mental distress.

At first the Chinese abandoned to death by freezing any of the sick or wounded Americans who could not maintain the pace. The prisoners observed what was happening and began carrying about 45 of their wounded buddies on stretchers which were rigged out of empty rice sacks.[32] But just moving forward, without the burden of carrying another man, required all of a soldier's stamina.

Survivors of similar forced marches reported that when each night's ordeal was over, the Americans would exit from a dream world and return to normality. They remembered nothing that had happened since their miserable journey began at nightfall the previous day.[33] During the daylight hours the POWs were shoved into caves or local houses. The Communists had no intention of sheltering their prisoners. Their only purpose was to hide them from U.S. planes passing overhead.

Such a demoralizing situation called for leadership and character. Years earlier, in his boyhood diary, Kapaun had recognized the importance of setting a good example. One of his radio broadcasts from Japan had emphasized the same ideal. Now was his chance to live up to his words.

Whenever the column of POWs paused for a short rest, Kapaun hurried up and down the line, a prayer here, a smile there, exhorting the exhausted men not to give up. Sometimes the prisoners were too weary to help the wounded and refused officers' orders to carry the litters. The men could not be left to die by the snowy wayside, so Kapaun and others shouldered the makeshift stretchers. The POWs watched the chaplain struggle to his feet, and his example eventually shamed the recalcitrants into picking up their buddies.

A few prisoners found out that Kapaun was suffering from frostbite. They offered to take his place in carrying the litters, but he always declined. Finally they asked why he refused to rest more often. Kapaun simply answered that he liked helping people and doing that was his reward.

"Father never complained and kept on struggling," said Lieutenant William A. McClain. "The Chinese guards were not sympathetic with our plight and kept yelling and prodding us with their bayonets to move faster."[34] The prisoners who survived the cruel trek were certain that only Kapaun's faith in God pushed him on, mile after mile.

During the period when the Americans were being herded toward prison, the Chinese officials interrogated many of the U.S. officers. They knew that Kapaun was a captain, but they did not bother to question him. The reason was that the Chinese did not consider him to be a "military officer."[35] In their eyes a chaplain was a noncombatant, in the same category as the political commissars who were attached to Communist military units.

What the guards failed to consider was that their oversight provided Kapaun with the time and the opportunity to boost the spirits of the captives. While the Chinese spent their time trying to get information from the American officers, Kapaun was able to circulate more freely among the enlisted men, encouraging them and praying the Rosary frequently.

The average age of the soldiers who were captured at Unsan was 21 years. Recognizing that these young POWs needed his stabilizing influence, Kapaun decided that some humor might help. Shortly after they became prisoners, an enlisted man from North Carolina asked him what he expected that the Chinese would do. "Probably shoot the officers and let the enlisted men go," Kapaun replied.

One night the enemy loaded some of the U.S. soldiers, Kapaun among them, on to captured American trucks. He found a spot midway in the steel bed of one of the vehicles. Others were crammed in around him, and as they traveled through the mountains Kapaun repeatedly led them in prayers. The guards warned him several times that he must stop praying, but he ignored their demands.

The engines of the U.S.-manufactured trucks did not perform well on North Korean gas, and the ride over the rutted dirt roads was a bumpy and frequently interrupted journey. The next morning, after the trip ended, Kapaun fell while he was getting off the truck. No doubt his legs were stiff from being cramped throughout the cold nighttime drive.[36] More likely the real reason why Kapaun stumbled was that his feet already were suffering the first stages of frostbite.

Besides suffering from the unusually severe weather, the prisoners could barely tolerate the little food which the guards distributed. It was far different from the normal American diet. Sometimes they ate unsweetened sorghum called koeliang, splintered kernels of corn, or occasionally cabbage soup. Even worse, the men received water only once a day. It was hardly a surprise that within a few days the captives began to lose weight and grow weaker.

The Chinese also seized the prisoners' water purification tablets, so trouble began almost immediately after the thirsty men swallowed gulps of ditch water.[37] Even more debilitating were the constant attacks of hepatitis and diarrhea.[38] The half-cooked corn intensified intestinal irritations among the POWs and except for a few consoling words, Kapaun could do little to help.

On many such marches the discomfort from diarrhea often became unbearable, but the Communist soldiers refused to stop to allow the prisoners to relieve themselves. With their strength declining, the desperate POWs followed a plan to deal with the problem. First they stumbled through the darkness beyond the head of the column and pulled down their pants while the other prisoners moved past them. Then they hurried to regain their place in the line of march before the rear guard caught them.

That exhausting and painful procedure took place again and again. All of the Americans were aware of the alternative. If a guard found someone squatting by the side of the path, he often would knock the prisoner sprawling with his rifle butt and leave him alongside the path to freeze in the dark.

The fate of some prisoners was even worse. "There were many stragglers who would fall behind the column, and guards would fall back with them," said a survivor of a similar march. "After the column had moved on we would hear shots and the guards would then catch up with the column, but we would never see the prisoners again. In some cases we would hear screaming prior to the shots."[39]

By the time Kapaun and the other cavalrymen who had been captured at Unsan reached Pyoktong on the Yalu River on November 16, 1950, dozens of the approximately 600 in the line of march had perished. Lieutenant Walter L. Mayo, Jr. estimated that about 50 in his group fell behind and died.[40] The survivors had gone back and forth over twisting mountain trails for more than 300 miles. Their strength had ebbed away; some men lost more than 60 pounds in barely two weeks.

That nightmare, and those of hundreds more military and civilian captives in similar forced marches during the Korean War, have been compared to the better-known and infamous Bataan Death March in World War II.

The first stop in Pyoktong was a huge hall, where the guards gave some food to the Americans and moved them into buildings on a nearby pig farm.[41] During this period the Communists decided that it was time to bring Kapaun in for interrogation.[42] However, their questions failed to intimidate him, and the officials decided that Kapaun could keep the religious oils and stole which he used to function as a chaplain.

Kapaun even gained permission to visit the wooden houses where the Chinese had dispersed the prisoners. It shocked him to find sometimes up to 35 men jammed into a tiny room. There was no place to say Mass, but Kapaun still managed to lead the Rosary prayers every day. Just being with their chaplain reassured many young POWs.

Their prison home, Pyoktong, was a small town nestled on a peninsula which stuck out into the backwaters of the Yalu. However, Kapaun and the other POWs stayed there only briefly. Their hasty departure was the result of a bombing attack by American planes, which occurred shortly after the POWs arrived.

The air raid set fire to half of the town. When the attack was over, the Chinese soldiers, panic-stricken and outraged, drove the prisoners out of their buildings.[43] Firing their weapons to harass the walking wounded, they forced the Americans up the ice slopes of the adjacent hills. The prisoners sat there shivering throughout the night and smoking cigarettes made from dried oak leaves.[44]

The next morning the worn-out POWs were on the road again. As Lieutenant Raymond M. Dowe, Jr. raised the front of one of the stretchers, he noticed that the soldier who was lifting the back end was a grey-eyed man of medium height with the beginning of a reddish-brown beard. When Dowe turned around to introduce himself, the prisoner extended his hand and said simply, "Kapaun." Dowe exclaimed, "Father! I've heard about you." A smile crossed Kapaun's face and he half-whispered, "Don't pass it along. It might get back to the Chief of Chaplains."

This time the prisoners and their homemade litters were headed for a place in the mountains called Sambakol. Carrying anything was agonizing; the poles which supported the fragile stretchers dug into the shoulders of the wasted litter-bearers. No one volunteered for the exhausting task of carrying the wounded POWs.

Kapaun never ordered anyone to pick up a stretcher. Whenever a brief break in the march ended, he merely called out, "Let's pick 'em up." All along the line of march the soldiers responded, hoisting their wounded buddies and trudging ahead in the snow.[45] Kapaun knew that the other prisoners were watching him. In spite of his frozen feet, he forced himself to do the job.[46]

Sambakol was a small farming community located several miles southwest of Pyoktong. The Americans who were being held there did not refer to the town by its geographical name. To them the prison was simply "The Valley."

NINE

The Valley

The legend of Emil Kapaun, already flourishing because of his heroism on the battlefields of Korea, reached maturity in The Valley and Camp No. 5 at Pyoktong.

Even before the prisoners had completed their freezing journey from Pyoktong to The Valley, Kapaun's character was being tested again. Chaplain Kenneth C. Hyslop, a Northern Baptist minister, grew weak and fell behind the line of march. Unable to eat because the Communists had kicked in his ribs when they captured him, Hyslop was dying.

Kapaun heard about the plight of his stricken colleague and found him in the dark. He comforted Hyslop throughout the night, remaining at his side as the chaplain slipped into a coma. When death ended Hyslop's ordeal, Kapaun made sure that his Christian colleague received a decent burial.[1]

As soon as they reached The Valley the Americans saw that their new home was a God-made prison. Mountains up to 8,000 feet high surrounded an open area, which was about three miles long and less than a mile wide.[2] North Korean families had lived there, but the Communists chased them away before about 750 prisoners and their guards marched into the little town.

It was not a conventional penal colony. Instead, the existing structures—small homes built with mud walls and straw roofs,[3] and hardly modern by western standards, chicken coops, and a former elementary school—had been converted into crude housing for the captives.[4]

116

Camp No. 5, Pyoktong, North Korea

Because The Valley was far above sea level and the mountains cut off much of the sunshine, the temperature in that part of North Korea often dropped to 40 degrees below zero during that winter of 1950–51.

The buildings in The Valley afforded scant shelter from the bitter winter weather. If they had any heat at all, it was the traditional, but archaic Korean method of distributing warm air. The heating system in the houses relied on underground clay pipes leading from the kitchen stove throughout the home.[5] Depending on the intensity of the wind outside, sometimes the smoke which occurred when the morning and evening meals were being cooked remained in the kitchen. At other times, however, it passed through the pipes under the adjacent rooms, but that made those sections of the building unbearably hot. The smoke cooled as it passed beneath other areas and, there being no other source of heat, the rooms which were the farthest away were extremely chilly.[6]

The Communists did not supply blankets, so the POWs who lived in the coldest rooms huddled together, shivering in the remnants of their lightweight uniforms. Even though men in some of the prisons gave their heavier clothing to their buddies who lived in parts of the houses which the heat never reached, several Americans froze to death.[7]

The Chinese staff separated the wounded GIs from the others and assigned them to one of the commandeered huts in The Valley. Kapaun pleaded that these men needed him and he should stay with them, but to no avail. The chaplain continued to argue until the guards threatened him and compelled him to leave.

The next morning they herded all of the American officers into a compound at the north end of the camp.[8] Kapaun objected again and insisted on being quartered with the enlisted personnel. The guards were more forceful this time; they prodded him with their gun butts and forced him to remain with the captured officers.

Just having Kapaun among them boosted some soldiers' spirits. Captain Robert E. Burke recalled that "...as we approached the house where we were to be interned, the sun appeared and soon the clouds completely disappeared. The sun referred to was not the celestial body but the warm friendly greeting of the MAN of God."[9]

Kapaun discovered that if he seemed relaxed everyone felt better. So he grinned and introduced himself to newcomers, "My name is Kapaun, glad to have you share our paradise." The oppressive conditions in The Valley did not disturb Kapaun's demeanor. He and Mayo often exchanged a grin and a couple of catch phrases: The Chaplain spoke the Latin words, "Ni illegitimi carborundum esse," and Mayo replied with a rough English translation, "Don't let the bastards get you down."[10]

In the first weeks of their captivity few details about Kapaun and the other survivors of the fighting at Unsan reached U.S. authorities. During November 1950, however, the enemy decided on a propaganda gimmick. They would free a handful of the Americans. When the rest of the world heard of this good deed by the Chinese, perhaps they would think more kindly about people who believed in Communism.

Kapaun seemed to sense what was about to happen. One morning he told Private Peter Busatti, "Pete, you won't have to worry too much now." When the incredulous Busatti questioned him, Kapaun continued, "Because you'll be going home soon." Busatti laughed and replied, "It's O. K., Father, I'm not scared, because you're around and if I die I might get to heaven."

Busatti could not forget Kapaun's remarks and prayed that they would come true. Two nights before Thanksgiving, Busatti and the other POWs were trying to sleep. About 2 A.M. a guard entered their frigid hut and flashed a light on a paper that he was holding.

The Chinese soldier called out Busatti's name. As the startled prisoner arose and began to dress, the first thought to cross his mind was that the guard was planning to take him outside and kill him. Then, after recalling Kapaun's confident prediction, he was still scared but now calmer.

The next day Kapaun's prediction proved true. The Chinese released 26 wounded prisoners and Busatti.[11] One POW who was freed carried the welcome news that Kapaun was in good condition.

The emaciated Americans who remained behind began to realize that their hopes of leaving The Valley alive were fading. Trying to survive on their meager rations was becoming impossible. The Communists had reduced their meals to 450 grams per day.[12] In short, the captives were starving to death.

To make matters worse, it was necessary to soften the cracked corn and millet before the POWs could eat them. In doing so, whatever vitamins were contained in those foods disappeared in the long cooking process. One after another the prisoners began to get pellagra and beriberi from their inadequate diet.[13]

Kapaun came to the conclusion that there was only one alternative to starvation. He had to find a way to steal food from the Communists, not only for himself, but for the other captives, too. But taking someone else's property violated the Ten Commandments, a prisoner reminded him. Kapaun replied that "Thou Shalt Not Steal" did not apply to men in these desperate straits.[14]

The solution, Kapaun decided, was to sneak out of his hut in the middle of the night, prowl around the camp and search for food. Before he left, he prayed for guidance from Dismas, the so-called

"Good Thief." The chaplain remembered how the Gospel of Luke told of two criminals who were crucified with Jesus. One admonished Jesus for failing to save himself. The second man, Dismas, reminded the other insurgent that they deserved their fate, but that Jesus had done nothing wrong.[15]

When Kapaun returned from his nightly forays and surprised the prisoners with sacks of grain and pocketsful of salt, it was evident that his prayers were being heard. Pretty soon other men began to petition the "Good Thief" to help them, too.

Even with a prayerful start Kapaun's missions were risky. Somehow he had to evade the sentries. The chaplain was well aware that if he were apprehended it would mean a severe penalty. A favorite punishment which the Chinese inflicted on a captive was to force him to stand on a frozen river for up to five hours.[16] Sometimes they made the man remove most of his clothing before sending him out on the ice. But the guards almost never detected Kapaun, and his efforts to find garlic, peppers, and other foods were amazingly successful.

One chilly night Kapaun sneaked out of the building where he lived with 19 other POWs. He crept over to a shed and broke into it. There was nothing edible there, but to Kapaun's surprise the shed backed up against a Korean corn crib. The chaplain found that he could reach his arm into the adjoining enclosure and when he did, his prayers for food were answered.

"Perhaps I shouldn't say it but he was the best food thief we had in the camp," Captain O'Connor declared. "Once he came back with a sack of potatoes. How he got it I'll never know. It must have weighed at least 100 pounds."[17] Occasionally The Valley's clerical burglar even persuaded the guards to give him some rock salt.[18]

The prisoners employed every ruse to snatch more food from the enemy. The Communists' customary method of providing supplies to their captives turned into another chance for Kapaun to show his daring. The guards would send a handpicked group of POWs to pick up rations from an open shed which was located at the far end of The Valley.

As the men formed into ranks to march to the supply building, Kapaun sneaked in at the end of the line. When the work party neared its destination, he disappeared into the bushes and crawled around to the far side of the shed. What happened next had been planned. The Americans suddenly started fighting among themselves and temporarily distracted the guards.

Kapaun seized the opportunity. The chaplain darted into the building and grabbed a sack of cracked corn. Then he slipped back into the surrounding undergrowth and waited until he could carry his spoils back to the area where the POWs lived. The food that Kapaun stole helped ailing Americans, so he had no qualms about taking it.[19]

Other prisoners also pilfered food, but some of them kept it for themselves. Kapaun noticed what they were doing, yet he handled the problem without admonishing them openly. Late one night, he brought the captives whatever he had just stolen. In front of the others, Kapaun publicly thanked God for a new supply of food "which all can share equally." The message was clear and the hoarding soon ended.

Thanksgiving arrived in The Valley, but the guards hardly regarded an American holiday as cause for a feast. The Communist cooks prepared a soup that day by boiling nine heads of cabbage. Then they apportioned it among 500 prisoners.[20] No wonder that Dr. Sidney Esensten, another POW, wrote later that Kapaun and the other Americans had lost up to 20 percent of their weight during the first month of their captivity.[21]

Under supervision of North Korean sentries, groups of prisoners climbed the hills around The Valley looking for anything that would burn, even twigs and scraps of scrub oak.[22] It was the only fuel available for heating food and boiling water. However, even their most diligent efforts sometimes yielded only enough wood for a few hours of cooking every day.

The guards who accompanied them on those assignments had no sympathy for the Americans. If an emaciated captive stumbled under a load of wood they either kicked the man until he staggered to his feet or left him to die by the side of the trail.

Those searches for firewood also provided an unexpected opportunity for the prisoners to send an ingenious signal to the American planes that sometimes flew overhead. The men pretended to be working, but actually they deliberately formed an arrangement of haystacks on the side of a hill. When seen from the air they spelled "P-O-W." Unfortunately, the Communists discovered the plan before the American pilots noticed the sequence of letters. The scheme succeeded only in infuriating the North Korean major who was in charge of watching the prisoners.[23]

Kapaun participated in the wood-gathering expeditions whenever he could.[24] He looked for twigs, but the chaplain also had a second, secret motive. Part of the path into the hills was the same as the route to the supply shed, and it took the chaplain past that section of The Valley where the American enlisted men were being held.

Many of the enlisted POWs had served with Kapaun in the 8th Cavalry. He was their beloved Father Kapaun. They knew that he often joined in the work details which passed near their enclosure.

If they saw a group of Americans approaching, the bedraggled enlisted men lined up along the fence to await their chaplain.

The prisoners could recognize Kapaun from a distance: medium height, a sharp pointed nose, a gaunt man who had become full bearded. One of his most distinguishing characteristics was not physical, but rather the knit U.S. Army cap that he usually wore atop his thinning reddish-brown hair.[25]

As Kapaun walked alongside the clusters of young enlisted men, he paused and gave them what they wanted: a smile to one, a verbal pat-on-the-back and a prayer with the next prisoner. If he had an extra moment or two he detoured from his usual route and visited the sick and wounded. The smallest sign of hope and good cheer meant a great deal.[26]

Whenever the chaplain received news that an enlisted man had died, he would return to the officers' area and ask someone to go back and assist him with the burial. No one was eager to help, but it also was a chance to scrounge for food, so Major David F. MacGhee frequently joined the chaplain.[27]

Something else was on Kapaun's mind as he greeted the enlisted POWs. He also listened attentively. Whatever scraps of information Kapaun learned about what was happening in the prison he could pass along to other men. Of course, those brief conversations also enabled him to tell the prisoners some good news, if there were any.

The captives, not only the Catholics but also those of other faiths and men with no religious convictions, were Kapaun's congregation behind bars. Everyone called him "Father Kapaun." The young POWs relied on his guidance. The chaplain, on the other hand, enjoyed his greatest satisfaction just from helping them. He stressed one idea again and again: Do not believe the lies that the Communists tell us about God and the United States.

While some prisoners languished physically and slowly gave up any hope of surviving, Kapaun kept busy performing tasks that absolutely had to be done. Many were so repulsive that everyone avoided them. Perhaps the worst were cleaning the latrines and helping the men who suffered so badly from dysentery that they constantly soiled their ragged clothing as well as themselves.

Kapaun removed their foul garments and bloody bandages and carried them to a stream which flowed through The Valley. The surface frequently was frozen, but he invariably smashed a hole in the ice and washed the dirty shreds of cloth in the icy water.[28] At other times Kapaun found cotton undershirts somewhere and tore them into fresh bandages.

The handworking skills that Kapaun had learned during his childhood in Kansas became useful again. He became adept at bending pieces of scrap metal into new forms. Although he worked outside in January without gloves and used a rock for his only tool, Kapaun pounded and twisted chunks of metal so carefully that the pots which he created were almost free of leaks.[29] The rice that Kapaun stole, the twigs that he gathered, the cooking pots that he shaped, together they were the means that allowed him to furnish a hot meal to his fellow prisoners.

Several American officers traded their watches to the North Koreans in exchange for tobacco. Then they supplied some of it to Kapaun. The next day he surprised the POWs by returning to his old habit of smoking oak leaves or dried garlic stuffed into strips of Communist newspapers. Everyone wondered what had happened to his share of the tobacco. The chaplain admitted that he gave it to his sick and wounded friends.[30] Because he thought that it was necessary, Kapaun also did business with the Communists, swapping his watch for a blanket. Then he cut it into pieces and made socks for the weaker prisoners.

Kapaun cajoled some POWs and prayed with others. If it helped, he told them jokes. He held the prisoners' fragile bodies when delirium overtook them. The chaplain let them smoke his beloved pipe stuffed with cabbage leaves. "We always knew that this man was a real friend," a survivor of The Valley declared.

In a thousand ways Kapaun infused in the captives a desire to hang on, to live. "It was his actual deeds that gave the prisoners such a tremendous impact as they watched him living by God's law. In a few words, Chaplain Kapaun practiced what he preached," said Lieutenant Ralph Nardella.

Amid below-zero weather, starvation, and constant sickness, just staying alive had become a daily struggle. "By his example he sometimes forced the little bit of good remaining in these starving men to the fore," declared another prisoner, Sergeant Charles B. Schlichter.[31] Kapaun coped with imprisonment better than many other captives. "When others were getting meaner the priest was only kinder," said another American soldier. "The longer we were in the valley, the rougher it got, and the rougher it got, the gentler Father Kapaun became."

Conditions in some prisons in North Korea were so extreme that a few POWs, angered because other men stank from their own excreta, rolled their helpless comrades outside the huts and let them freeze to death. Kapaun insisted that there was some good in everyone, but sometimes his beliefs were hard to prove.

In spite of the ceaseless efforts of Dr. Anderson, Dr. Esensten, Kapaun and other valiant prisoners, the Americans were dying one by one. Pneumonia was rampant. Usually the only medication that the Chinese supplied was cough drops and they could not control the illness.[32] Severe diarrhea was another problem. Often it could be stopped if a man swallowed a mixture of gunpowder and charcoal made out of baked dog bones. "It put a plug in you," many believed. But relief was only temporary and ended abruptly.

On occasions the American physicians had to perform operations, but they had no medical instruments after they were captured. The prisoners finally created them by removing the steel arches from their combat boots and sharpening the metal.[33] Operations with these improvised scalpels were agonizing because the doctors frequently had no anesthesia to give to their patients. Penicillin also was rarely available.[34] Worse yet, the camp administrators were known to deny medicine to a sick POW unless he first confessed to anti-Communist activities.

The shock of their capture, especially when the war seemed almost over, and their harsh, primitive confinement were too much for some men. Many whose wounds were not attended never recovered and died within a couple of months. Observers noticed that the youngest of the remaining captives slowly began to lapse. Largely cut off from the watchful eye of Kapaun and tougher noncommissioned officers, too many of the enlisted men began to develop "give-up-itis."[35]

Those prisoners started downhill by skipping their evening meal. That, they hoped, meant fewer frantic trips to the latrine and a more comfortable night.[36] Then they pulled the blankets over their heads and curled into a fetal position. Those prisoners were slowly shutting out the rest of the world.

Unless a determined person such as Kapaun could jolt those men out of their stupor, the sequence of their behavior indicated that their death was predictable—and usually within a matter of a few weeks. Coaxing or reasoning seldom helped. There was only one way to prevent the inevitable. Someone had to yank those prisoners to their feet or anger them until they jumped up; then forcefeed them and if they spit out food, shove it back into their mouths.[37]

Stripped of most material sustenance, many POWs needed a reason to stay alive. Unfortunately, too many Korean War prisoners had grown up without a spiritual anchor to sustain their lives. Some observers attributed this failing to the absence of strong values in the prisoners' families and schools during their childhood. What others lacked Kapaun possessed in abundance. It was character. By his example the farmer/priest from Kansas earned the esteem of all of the captives as well as their Communist guards.

One time after a Chinese official gave some tobacco to a high-ranking prisoner, the American jumped up and shouted to the men around him, "Three cheers for Comrade Hu. Hip hip hurray, hip hip hurray!" Kapaun heard the words and they angered him. He would not tolerate such fawning over a Communist. He immediately berated the American officer in front of the other captives, and the embarrassed man walked away.[38]

The Chinese and North Korean staff in The Valley not only grudgingly respected Kapaun, but they also feared his religious influence. They told him so. Therefore, the Communists became suspicious when he asked for permission to accompany Dr. Anderson on his rounds to check on the ailing prisoners.

"What these men need is medicine, not prayer," a Chinese official said to Kapaun. "Since they aren't getting any medicine, a little prayer won't hurt," the chaplain replied. "No, you will not be permitted to spread your poisonous Christian propaganda here," the Chinese stated, ending the discussion.[39]

Kapaun did not hide the fact that he was a Catholic priest. The religious stole around his shoulders openly identified him. What rankled the Chinese even more was that Kapaun was a leader among the POWs. They knew that at night groups of the Americans waited in their darkened huts as Kapaun moved stealthily from one building to another to meet with them.

Even though the Communists had banned religious activities,[40] the chaplain led regular prayer services. Surprisingly, under Kapaun's prompting, the captives asked not only for their own freedom, but also that their captors would be delivered from materialistic Communism.

The guards called Kapaun an agitator and circulated rumors that the American enlisted men did not want him to visit them. That did not stop him, even though the enlisted POWs were more difficult to reach because they were held in a lower area of The Valley. One time the sentries caught Kapaun on his way to pray with other prisoners. The Chinese cautioned him: "There is no sense in your risking your life in this manner; prayers won't help these men." But their warnings fell on deaf ears.

The first Christmas in a bleak Communist prison arrived for several hundred prisoners in The Valley. As Kapaun assembled the POW officers to celebrate the holyday,[41] the squalor of their compound reminded them of the cave where Jesus was born. New Year's Day was even more disheartening for some POWs in another prison camp. The Chinese allowed them to buy a sick cow for a special meal, but then the guards kept most of the meat for themselves.[42]

A startling turn of events, however, demonstrated that the Communist leaders could not suppress the spirit of Christmas. The chief officials in The Valley decided to show the prisoners how well they had indoctrinated the Korean children. The Communists brought the Americans to a small building where they had gathered local boys and girls, from about seven to ten years old, to perform for the captives.

This was not holiday good will. Instead, the event was planned as a propaganda show. Everything that the children did contained a Communist message—hammer and sickle songs, harvesting the crops dances, distinctive clothing—all intended to glorify the proletariat and the Communist workers.

When the performance stopped and it was time for an intermission, the prisoners slowly, softly began to sing in unison: "Silent night, holy night..." As their prayerful chorus carried throughout the building and on to the stage, the volume of sound around them began to increase. One after another, more voices were added. Young, high voices joined in "...all is calm, all is bright..."

The Americans looked around, amazed. The happy Korean children knew that it was Christmas! They were singing with the prisoners! As the combined voices of the American men and the Korean boys and girls converged in the closing words of the beautiful Christmas hymn, "...Sleep in heavenly peace," the Communist guards realized that their propaganda scheme had turned against them. They blew their whistles and hustled the youngsters off the stage. The performance was over.[43] But the prisoners were smiling. It was obvious that the world was not all bad. Even in The Valley, at Christmastime there were still reasons to hope.

Shortly after New Year's Day 1951 the Communists decided to move the prisoners out of The Valley and march them back to Pyoktong. Many were ill and others still were suffering from wounds. For all of them it was another grueling wintertime journey toward the freezing Yalu River and their grim destination, Camp No. 5.

Dr. Esensten and Kapaun trudged along near the front of the column. Men in the rear frequently called out for medical help and Esensten headed back to assist them. Kapaun usually accompanied him, for this was a chance to boost the spirits of everyone along the route of the march. Sometimes words were not enough and Kapaun had to coerce them into helping one another.[44]

By one estimate almost 40 percent of the American soldiers who were captured in the Korean War died in Communist prisons.[45] Hundreds perished at camps in North Korea during the horrifying winter of 1950–51. Yet only about 20 of the men who were held in The Valley died and some of those succumbed to wounds which they had received before they were captured.[46]

What were the reasons for this relatively high survival rate? The dedicated efforts of Doctors Esensten and Anderson and other determined Americans were part of the explanation. But in some immeasurable way Kapaun was the answer to why so many emerged from The Valley and eventually returned to freedom.[47]

His presence among the Americans was the ray of warm sunshine that flooded their tomb and preserved a spark of hope. The faith that Kapaun kept alive overcame shortages of food and medicine, despair, the inescapable cold weather.

The extent of Kapaun's influence became clear after the survivors were repatriated in 1953. Lieutenant Raymond M. Dowe, Jr. wrote a long report about life in the prison at Sambakol. To him, however, the place was not simply The Valley—he called it "Father Kapaun's Valley."[48]

TEN

Camp No. 5

Anyone flying over Pyoktong looked down on a typical North Korean waterfront town. About 10,000 persons lived there in conventional small wooden houses. A pagoda, a church, and some shops served the remote community. Surrounded on three sides by the Yalu River and mountains and barely two miles from the border with Communist China, the town at one time had been a summer resort.[1]

From the ground, however, it was obvious that this ordinary community was not what it appeared to be. It included a prison which the Communists had named Camp No. 5. Ringed with barbed wire and sentry posts and staffed by Chinese administrators and North Korean guards, the camp contained about 30 Japanese-style wooden buildings.[2]

The POWs who marched into Pyoktong in the middle of January 1951 immediately recognized Camp No. 5 as a frigid, disease-ridden pesthole. Many of them, including Kapaun, eventually died there. It was the first of 20 such places in North Korea where American soldiers and a few civilians were held in captivity during the Korean War.[3]

The return journey through the snow-clogged mountains between The Valley and Pyoktong had cost the lives of nine of the captives. It was a harsh winter, but some of the prisoners arrived without overcoats or boots. Although the guards already had stolen many of their possessions, along the way the guards had confiscated the prisoners' footwear and replaced it with thin sneakers.[4] The POWs saw that many buildings in Pyoktong had not been repaired after the

128

American bombing raid which had forced them to leave during the previous November.

In the first months of 1951 Camp No. 5 was the site of a psychological battle. It pitted the weary minds of the POWs against a tightly controlled system of Communist indoctrination. Even though Kapaun's military grade was captain, and other captives outranked him, he nonetheless was a universally accepted commander of the defense of the prisoners' religious beliefs and welfare. The strongest person in any group usually influences the behavior of all, and Chaplain Kapaun was one of the dominant voices in the camp.[5]

As soon as the captives arrived, the Chinese officials instituted an ideological campaign against the Americans, directed especially at the minds of some younger, less-educated enlisted men. Their objective was to reduce the POWs from disciplined, but hungry, human beings to snarling animals fighting each other over scraps of food. The Communists knew that if they succeeded in eradicating the prisoners' spirit and will to resist it would be easier to divide and conquer their captives. That, they assumed, would prove that Communism was superior to any Western-style religion and that democracy was a failure.

The guards started by separating the arrivals into pre-selected categories. First they put Kapaun and the other officers off by themselves on a hill overlooking the town.[6] That limited their ability to maintain any influence over the enlisted men. The next step was to segregate the enlisted men, holding the sergeants separately from the rest of the soldiers. The black and Hispanic soldiers also were transferred away from the remaining captives.

The Communist plan for separating the prisoners had two purposes: to promote dissension among the Americans and to prevent them from hatching plans to escape.[7] As a result the Chinese frequently moved the POWs from house to house and broke up the groups who roomed together in order to prevent the prisoners from forming coalitions against them.[8] The Communist officials decided that by separating the Americans into selected groups, they also could try to identify a few who were susceptible to persuasion based on racial, religious, or economic arguments.

Kapaun was upset when he found that the guards had isolated the sick and wounded. He became more aggravated when he saw that they had left those POWs unprotected in the bitter cold. The chaplain decided that something had to be done about this situation. He located one of the Chinese supervisors and demanded that the stricken men be sheltered, but the Communist paid little attention.

The enemy soldiers forced all of the American officers into two huts. But the buildings were in such poor condition that only a couple of rooms were habitable. The usable space barely provided standing room. Even though the temperatures were well below freezing, it was apparent that someone had to begin making repairs immediately so other rooms could be used.

Most of the prisoners were too hungry and exhausted to volunteer to help. Moreover, food was the most immediate need that first night in Camp No. 5. Kapaun's first task was to find something for the men to eat, and after he dealt with that problem, he and Captain McClain started patching up the huts.[9] Other POWs joined them in pulling nails, pieces of tin, and even broken boards from the rubble. Eventually, they repaired the damaged buildings.

Kapaun made a mental list of what must be done to improve their living conditions. The next project was the construction of an outdoor fireplace so that the prisoners could cook some of their food. At first, the chaplain had no idea where he could find enough bricks and other building material. He started scrounging among the ruins of a bombed-out church adjacent to the officers' housing and soon located everything that he needed.

As Kapaun observed the sagging spirits of his fellow prisoners, he decided that what they needed the most was hot coffee, or at least some warm liquid that reminded the men of American coffee.

The chaplain obtained the water easily. He simply went over to a stream that flowed through the camp and smashed a rock against the frozen surface until he could reach down for some of the water. The chaplain already had the pan that he needed to boil the liquid, having shaped one out of a piece of corrugated scrap metal.[10]

The difficult ingredient was a supply of coffee beans. The Americans had none and Kapaun knew that if the Chinese had any, they would not give it. So he decided to substitute a few burnt crusts of sorghum grain. About 5 A.M. each day, an hour or more before the whistle blew to awaken the other POWs, the chaplain left his hut to begin working. The temperature might be 20 degrees below zero, but he started an outdoor fire with twigs, corn husks, and sometimes bits of pine. Then he brewed his make-believe beverage. Finally, with a cheery "Good morning. Hot coffee?", Kapaun entered the gloomy prison houses at daybreak and poured a small amount into each man's bowl. Their wan smiles were his reward.[11]

The captives who required the most care were in a separate building which the POWs called the "death house." These helpless occupants required constant help. They soiled their uniforms frequently and Kapaun realized that he had to find a way to keep their clothing clean. He needed a wash tub, but nothing was available except a rusting, leaking old oil drum.

Kapaun solved this problem in the same enterprising manner as he had fixed a leaking bicycle tire. He melted the rubber from the sole of an overshoe and applied it to seal the homemade wash basin. Then the chaplain not only washed the men's ragged clothes and filthy bandages, but also dressed the pathetic human hulks. Their "death stares" vanished momentarily and tears swelled in their eyes. The men smiled and gasped, "Thanks, Father." With such dedication, Kapaun was able to keep some of the POWs alive.

Before long the prisoners realized that their chaplain was more than merely a religious leader. To the American doctors he was someone who knew the health problems that everyone was facing. Kapaun also was a practical-minded person who tried to overcome the difficulties of living in prison. Many captives considered him to be a jack-of-all-trades. "Father Kapaun, a man who could do almost anything with his hands, was the camp favorite," wrote war correspondent Frank Noel after his release from imprisonment.[12]

Dozens of POWs in Camp No. 5 and other North Korean prisons were equally versatile. They learned to glue eight pieces of paper together to form a playing card, using a paste made from sorghum and later trimming the edges around the paper. Pieces of waste material were turned into checker games; something hard and round became a baseball; arch supports were sharpened into blades. Watches and pens served little purpose in prison, so the prisoners swapped them for foods such as yud, which was an oriental toffee, and eggs.[13] The Americans also had not lost their taste for smoking and some gave up a day's ration of food for one cigarette.[14]

By controlling the amount of water and meals which the captives received the Chinese tried to soften them up and convince them to accept Communist indoctrination. Americans who cooperated lived better, especially those who listened carefully to their captors' lectures. They were the so-called "Progressives," but there were not many of them. Noel believed that most of the "Progressives" faked their approval of the Communist ideology.[15]

The Communist officials, however, treated harshly any "Reactionaries" who opposed the Marxist ideology.[16] They not only beat these men and forced them to stand on ice for several hours, but the Communists also refused to give them their meals. Even the prisoners who did not resist openly found that in Camp No. 5 the amount of food which they received was hardly enough to keep them alive.

Hungry, confused, and physically weakened, the Americans had become the targets of a well-organized plan of Communist propaganda. "Political education" was the Chinese/North Korean description. The Chinese bombarded the POWs with atheistic slogans such as "God cannot help you, only the CPV can save your precious lives." If a man seemed slow to accept the instructors' reasoning, the Chinese told him, "You don't understand the problem, comrade."[17]

Some of the Chinese lecturers had studied in the United States and they strengthened their arguments by referring frequently to American sports, economics, and politics.[18] Although a handful of the prisoners signed peace petitions and made radio broadcasts favoring Communism, the majority of them either silently disregarded the Marxist ideas or were not equipped intellectually to evaluate them. Moreover, politics bored many of the POWs.

The instructors harangued in English, having learned the language either in the United States or in Christian schools in China and Korea. One of them had attended an Episcopalian college. He made the mistake of publicly calling Kapaun "Father." That disturbed his superiors and, worried that the captured priest might turn this man against them, they removed him from any further contact with the chaplain.[19]

For propaganda purposes, the Chinese officials desperately wanted some of the Americans to confess to war crimes. However, unlike the North Koreans, they did not rely entirely on brutality to force captives to admit their guilt. Instead, the Chinese compelled the POWs to memorize Communist documents for week after week and prohibited them from reading anything else. The Marxist ideology also encouraged prisoners to criticize themselves and to inform on other POWs. The objective was to induce the Americans to distrust each other, and in some cases they did.

"Your life depends on your attitude," the Communists cautioned Major David F. MacGhee during his interrogation.[20] The whole idea was to spread disunity among the captives. The Chinese were intent on breaking down discipline among the prisoners and thought that humiliating the senior American officers would accomplish their purpose. They often forced them to read aloud publicly from the writings of Karl Marx[21] and to carry out the orders of the younger American officers.[22]

Fear spread throughout the camp, but Kapaun and the other Americans soon realized that they were not the only ones who were afraid. The guards, too, were scared. The Communists' philosophy had caught them in a totalitarian web in which they both informed on their comrades and in turn, the same individuals betrayed them.[23] The Communist officers adhered so strictly to Marxist doctrine that after a while the POWs figured out exactly what their captors were going to say.

Lieutenant Mayo described the Communist program to indoctrinate Kapaun and the other Americans at Camp No. 5:

> First they had to eliminate a person's belief in himself,
> a belief which is based on the very uniqueness of a human
> being. The ability to think, the capability to recognize right
> from wrong, truth from falsehood, a conscience.

> By manipulating the environment, increasing or de-
> creasing the food ration to reward correctness or punish bad
> behavior, solitary confinement or physical punishment, they
> sought to instill fear and a sense of impotency and despair.
> Then by forcing a person to bend, little by little to equivo-
> cate, to rationalize, they could shape him as they wanted.

> Not only had an individual's ability to follow the dic-
> tates of his conscience to be eliminated, but also his faith
> and trust in his fellow man. Understanding, compassion,
> empathy and trust had to be replaced by suspicion, hatred
> and isolation. Faith in our country, belief in its principles
> was attacked by a clever mixture of blatant lies, half truths
> and subtle shadings.[24]

That was the harsh environment in which Kapaun sought to
preserve the religious beliefs of the men around him. Mind-condi-
tioning lectures began early each morning and everyone was forced
to attend. The Chinese instructors continued to place the blame for
the war on Wall Street capitalists, claiming that they started the
fighting in order to raise stock prices as a prelude to World War III.

During the winter the Chinese assembled the POWs indoors,
sometimes in a farm house, to hear lectures twice a day about Communism. When the weather became warmer the captives sat outside in the dirt while the instructors preached their Marxist slogans
again and again.

The repetition became so incessant that any prisoners who
wore hats pulled the flaps over their ears. When the Chinese found
out that these men were not trying to protect themselves from the
cold, but instead they wanted to shut out the ceaseless propaganda,
the guards punished these Americans in their preferred way: forcing them to stand at attention for hours at a stretch.[25]

Ironically, the Communists held some of the "political education" talks near the 15 steps that led into the bomb-damaged church
in the officers' compound. That was the place where a few weeks
later Kapaun conducted an Easter morning service which many
survivors regarded as a high point of their imprisonment.

The captives in the North Korean military prisons adopted various strategies for coping with the efforts to indoctrinate them. Ridicule was one course of action. Citing two American comedians who were well known at that time, a prisoner prefaced his remarks about Communism this way, "According to the great doctrines taught us by the noble Stalin, Lenin, Marx, Engels, Amos and Andy...."[26] When his captors ordered another POW to complete a document, he reportedly quipped, "I filled out something like this before and I ended up in the army."

Humor was particularly effective because the Chinese did not know how to handle it. A prisoner befuddled the enemy when he imagined that he was riding a make-believe motorcycle around the camp. The guards reacted by taking him and his phantom motorcycle into custody. After being questioned about his antics, the man reappeared a few hours later. The prisoner reported that the Chinese officials had warned him that it was against the law to ride a motorcycle without permission and he must give up his vehicle if he wanted to avoid going to jail.

Another POW ran around wearing a headband with a feather and claimed to be a blood brother of the Mohawk Indian tribe. When the guards interrogated him, the man simply explained that he was celebrating National Tom-Tom Week.[27]

Kapaun took a different tack. He was willing and able to stand up to the Communists who lectured the POWs. In fact, he questioned the instructors about their doctrines, and they embarrassed themselves when they could not explain their arguments.

A short Chinese major named Comrade Sun was the chief protagonist. He ranted and raved for hours in front of groups of disinterested prisoners. Sun clearly hated the Americans and the ideas which they held sacred. After each talk about the theories of Communism, he forced the POWs to comment on what he had said.

That was the moment to be cautious. Sun was a volatile individual and woe to the American who crossed him. He would pounce across the speaking platform in the manner of a wounded animal if anyone challenged his viewpoints. The prisoners knew that the Chinese penalized anyone who spoke his mind by sentencing him to weeks of solitary confinement in a freezing hole in the ground.

Although Kapaun did not provoke controversy, he also did not avoid it. The chaplain sat quietly in the dirt among the other prisoners, but when the opportunity presented itself he asked pointed questions which were intended to refute Sun's statements. His calm and logical manner enraged the Chinese officer. The frustrated Sun accused him of spreading propaganda against the Communists.

Kapaun only smiled and replied, "No, it is not anti-Communist propaganda, it is Christian love and I shall pray for your soul."[28]

Accustomed to outmaneuvering poorly informed prisoners, the Chinese could not accept the fact that Kapaun so openly rejected their Marxist principles. They dragged their antagonist in front of the other Americans. The Communist officials tried to frighten him, but he did not waver. They would not forget that it was the prisoners' religious leader who had outtalked them.

Years later Lieutenant McClain analyzed the chaplain's strategy:

> Father Kapaun never backed down from the Chinese in discussing any subject of their choosing. He would never antagonize or engage them in a debate, but when the opportunity came he was more intellectually armed than they were. He was always the gentleman and never displayed emotional strains. The Chinese seemed to both fear and respect him for his actions and they were not oblivious to his devotion to his fellow prisoners.[29]

When the Chinese argued that religion exploited the masses of the people, Kapaun singled out the English-speaking instructors. He asked them if their missionary teachers had done the wrongs which the Communists alleged. Sometimes the staff at the prison retaliated by harassing the Americans. "Where is your God now? Let him come and take you from here," they taunted Kapaun.[30] "See if he can feed you. You should thank Mao Tse Tung and Stalin for your daily bread. You cannot see or hear or feel your God, therefore, He does not exist."

Kapaun responded that God was as real as the air that they breathed, but could not see. He was more explicit another time: "One day the Good Lord will save the Chinese and free them from the scourge that has set upon them. The Good Lord, as He fed the thousands on the mountain, will also take care of us. Mao Tse Tung could not make a tree or a flower or stop the thunder and lightning."[31] The frustrated Chinese could not overcome Kapaun's arguments and they finally gave up trying.

The chaplain not only expressed his religious belief verbally, but he also worked to assure that the prisoners practiced their faith. If they swore he scolded them. When Kapaun met with a group of prisoners, he asked them to thank God for His favors, even if they were not aware of any.

The guards wanted to restrict Kapaun's religious activities, so they confiscated his rosary beads. They thought that would stop him from praying. However, he was as handy as ever and made another set from strands of barbed wire. The chaplain did not mind deceiving the guards in order to accomplish his purpose.

He sometimes gave the appearance of working, moving around the camp while carrying an old bucket. Its only purpose was to distract the guards so that he could meet and pray with groups of the prisoners.[32]

On many nights the captives huddled in their huts awaiting Kapaun's arrival. Suddenly the door opened and a stealthy figure appeared among them. "Evening prayers, gentlemen!", the chaplain announced in the dark. The services had to be brief because there were several groups to visit. Kapaun read quotations from the Bible, recited the Our Father with the Protestant soldiers and inquired about everyone's health. Then he was gone, on his way to another hut.

Even without seeing his face in the shadows, the prisoners always knew that their nighttime visitor was Kapaun. They recognized his flat mid-western voice and the outline of the peculiar knit cap which he had created from the sleeve of an old sweater.[33] Kapaun's fatigue uniform was torn and dirty and he looked like every other half-starved POW. But in the words of Lieutenant Dowe "...by his very presence he could for a time turn a stinking mud hut into a cathedral."[34]

Several prisoners who survived Camp No. 5 remembered the same details as Major MacGhee:

> As time went by, a strange transformation occurred in the Chaplain's appearance, he began physically to look like Christ. His features became more and more ascetic through emaciation, and his long straggly hair turned to reddish-brown. The resemblance was not the product of any one man's imagination; it was so pronounced that the men kidded him about it.

When that happened, MacGhee noted, Kapaun turned away "...in any agony of embarrassment."[35]

The Chinese could not figure out how to handle this forthright clergyman. They appeared to trust Kapaun, but they were aware that they could neither scare, nor cajole, nor humiliate him. Most of all, the enemy officers saw how the prisoners admired the chaplain and they wanted to limit his influence over the other Americans.[36]

They told the enlisted POWs that Kapaun was a capitalist propagandist, but none of them turned against him. The guards also accused him of leading counterrevolutionary activities. The chaplain just smiled at those charges, and that enraged the Chinese.[37] They were resolved to find any excuse to put him in jail.

Early in the spring of 1951, the Communists finally thought that they had grounds to punish Kapaun. It happened after the Chinese picked out a pair of American officers and tortured them in order to extract information. They hung the captives from ropes until their wrist joints pulled apart. The two men finally broke under the pain and told their captors what they wanted; that Kapaun slandered the Chinese, advocated resistance to the propaganda program, was hostile toward his captors, and threatened that any American who cooperated with the enemy would be court-martialed.[38]

All of the prisoners were certain that the accusations were false. Yet when the two brutalized officers returned to their hut, uncertain how the other prisoners would accept them after their ordeal, Kapaun was the first to rush forward and comfort them. "You never should have suffered for a moment trying to protect me," he said.

Everyone worried that Kapaun would face a trumped-up public trial, conviction, and punishment. However, that did not happen. Instead, the guards hauled him before a group of Chinese officials. They browbeat Kapaun, but did nothing else. The POWs realized then what many had suspected. The Communist leaders of the camp were afraid of him.[39] The enemy soldiers feared a mass rebellion among the Americans if they publicly mistreated the beloved religious leader.

Even though all the Americans looked up to Kapaun, he suffered as much as anyone from living conditions in Camp No. 5. Their quarters were especially depressing. Most mud-walled Korean houses contained three or four rooms, but often the rooms were as small as seven feet by ten feet. Lieutenant Joseph A. Magnant recalled that into such a tiny space the guards crammed a dozen or more of the lice-infested captives.[40] To make matters worse, the buildings sometimes were in danger of collapsing because the POWs had stripped them of everything that might be used for firewood.

There was barely standing room, yet somehow each POW had to find a space to sleep on the dirt floor. Blankets were not available until months later, so Kapaun and the other captives in his hut improvised a novel way of keeping warm. Each man slept with his feet in the armpits of the two POWs on either side of him.[41] Nevertheless, occasionally a prisoner awakened and found that the man who had rested next to him during the night had frozen to death.[42]

Such close quarters were a natural breeding ground for disease. Skin infections passed quickly from man to man. Pneumonia was widespread. Even when sleep was possible, attacks of diarrhea frequently interrupted nights in the unlighted huts. One captive and then another would stumble over their comrades toward the door and outside into the open. Dysentery struck some prisoners so quickly that they soiled their garments before their brains could warn them.

Diseases spread easily because for many months the POWs seldom had any soap to wash themselves. Except for stripping off their tattered uniforms and washing their bodies and clothing in snow or icy water, the prisoners almost never had an opportunity for any personal hygiene. As a consequence, body lice attacked hundreds of POWs.

Infestations of lice particularly overwhelmed those who were too feeble to spend the two hours every morning that were necessary to delouse themselves. It was a loathsome task to remove the tiny insects from another man's body, but Kapaun never hesitated to help his unfortunate comrades. Any diversion helped, so he started counting the dead lice. Other officers soon did the same.[43]

Although some prisoners criticized men who were unable to care for themselves, Kapaun would not join in scolding them. Everyone griped sometimes, but whenever Kapaun complained he spoke only about some injustice which was hurting someone else.

Sickness swept through all of the prisons in North Korea, but the Communist administrators were reluctant about cooperating with the captured U.S. Army doctors. The American physicians offered advice, but the poorly trained Chinese medical personnel either were too proud or too ignorant to accept it.

It surprised the American doctors to learn that the Chinese were inserting small pieces of chicken livers during operations on sick prisoners.[44] When Dr. Esensten asked for information about the procedure, a Chinese official in Camp No. 5 replied, "You are not here to study medicine. You are here to study Communism. When America is liberated all the American doctors will have to go back to school to learn whom to save and whom not to save—those who are for the people and those who are against the people."[45]

The overall well-being of the captives in the camp could have been improved. However, "Dirty Hands," the political chief of the Chinese medical staff, controlled all decisions regarding health care.[46] If, for example, a prisoner had symptoms of dysentery and night blindness, or any combination of sicknesses, "Dirty Hands" authorized enough medicine to treat only one of the ailments.[47] The Chinese held the handful of American doctors separately from the other captives, making matters worse because it prevented them from treating the hundreds of enlisted prisoners.

An exception was Dr. William Shadish. The Chinese had assigned him to live alone in the enlisted men's compound. His tiny building contained only a dispensary and a small bedroom. Except for those occasions when a prisoner came for medical attention, the guards had warned Dr. Shadish not to associate with the other Americans. Isolated both mentally and physically, he was trapped in a special kind of captivity.

One day as he sat outside his hut, Dr. Shadish noticed that a man wearing a tattered GI uniform was walking toward him. The other person obviously was an American, yet the doctor did not recognize him. The prisoner approached to within 100 feet; then he raised his arm and called out, "Good morning, doctor, how are you? I am Father Kapaun." The physician waved and shouted back, "Good morning, Father, how are you?"

Kapaun appeared in the distance from time to time and called out to Shadish. On some days that was the only conversation that the doctor had. Except for those few words, the two men never met. Yet, years later Shadish remembered how those hearty greetings had periodically lifted his sagging spirits.[48]

Captain Robert E. Burke described how Kapaun conducted himself during that period:

> By February and March, 1951, the majority of us had turned into animals, fighting for food, irritable, selfish, miserable. The good priest continued to conduct himself as a human being. When the chips were down, Father proved to be the greatest example of manhood I've ever seen in my life. Although not every man slipped into primitive and savage existence, our good priest stood head and shoulders above everyone.[49]

The unhealthy conditions in the prison at Pyoktong, including an attitude which a few men held of "What's the use of trying? I'm not going to live anyway," were killing the prisoners in growing numbers. Historians estimated that 1,700 occupants of Camp No. 5 died during the first six months of 1951.[50] At times corpses were stacked eight feet high,[51] because during the winter months, the ground was frozen and Kapaun could not assist in burying the bodies until warmer weather thawed the soil.

The food which the Chinese gave the POWs during that period contained only about 1,200 calories per day. To that meager ration the Communists added insults: "Don't thank God for your food," they taunted the prisoners, "thank Mao Tse Tung."[52]

When the toll in Camp No. 5 began to average 24 deaths every day at the end of February,[53] the Chinese overseers finally became alarmed. They summoned the American doctors and announced that they would supply more medicine. The guards also added barley and pickled peppers to the prisoners' diet and agreed that they would provide better food. That sounded hopeful, but all the captives in North Korea had grown to be wary of any assurances from the Chinese officers. They had learned from experience that their captors often made promises and failed to keep their word.[54]

Even a burial party might lead to something to eat. As the prisoners carried the body of their deceased comrade they looked around for wild raspberries or root cellars where the Koreans stored rice in 100-pound straw sacks. Once Kapaun was part of a funeral detail which found such an enclosure and the POWs broke into it.

As they headed back to camp with their concealed and much-needed plunder, a prisoner asked a familiar question, "Father, doesn't the Good Book say thou shall not steal?" Kapaun's reply eased the man's conscience, "I know that the Lord will forgive this transgression as we take this food not for ourselves but to save others."[55]

The prisoners thought that at last their appetites would be satisfied when a little black pig took a wrong turn and wandered into their compound. As the other POWs watched, and prayed for fresh meat, Kapaun decided to kill the animal. He closed in on the pig, a rock clutched in his upraised fist. Then he brought his weapon crashing down.

What was intended as a fatal blow missed its mark, bouncing off the pig. Frightened, but uninjured, the animal shrieked, loudly enough that a Chinese guard hurried over to investigate. The prisoners' hopes for a tasty meal vanished as the pig sped off in one direction and Kapaun ran the other way.[56]

Meat was on every man's mind. Unfortunately all they could do was talk about it. There was one exception, and Kapaun could claim credit for it. On the night before March 17, he prayed to St. Patrick and asked him to help the starving POWs. His prayers were answered the next day. The Chinese brought a case of liver into the POW compound. The meat was spoiled, but it was the first that many Americans had tasted in several months. And, as if St. Patrick were offering Kapaun a bonus for his feast day, a guard tossed a bag of straw-like Korean tobacco into a group of prisoners.

The surprise delivery of rotten meat notwithstanding, the prisoners were so desperate for vitamins that by the beginning of spring 1951 they began to boil dandelions, sheep sorrel and green weeds and eat them. The soybeans that the Communists distributed actually were a source of proteins. However, the POWs believed that they caused diarrhea and were reluctant to swallow them. Instead, their daily ration usually consisted of two bowls of millet or corn.

Kapaun regularly gave some of his own food to the weaker prisoners.[57] Consequently, his physique was hardly more than wrinkled skin stretched over his bones. The chaplain's appearance was even more conspicuous because he deliberately wore an extra large overcoat. The coat was warm enough, but the real reason why he used it was the unusually big pockets. Kapaun stuffed the pockets with whatever food, perhaps garlic or rice, that he had stolen, yet the guards could not see that he was hiding anything.[58]

Time was far more plentiful than food in Camp No. 5. Wintertime daylight began to fade around 4 P.M. and the prisoners faced long, cold nights in their grimy huts. Conversations about their families and home cooking helped to ward off despair. One man enjoyed discussing his thoughts about baked alaska.

The chaplain supplemented the fictitious menu by describing the full ten-course meals that his mother prepared for the holidays in Kansas: roasted goose, chicken noodle soup, angel food cake, and that Bohemian specialty, kolache. The eyes of the hungry Americans glistened with delight.

Occasionally prisoners in some of the camps tried to raise their morale by sing-along sessions late into the night.[59] At those times it was hardly surprising that sooner or later every discussion among the POWs turned to going home. Each man savored his own hopes. Kapaun announced that after the war ended he planned to collect his back pay and donate $1,000 to charity,[60] reclaim his car which was still in Japan, and visit his family and his fellow prisoners, all in that order.[61]

The Chinese discouraged any thoughts of an early release. In fact, they cautioned the POWs that if they did not accept Communist political indoctrination they would be detained for up to 30 years. Commandant Ding urged the captives in Camp No. 5 to study hard with open minds.[62] Should they remain obdurate, the Chinese warned Lieutenant Mayo, the Americans would be buried "...in a deep hole so we would not stink the area."[63]

Still, the prisoners grasped for straws of hope which might mean that their release was near. Sometimes they could hear huge explosions far to the south. The men wanted badly to believe that the sounds were friendly artillery fire. The noises actually came from American bombers attacking roads and bridges throughout the Communist supply lines. Dreams of freedom made it easy to assume that rescue forces were on the way.

"The guns sound closer tonight," Kapaun speculated one time. "They're coming. They'll be here soon. The moon is full tonight. By the time it's full again, we'll be free." Was his enthusiastic statement merely wishful thinking intended to bolster the spirits of his companions?

If and when U.S. tanks roared up to the gates of the camp Kapaun already knew what his reaction would be. "What are you thinking of, Father?" a prisoner asked when he saw Kapaun smiling broadly. "Of that happy day when the first American rolls down that road," he answered. "Then I'm going to catch that little so-and-so, Comrade Sun, and kick his butt right over the compound fence."[64]

The Americans who suffered together in the prison at Pyoktong came to know each other pretty well. Dr. Esensten later offered his thoughts about Kapaun:

He was almost a Jekyll and Hyde in his personality and his relationship with the men. He was very liberal thinking and very prone to forgive any discrepancies committed by both the officer and enlisted men in relationship to their association with the Chinese and any type of activity which was the least bit friendly toward our captors.

But yet, in his religious viewpoints, he was a very dogmatic individual, with no leeway whatsoever in the doctrines of the church. He felt that anybody who believed in a religious philosophy should accept this positively without qualms, unquestionably without consideration for leniency, and anyone who partially participated in religion should not belong.

He said that if you belong to this religion, you must accept all of its doctrines. You must fulfill the rituals of the religion plus its holidays without asking for relief regardless of whether they seem markedly out of context in the modern world. We always lost in the attempt to liberalize his thinking of religion by throwing out quotations from the Bible and ending up saying this is my creed and my belief and here it is in black and white.[65]

Kapaun did not push his Catholic doctrines on anyone, but the way he conducted himself was persuasive. Other prisoners estimated that 15 of the American officers converted to Catholicism as a result of the chaplain's example.

By now the Communists recognized the extent of Kapaun's influence. Since neither punishment nor threats deterred him they had to find another way to thwart him—if they could do it at all.

ELEVEN

The Dying Place

Although he did not plan it, Kapaun was a principal cause of his failing health and ultimate death. By offering pieces of his clothing to Sergeant Gilbert Christie and others and giving away portions of his food he unwittingly weakened his resistance to pneumonia and other diseases.

A couple of minor injuries made matters worse. A chip flew up and struck Kapaun in the eye when he was chopping wood. The American doctors were unable to give him any medicine and the wound became infected. The best that Kapaun could do was to cover his eye with a homemade patch. Another mishap occurred when he twisted his ankle while scrounging for scrap metal among the rubble of the bomb-damaged buildings.

Neither injury was life-threatening, but they were painful and slowed him down. Yet Kapaun would not allow these accidents to interfere with his regular schedule. His determination to continue working reinforced what the POWs already knew. Their chaplain was spending his strength to help them.

In spite of the risks of punishment, Kapaun used a ruse to keep in touch with the enlisted POWs in the lower part of Camp No. 5. Late in the afternoon he would shoulder a wooden frame from which hung a pair of five gallon cans. Then he began walking toward the prison gate, seemingly intent on filling the containers with water from the Yalu River and bringing them back into the officers' compound. The sentry always challenged Kapaun, but he shouted the Chinese words for cold water and the guard motioned for him to pass.

Instead of heading toward the riverbank, Kapaun changed direction and hurried to the huts which held the enlisted prisoners who were sick. He prayed and joked and shared his tobacco with them. Then, after darkness fell, the chaplain picked up the yoke and containers and brought them back past the sentry and into the officers' section of the prison. If Kapaun found that an enlisted man had died he returned later to bury the body or cover it with rocks if the ground were frozen.

One evening Major David F. MacGhee noticed that Kapaun had returned to the officers' area carrying the cans. He stopped him and asked for a drink of water. "I'm sorry, David. I don't have any water, just the love of Jesus Christ," the chaplain replied. At that point Kapaun tipped over each of the cans, revealing that neither had a bottom in it.

"What gives?" MacGhee inquired. "You must never cheat the Lord," Kapaun answered. "He knows what you do and you must be faithful to His word! I am sure that the guard knows also and God knows about both of us."[1]

The Chinese suspected for some time that Kapaun was breaking their rules, especially the one which prohibited moving around the camp at night. Even though on several occasions the guards apprehended him and took him in for questioning, many of the survivors who lived with Kapaun and knew him well stated that the Chinese officials did not abuse him. That evidence notwithstanding, W. W. Smith claimed that more than once he saw the chaplain being beaten.[2] Another prisoner confirmed that the guards mistreated Kapaun.

Herbert Miller, whom Kapaun had rescued at Unsan, remembered that the chaplain's face was black and blue after the Chinese caught him one night sneaking from hut to hut.[3] On a different occasion, Kapaun sneaked out to find some firewood, and the guards found him stealing pickets from a wooden fence. They punished the chaplain by stripping off his outergarments and forcing him to stand for hours in the bitter cold. However, he avoided the even crueler, but often used punishment of solitary confinement for weeks in a hole in the ground.

If the weather permitted, Kapaun sat outside his hut during the day. Not only the Communist officials, but everyone else knew why he was there. With his religious stole around his neck, his pipe jammed between his teeth, and a twinkle in his grey eyes, Kapaun waited for the chance to talk to the other prisoners. Sometimes the conversation was just prison-camp banter, but more often the POWs bowed their heads and Kapaun led them in a quiet prayer.[4] A newcomer might even be greeted with simply, "Let us pray." Kapaun's message continually assured the prisoners that, despite all their adversities, they were fortunate to be alive and that the Lord would take care of them.

North Korean and Chinese troops worked together in running Camp No. 5 until March 1951. At that point the Chinese assumed complete responsibility and improved living conditions slightly.[5] They even eased their total prohibition on any religious expression,[6] after the Americans protested severely because they could not hold any public prayer services. The commandant of the camp finally relented and allowed the men to pray together once a week.[7]

In many of the military prisons in North Korea, captives of all faiths began to practice their religions openly. A few of the Americans had concealed their Bibles when they were captured and now they could assemble to read passages from them. The Masonic prisoners gathered for prayer meetings. However, even though the Chinese were more tolerant, they still warned the captives that religious activities must be confined to Sundays.[8]

Chinese officials carefully monitored all religious gatherings. If what the staff at Camp No. 5 overheard conflicted with their ideology, they demanded changes in the religious services. However, Kapaun discussed the problems with the Chinese officers and was shrewd enough to resolve them in a way that pacified his adversaries, but did not compromise his beliefs or his ability to continue his spiritual work.[9]

A case in point was Kapaun's helmet liner, which had a white cross painted on the front. Warrant Officer McCool noticed that it had been on the ground throughout the winter and spring. McCool asked the chaplain why he was not wearing the liner.

"Mac, if I wear it, it will only antagonize the Chinese, so I won't, but the fact that it is lying on this garbage heap causes every man to see it and to remind them of their God," Kapaun answered. "You know, Mac, I often wonder just how many silent prayers are offered at this old heap. God moves in strange ways."[10]

On spring evenings many of the American officers gathered in the small courtyard near the hut where Kapaun lived. He stood in front of the group and talked in down-to-earth language about the life of Jesus and His crucifixion.

"This would be extremely beautiful, especially on nights when the full moon shone down upon the silent figures standing and kneeling in front of this one lone figure standing on the porch," Dr. Esensten recalled. "It was almost as if one big spotlight centered upon the Father." Somehow the presence of God became more real to the beleaguered Americans.[11]

As soon as the Communists agreed to modify the restrictions on religious activities in the POW camps in North Korea, Kapaun and others started to prepare for a special service on Easter.[12] At first the administrators of Camp No. 5 objected, but changed their minds when the prisoners reminded them that the Communists had proclaimed freedom of religion.

On that gray Easter morning, March 25, 1951, daylight reached Pyoktong about 6 A.M. The calendar said that it was spring, but there were some clouds[13] and the weather was cold enough that ice was still clogging the backwaters of the Yalu River. About 60 men, all of the officers in the camp except those who were too weak to leave their huts, bundled up and shuffled over to the foot of the stairway leading to the partially destroyed Christian church.[14] Ironically, the Easter service was held in the same place where Chinese instructors sometimes lectured the Americans about the superiority of Communism.[15]

With the surrounding hills as a backdrop, the setting in the upper part of the camp was a natural amphitheater. The congregation was a ragtag lot of gaunt, foul-smelling and bearded men of several religious faiths, not all of them Christian. They wore an assortment of tattered American and British uniforms, and a few dressed in hand-me-down pieces of clothing which they had obtained from the Communists. English-speaking Chinese guards hovered in the background, ready to report on whatever happened.[16] One woman, the sister of a Chinese official who had been a Christian, watched from the sideline.[17]

The thin, bearded U.S. Army chaplain who led the service was strong in spirit, but broken in body. A black patch still covered his injured eye. Handicapped by an infected leg, Kapaun supported himself with a homemade cane as he faced the assembly. At the very beginning he showed that this gathering was special. Well aware that the Chinese were watching carefully, the chaplain nevertheless held aloft a small crucifix that he had made from two pieces of wood.

On that Easter morning there was something symbolic about a group of American prisoners praying in that distant Asian country near an isolated set of steps that led skyward. Having survived the dull, chilling winter, each of the captives yearned for an uplifting spiritual message. They badly needed encouragement, for little information was available about when, or if, the war might end or how soon they might see their families.

The words that they sang that Easter expressed their deepest thoughts:

> Faith of our fathers! Living still
> In spite of dungeon, fire and sword:

As their voices carried the phrases of the familiar Christian hymn into a strong wind blowing across the Yalu from Manchuria, the Americans recognized clearly the meaning of those lines. Their ordeal tested their faith in God, their country, and themselves every day, but an oppressive enemy prison had not extinguished their strongest beliefs.

Kapaun's sermon was especially meaningful. He spoke quietly about the suffering and crucifixion of Jesus. What these men had endured helped them to understand more easily. Then someone requested that Lieutenant William Whiteside sing the Lord's Prayer, and everyone's faith rushed to the surface.[18] Dr. Esensten later described everyone's emotions:

> This was extremely beautiful, the words being lofted into the cold air, of fortunately a nice sunrise. There was nobody there who did not feel the thrill of the music, the meaning of the words, the solemnness of the occasion, the goose pimples up and down their bodies and the feeling that this brought them much closer to home than they had felt for many, many months.[19]

It was equally appropriate that these Americans decided to sing the "Battle Hymn of the Republic." As Kapaun had reminded them, this Easter once again celebrated the Resurrection of Jesus. They, too, should look ahead to the joyful day when their dreams of release from captivity would be fulfilled.

> Mine eyes have seen the glory
> of the coming of the Lord.
> . . . .
> . . . .
> Glory! Glory! Hallelujah!
> Glory! Glory! Hallelujah!
> Glory! Glory! Hallelujah!
> His truth is marching on.

One of the prisoners had confided earlier to Kapaun that he wanted to become a Catholic. The chaplain chose Easter morning as the time for a public, but unusual baptism. Since no woman was available to serve as the man's godmother another captive agreed to assume that role. From then on the newly admitted Catholic happily looked forward to the day when after being freed, he could walk into his local church with his wife and twin daughters.

Kapaun asked the other men to be patient for a few minutes while he and the Catholic prisoners recited the Rosary and the Stations of the Cross. The Catholics made their confessions, too, but at that point the chaplain broke down and cried. He was overwhelmed by disappointment because he was unable to offer Holy Communion to the men.

A prisoner loaned his prayerbook to Kapaun, who read aloud to everyone. The chaplain also spoke briefly, assuring the men that he was no better than they were and that he would not presume to instruct other prisoners about how they should behave.

Someone suggested that the prisoners sing "America the Beautiful." As they bravely joined their voices that chilly morning the words expressed the thoughts of many of them:

America! America!
God shed his grace on thee,
And crown they good with brotherhood
From sea to shining sea.

The Easter services which Kapaun conducted left many enduring memories. Dr. Esensten, who was released two years later, said, "The feeling of the moment was indescribable and was almost akin to the feeling of inner joy as we sighted the American flag for the first time again as we were taken across the line at the exchange center."[20]

The prisoners who spent that morning with Kapaun could see that he was becoming weaker. The chaplain had been limping for weeks, but he jokingly brushed his ailments aside as a problem of oncoming old age.[21] The next Sunday Kapaun led the captives in another religious service. As he talked about the words of the Epistle, "And this is the victory that overcomes the world—our faith," his voice faltered and he collapsed in front of the group.

Few of his comrades realized that Kapaun had been suffering terrible aches in his bones. As soon as they learned about his condition, the American doctors recognized that it was a by-product of not having enough to eat. Pain brought on by hunger overcame some prisoners so forcefully at night that they screamed and beat the ground in agony. Tears filled Kapaun's eyes, but he never whimpered or complained. His will broke after he fell asleep. Only then did anyone hear him moan.

Kapaun knew, however, that pain was not his worst problem. His lower leg had become discolored, swollen to twice its size and extremely hard. The condition was getting worse and finally forced the chaplain to seek help. Supporting himself with a cane, Kapaun hobbled over to see Dr. Esensten and asked him what was wrong.[22]

Doctors Esensten and Anderson diagnosed the condition as a blood clot and severe thrombophlebitis. For a time they considered whether they might have to amputate Kapaun's leg. When the Chinese officials heard this, they refused permission. "Let God save him! He was a man of God!", the Communists announced.[23]

The bad news hardly surprised Kapaun. Nevertheless, he was not prepared for the treatment that the American doctors prescribed. They insisted that he return to his hut, elevate his leg and apply heat. If the chaplain was to recover he had to stay off his feet for two weeks. The doctors informed him that he must accept help from his friends. For Kapaun, who had unselfishly devoted himself to aiding so many prisoners, it was hard to be on the receiving end.

The spirit of helpfulness that Kapaun had instilled in other POWs now worked to his advantage. The prisoners built a trapeze and hung it from the ceiling so that the device could raise his leg. They removed some of the bricks from the damaged church, heated them and wrapped them close to the swollen limb. Other men made sure that he always received enough to eat. POWs who had hidden aspirin tablets for themselves gave them up in order to alleviate Kapaun's pain. All the attention bothered the chaplain and he protested that his comrades spent too much time caring for him.

The most difficult part of the cure was as much psychological as it was physical. Kapaun had trouble urinating and making bowel movements. That was a common problem in prison, and the men had constructed a special commode for their friends who had trouble caring for themselves. Kapaun knew about this device because he often had assisted others in using it.[24]

Kapaun's self-assurance suffered, however, when the prisoners had to carry him outside to the makeshift toilet. Even though his friends waited nearby he remained at the commode for an hour or more sometimes and refused to ask for assistance. The chaplain's reluctance to accept any help worried the other Americans.

The intensive care which Kapaun received improved his condition within two weeks. At first the doctors allowed him to stand with the support of homemade crutches, but when he tried to walk he fell frequently. The warmer spring weather had a curative effect, enabling the chaplain to regain his strength by sitting in the sunshine for a few hours every day. The thrombophlebitis lessened and his overall health should have become better, but it did not.

Unfortunately, another problem, a serious case of diarrhea, developed almost immediately. The POWs had carefully hoarded sulfa tablets for situations such as this. When they found out that their beloved chaplain needed medicine they contributed whatever pills they had saved.

Dr. Esensten devised a scheme to get more medicine. He rounded up several prisoners and instructed them to visit Dirty Hands and the rest of the Chinese medical staff. Each man should complain of diarrhea. However, instead of taking the medicine which Dirty Hands distributed they were told to bring it to Dr. Esensten.

The doctor gave it to Kapaun. The plan worked. After about six days, his attacks of diarrhea began to subside.[25]

The staff at Camp No. 5 knew that Kapaun's infected leg and his round-the-clock trips to the outdoor commode had weakened him. Their adversary needed help and they had the means to provide it. Supplies of medicine were passing through North Korea en route to the battlefront in the south, but the Chinese would not distribute any for Kapaun.

In deciding whether they would aid a sick prisoner, the Communists considered factors which had no bearing on his illness. A Chinese official commented that the Americans did not know the right persons who should be given medical help. In other words, they were not political realists.[26] While POWs who collaborated with the enemy received penicillin or sulfanilamide,[27] the Chinese doctors deliberately ignored those who opposed the Communist system, such as Kapaun.

War correspondent Noel affirmed the conclusions of the American physicians in Camp No. 5: Kapaun's failing health could have been prevented with basic medical care. But the Communists stood by idly when he began coughing heavily and his eyes glistened with fever, the classical signs of pneumonia. Except for a few aspirin, the American doctors had no more medicine to give him.

A turn for the worse occurred one warm day in mid-May. The American officers were eating their evening bowl of corn when a messenger brought word that Kapaun had become sicker. He was calling for Lieutenant Mayo. Several POWs rushed to the chaplain's hut where they found him lying on the floor, breathing heavily. Despite the fact that he was talking rationally, Kapaun obviously was in great pain.

Then Kapaun's will snapped and he began to weep. His tears, he explained, were tears of joy, because he expected to be with God in a short time. His suffering had revived Kapaun's memories of that sermon from the Second Book of Macabees which he had preached years earlier at a funeral in Pilsen. Kapaun sadly repeated the story of the woman whose seven sons had died rather than renounce their religious faith.

Lieutenant Mayo remembered the scene:

> Father looked at us and said he was crying for the same reason. He said that he was glad that he was suffering because Our Lord had suffered also and that he felt closer to him. By this time we were all crying. Everyone in the room, who had seen scores of people die in the past few months and who thought they were pretty hard.[28]

An English-speaking enemy officer entered Kapaun's hut at that critical point. He angered everyone by announcing that the Chinese had decided to transfer the chaplain. His new home would be their so-called hospital about half a mile away on a hilltop near Pyoktong.

Word had gotten around concerning the hospital's reputation. The prisoners called it "the dying place" because few men who went there returned alive. The hospital population remained steady at about 100 barely clothed, hardly breathing Americans. Their tattered clothing often appeared white from a coating of lice and maggots.[29] The Chinese sometimes brought in sick prisoners at night and removed their dead bodies the following morning.

The principal hospital building was a tile-roofed former Buddhist monastery with about 15 rooms. From a distance its appearance was deceiving because the outside was painted ornately with birds and animals. However, anyone who walked up the 30 steps to the front entrance instantly realized that the inside of the building was a deathhouse by every standard.[30]

There were no washing facilities or beds. The filthy occupants had to sleep on mud floors surrounded by their own excrement.[31] Ward 10, a unlighted room about 10 by 14 feet, housed captives with dysentery. No one cleaned the rooms; in fact, conditions were so horrid that Ward 10 became known as the "Death Ward."[32]

Time was growing short before the Chinese moved Kapaun to the hospital. Drawing upon his remaining energy, the chaplain, now a ghostlike figure, arose to give the last rites to a dying prisoner. He also found a scrap of paper and wrote the Our Father and Hail Mary. Then he gave the paper to one of the prisoners, who believed that was the last thing that Kapaun wrote.

Even as he spent his last few minutes among his close friends, his thoughts were with all the Americans. He asked one soldier to dedicate his life to the Blessed Virgin Mary. Warrant Officer McCool wanted Kapaun to forgive his sins. "He told me that he thought that he was going to die," McCool said. "After hearing my confession he sat up in bed and blessed me in Latin. He seemed to wander off and go out of his head."[33]

Kapaun also listened to another man's confession and gave him a card which contained the words of the 23rd Psalm.[34] For Kapaun the familiar passage from the Bible had become prophetic:

Even though I walk in the dark valley
I fear no evil; for you are at my side
With your rod and your staff
that give me courage.[35]

Moments later, Kapaun's breathing slipped ominously into a hoarse rattle. He deliriously babbled on about the joyful events of his youth. His grieving friends heard the familiar stories about his pals from Conception days, schoolmates from Pilsen, and those happy days on the farm with Enos, Bessie, and Eugene. At last Kapaun fell into a quiet sleep.

The other prisoners feared the worst, but several hours later he surprised them and awoke. The fever had broken. He was rational again, cracking jokes, sitting up, eating normally.

The euphoria ended as quickly as it began. The commandant of Camp No. 5 sensed that now was the time to deal with this thorn in his side.[36] Nevertheless, the American doctors assured the Chinese that they could restore Kapaun to good health. All they needed was the right medicine.

The officials in charge of Camp No. 5 refused to help. They had made up their minds to move Kapaun. The usual Communist diagnosis was that Americans became ill because they were an evil, immoral, and decadent race. In this case, the Chinese officials blandly announced that Kapaun's problem was that he had syphilis.

The prisoners who were gathered around the chaplain continued to argue. He need not be sent to the hospital; even without medicine they could take care of him. When the U.S. physicians went further and contended that taking Kapaun to the hospital might kill him, the exasperated Chinese finally shouted, "He goes! He goes!" They threatened to use their weapons, if necessary, to remove Kapaun.

The chaplain recognized that his time had come. Just before he departed for the hospital Kapaun met privately with a Protestant chaplain.[37] He was leaving his congregation behind and he wanted another clergyman to take care of them.

Kapaun also asked his closest friends to continue his work. He assigned Lieutenant Ralph Nardella to take responsibility for leading the Catholic prisoners in the Rosary and readings from the Bible.[38] Then he requested that Warrant Officer Felix McCool say prayers over his grave. The chaplain had held on to his ciborium and a list of the prisoners that he had baptized. He gave these to Lieutenant Walter Mayo, Jr. for safekeeping, adding "Walt, tell my bishop that I died a happy death."[39]

When a pair of English-speaking Chinese officers showed up outside his hut carrying a makeshift stretcher Kapaun accepted his fate with more composure than his distraught fellow prisoners.[40] The other Americans assured him that he would return, but Kapaun only grinned weakly and shook his head. Before leaving he smiled and turned to one POW who had experienced family problems, "When you get back to Jersey, you get that marriage straightened out or I'll come down from heaven and kick you in the tail."

Lieutenant Dowe's grief showed clearly on his face. "Don't take it so hard, Mike," Kapaun comforted his friend. "I'm going where I've always wanted to go. And when I get up there I'll say a prayer for all of you." Kapaun was so widely loved that another officer, Captain Fezi Bey, a Turkish prisoner, exclaimed, "To Allah, who is my God, I will pray for him."[41]

As his friends lifted Kapaun's emaciated body on to the litter for the trip to the hospital, everyone knew that he was starting a one-way journey.[42] Six of the Americans accompanied him. "Standing there watching Father Kapaun being carried off down the hill on that stretcher, I realized I would never see him alive again," one captive stated. "I also realized that he knew that more than anyone else."

Kapaun carried his stole and the gold-colored metal containers which held his holy oils. His face was haggard yet serene and his voice was calm. However, Dr. Anderson was sure that Kapaun was in great pain. The American physician recalled some of the chaplain's words:

> He hated Communism and he hated what the Communist ideology made the Chinese do. But he did not hate the Chinese.

> As he left he asked the Chinese officer in charge, a snaky looking and acting person who could only provoke revulsion—he asked this fellow to forgive whatever wrongs he might have done. I couldn't understand why Father Kapaun would ask this fellow's forgiveness, until I figured out that after all, it hadn't been easy for him not to hate his captors.[43]

Lieutenant Nardella walked at the rear of the stretcher as they approached the hospital. Kapaun looked up and said, "Ralph, when I do and I know I am going to die, I will be up in heaven and I will say a prayer for your safe return."

Years earlier, while a student, Kapaun had written about how an individual faces the time of death: "In that dreary moment we shall be stripped of friends. Yes, and those friends who have been so very dear to us."[44] As his heartbroken comrades were about to leave the hospital, they saw the chaplain glance up at the Chinese awaiting him. One man thought that he heard the chaplain quote from Luke's account of the crucifixion of Jesus, "Father, forgive them, they do not know what they are doing."[45]

The Communists figured that at last they had silenced this Christian thorn in their side. They thought that they had won.

Once a prisoner was sent to the hospital in Pyoktong, the Chinese officials would not permit any American doctors to visit him.

Considering the wretched physical condition of all of the POWs, Lieutenant Dowe estimated that two days of neglect was sufficient to kill any man.[46]

Sergeant Charles B. Schlichter saw the Communists put Kapaun into a filthy, unlighted room. No one else was there. They placed a small amount of food in the doorway, but they knew that he was too feeble to reach it. A Chinese doctor stood outside occasionally and peered into the room. Then he walked away.

Prisoners in the hospital could not receive any visitors. Jack Stegall was in the hospital at the same time, suffering from appendicitis. Stegall broke the rules and looked into Kapaun's room. He saw him lying alone on the dirt floor, too weak to eat. Stegall entered the room and called out to Kapaun. The chaplain did not have the strength to reply.[47] Joe Ascue also was in the hospital. He tried to feed cracked corn and millet to Kapaun, but it was too late to help him.[48]

Separated from the American soldiers whom he served so faithfully, far from his peaceful homeland among the farms of Kansas, Kapaun languished for two days. He died in the hospital on May 23, 1951. The day was the feast of Saint Demetrious, another man who had been murdered because of his Christian faith.

Between 1951 and 1953 the American prisoners buried thousands of their comrades, including about 1,600 in unmarked locations near Pyoktong. If the ground was too hard, the bodies were stacked one on top of another.[49] At other times, a detail of prisoners tied a rope around each corpse and dragged it across the frozen Yalu River to the burial site.[50] Kapaun's body, like many of the others, was put into a mass grave.

One of the reasons for Kapaun's deteriorating health and death was that he did not have enough food. However, if starvation was why a prisoner died, Comrade Sun would not allow it to be listed as the cause of death.

The burial party usually stripped the clothing from each man's body so that it could be given to other captives. The Americans had hopes of eventually retrieving the remains and returning them to the families of the deceased POWs. In order to identify each body, the burial detail put one U.S. military dogtag in the dead soldier's mouth, but when the Chinese learned about that procedure they banned it.[51]

The Communists denied one of Kapaun's final wishes. They prevented Warrant Officer McCool from saying any prayers at his grave.[52] In fact, that spring they plowed the field where Kapaun and hundreds of the prisoners had been buried. In its place the Chinese planted a garden.[53]

Some persons believe that in the end it was Kapaun who triumphed. A year after the chaplain died, Lieutenant Nardella asked for permission to lead a memorial service in his honor. However, the Communists refused the request.[54] They were still afraid of the spirit of Emil Kapaun.

Except for a terse message from the Military Ordinate of the Catholic Church in November 1950 that Chaplain Kapaun was missing in action, almost no one outside of Camp No. 5 knew what had happened to him.[1] Eugene and Helen Kapaun tried to stay in touch. They mailed a Christmas card, but it came back from Korea, undelivered.[2]

Kapaun's parents did not give up hope that their son would survive. Every weekday either Enos or Bessie Kapaun walked to their mail box alongside the dirt road near Pilsen, praying for another letter from him. None came during the remaining days of 1950 or any time the next two years. The parishioners of St. John Nepomucene Church offered special prayers for the return of their native son. Yet even without any further news, word of Kapaun's fate circulated throughout Wichita and nearby areas of Kansas, mainly through reports in the daily newspapers and the Diocese of Wichita's weekly newspaper.

The army ordered that the Distinguished Service Cross and the Bronze Star be presented to the still-missing chaplain. The award ceremony took place in Pilsen on October 18, 1952, and a capacity audience filled St. John Nepomucene Church. Enos and Bessie Kapaun received the medals and immediately handed them to Bishop Carroll. They had given their son to the Church, they said, and it should have his medals, too.[3]

The citation which accompanied the Distinguished Service Cross undoubtedly told the Kapaun family more than they had

156

known about the battle at Unsan and the chaplain's rescue of other soldiers. Part of it read:

> ...Chaplain Kapaun, with complete disregard for his personal safety, calmly moved among the wounded men, giving them medical aid and easing their fears. His courageous manner inspired all those present and many men who might otherwise have fled in planic were encouraged by his presence and remained to fight the enemy.[4]

It was impossible for any account of the chaplain's heroism to relieve the family's anxiety, for, as Bishop Carroll stated that day, "...no human ministration can assuage their sorrow; no mere words, however elegant, can comfort; no rewards, even those as noble and precious as received this morning, can compensate parents even for the temporary loss of their son."[5]

Even as the U.S. government and the residents of Kansas honored Kapaun at home, the soldiers still imprisoned in Camp No. 5 worked to preserve his memory. One of the most notable accomplishments was a crucifix carved by Marine Captain Gerald Fink. He was captured after Kapaun had died, but after hearing other Americans tell about the chaplain, he found some scrap firewood and resolved to create a memorial to Kapaun.

First Fink had to fashion some tools, a chisel out of a drain pipe bracket, a knife out of the steel arch of a boot, and a mallet. At one point he needed glass shards for minute carving so he smashed a window and used the broken pieces. After working for two and a half months Fink completed a cherrywood cross about 40 inches high bearing the scrub oak figure of a body some 26 inches long. When the Communist officials became suspicious that the figure represented Christ, Fink assured them that it really depicted Abraham Lincoln, and that information satisfied his captors.[6]

Fink's praise of Kapaun was as eloquent as his handiwork. He wrote later:

> If the meek shall inherit the earth, it will be because people like Father Kapaun willed it to them. I am a Jew, but that man will always live in my heart. He was a man among many who were not. I saw the biggest, huskiest and toughest men crack under the strain. Father Kapaun not only served Christians well but he served everyone else with equal goodness and kindness. Never thinking of himself, he was always doing something for others. He represented to me saintliness in its purest form and manliness in its rarest form.

The announcement which the chaplain's friends and family dreaded came on July 12, 1953. A letter from the War Department in Washington stated that Kapaun had died May 5, 1951, in Pyoktong, North Korea.[7] His mother was so distraught that she planned to travel to Pyoktong to recover her son's body. Father Arthur J. Tonne, who later became the pastor at St. John Nepomucene Church, struggling to change her mind, finally dissuaded her by arguing that if she went to North Korea, he would have to go, too, and they would both end up in jail.[8] Acquaintances in Pilsen wondered aloud why Kapaun did not try to escape from Unsan when being captured seemed almost certain. Then someone explained that his lifelong commitment to helping other persons would not allow him to flee.[9]

When the fighting ended in 1953 and the warring sides exchanged prisoners in Operation Little Switch and Operation Big Switch, four of Kapaun's closest friends, Lieutenant Nardella, Lieutenant O'Connor, Warrant Officer McCool and Lieutenant Paul O'Dowd, brought back the crucifix which Fink had carved. One of the repatriated men also reported that May 23, 1951, was the correct date when the chaplain died.[10] The army listed his cause of death as pneumonia.

News of the death of Chaplain Kapaun and the accounts of the former POWs about his courage and leadership stimulated widespread interest in his life. Tens of thousands of readers of *Our Sunday Visitor*, a Catholic newspaper, urged Hollywood to make a movie.[11] "Crossroads," a half-hour television broadcast in 1955 dealt with Kapaun's exploits in Camp No. 5, but Columbia Pictures, Metro Goldwyn Mayer, and United Artists all declined to produce a full-length film.

Columbia Pictures did release a movie which infuriated Kapaun's relatives and others who loved him. Titled "Bamboo Prison," it was the story of a jailed priest who was portrayed as a collaborator of the Communists. A Catholic columnist charged that the movie falsely showed Kapaun's life in prison, but the controversy subsided after the producer denied any comparison.

Many considered Fink's crucifix as the truest representation of Kapaun's life. It hung for several years at St. John Nepomucene Church and served as Bessie's most precious connection to her son whenever she attended Mass there. She became upset, however, when the Diocese transferred the cross to Wichita where it would be displayed in a new high school which was being named in honor of Chaplain Kapaun.[12]

Lieutenant Nardella spoke at one of the opening ceremonies at Kapaun Memorial High School and declared:

> This school is a fitting tribute to this great man. If those who enter the school can only learn to reflect on the qualities

that made Father Kapaun great, they cannot help but build a better America. The school itself is only a vehicle—it is the end product that will count, what comes out of the school.

Other honors followed, including the award of the Legion of Merit military medal and in 1989 the Prisoner of War Medal. The army recognized his extraordinary service by dedicating the Kapaun Barracks at the U.S. base in Vogelweh, Germany. His name became associated with a library in Spokane, Washington, a military chapel in Korea and Knights of Columbus councils in the United States. From a religious standpoint the most important recognition was the announcement by the Archdiocese for the Military Services, USA in 1993 that Kapaun could be called "Servant of God," the first step toward possible sainthood.

Perhaps the highest honors are the memories of those who knew him the best. Eugene and Helen recalled unhappily how they missed the opportunity to visit with the chaplain at a Christmas reunion of the Kapaun family in 1949, just before he left for Japan. Father Edward Malone, O.S.B., wrote about Kapaun's years at Conception College:

> Thinking of him now is somewhat like thinking of a mystery story after you have read the ending. Had you been more observant you might have spotted the clues the author divulged, which would have led you to guess the ending before you reached the last page. So it was with Father Kapaun. Now one remembers little things about him which were not significant then, but which might have let you know what sort of man he would be when the going was difficult, and he became involved in a crisis.

A former schoolmate, Father Aloysius Clupny, summed up his recollection: "He was the most wonderful man I ever met, a saint is the best possible description I can give. A go-getter—. No, I would rather say he was a go-giver." Praise, however, was not limited to Catholic clergymen. Protestant Chaplain Arthur E. Mills, a former prisoner of war, wrote to Enos and Bessie Kapaun:

> I've never known a braver man, a more devoted Christian leader, and more sympathetic listener, or a better friend. ...I've always prayed he would be spared, but God rewarded him in a greater way. ...Thank you for giving us your son. ... He is a hero, a saint if anyone ever was one.

Dr. Esensten, one of the chaplain's closest friends in Camp No. 5, showed that religious beliefs were not the only standard by which the other prisoners judged Kapaun:

I am Jewish. My feelings, therefore, for Father Kapaun were not clouded by any religious affiliation. My relationship to Father was based purely on a man to man, and I was completely and solely impressed by Father as a man. I have only the greatest admiration and respect for him. In my life I have met few to equal him.[13]

Chaplain Mills, Dr. Esensten, and the other Americans who suffered in Camp No. 5 probably offered the best perspective of how Kapaun conducted himself in those stressful times. Here is what some of them said:

William A. McClain, a prisoner of war, wrote:

Father Kapaun, in my opinion seemed to relish the opportunity to serve his fellow man in a deplorable environment. He mentioned to me that a situation such as we were in would bring out both the best and worst in men. Yes, Father Kapaun was the best and his strong beliefs in God, family and country enabled him to stand up and meet his Maker by carrying out his duties of assisting and helping all prisoners of war who knew him. His POW status was probably the ultimate challenge in his life and he met that challenge with distinction.[14]

From an article which was written by Raymond M. Dowe, Jr., a prisoner of war:

In his soiled and ragged fatigues, with his scraggly beard and his queer woolen cap, made of the sleeve of an old GI sweater, pulled down over his ears, he looked like any other half-starved prisoner. But there was something in his voice and bearing that was different—a dignity, a composure, a serenity that radiated from him like a light. Wherever he stood was holy ground, and the spirit within him—a spirit of reverence and abiding faith—went out to the silent listening men and gave them hope and courage and a sense of peace.[15]

Dr. Clarence Anderson, a prisoner of war, declared:

More than a human being, a hero, a saint—Father Kapaun was at first an enigma, as all simple men are. You wondered why he did some of the things he did. ...He was a man without personal motives, without any regard for his personal safety or comfort. He simply did what his moral and ethical code told him was his duty.[16]

Peter Busatti, who was captured at Unsan with Kapaun, expressed his feelings:

Is Father Kapaun a saint? As far as I'm concerned, he is. If I were able to send a note to heaven, I would say "Thanks to a great priest, a great soldier, and a great man—way up there in heaven. If anyone deserves heaven, it certainly is you, Father—I shall never forget you."[17]

What Emil Kapaun did for the other prisoners during the difficult days at Camp No. 5 was summed up by Robert E. Burke, a former POW:

Every man is proud to say, "I knew Father Kapaun—he saved my life, he made me fight to stay alive when dying was so simple"; it was easier to die than live in those days. Death was a welcome relief. We owe our present happiness to that heroic man who gave his all, who sacrificed himself for his fellow man, who worked himself to death.[18]

CHAPTER 1

CAPTURED BY THE COMMUNISTS

1. Whiting, Allen S., *China Crosses the Yalu: The Decision to Enter the Korean War*. New York: MacMillan, 1960.
2. Emil Kapaun to Eugene and Helen Kapaun, October 2, 1950.
3. Tonne, Rev. Arthur J., *The Story of Chaplain Kapaun: Patriot Priest of the Korean Conflict*. Emporia, Kansas: Didde Publishers, 1954, 143.
4. Kapaun to Bishop Mark Carroll, October 4, 1950, reprinted in *Wichita Eagle*, September 8, 1953.
5. Tonne, 185.
6. Tonne, 143–47.
7. Kapaun to Carroll, October 4, 1950.
8. Tonne, 183.
9. Kapaun to Fred Tuzicka, November 17, 1948.
10. *Advance Register,* Wichita, Kansas, March 9, 1951.
11. R. Jennings to author, February 13, 1992, February 15, 1992.
12. John P. Gannon to Rev. Dolan, S.J., undated.
13. Tonne, 148.
14. Kapaun to Tuzicka, October 14, 1950.
15. Robert Mack to author, November 14, 1991.
16. Kapaun to Eugene and Helen Kapaun, October 13, 1950.
17. Tonne, 164.
18. William A. McClain to author, December 15, 1992.
19. *New York Times*, February 26, 1992.
20. Sun Yup, Paik, *From Pusan to Panmunjon.* Washington: Brassey's (U.S.), 1992.
21. Toland, John, *In Mortal Combat.* New York: William Morrow and Company, Inc., 1991, 21.
22. Toland.
23. Cyrille W. Hanssen, interview by author, May 24, 1993.
24. John D. DiCerchio, interview by author, January 8, 1992; Don Summers, interview by author, February 13, 1992.
25. Tonne, 186.

26. Marshall, S. L. A., *The River and the Gauntlet*. New York: William Morrow & Company, 1953, 7.
27. Appleman, Roy, *South to the Naktong, North to the Yalu*. Washington: Center for Military History, U.S. Army, 1986, 688.
28. Blair, Clay, *The Forgotten War*. New York: Timesbooks, 1987, 382.
29. Spurr, Russell, *Enter the Dragon: China's Undeclared War Against the U.S., 1950–51*. New York: Newmarket Press, 1988, 140.
30. Hanssen interview.
31. Blair, 381.
32. 8th Cavalry Regiment, Periodic Operations Report, November 1 to November 13, 1950, National Archives Branch Depository (NABD), Suitland, Md.
33. Poats, Rutherford M., *Decision in Korea*. New York: The McBride Company, 1954.
34. Blair, 381.
35. Venske, Rodger B., *Confidence in Battle, Inspiration in Peace, The United States Army Chaplaincy, 1945–75*. Washington: Office of the Chief of Chaplains, 1977, 82.
36. Spurr, 134.
37. Appleman, 700.
38. Appleman, 689.
39. Appleman, 693, 708.
40. 3rd Battalion, 8th Cavalry Regiment, History, October 30, 1950, to November 5, 1950.
41. Spurr, 137.
42. Hoyt, Edwin P., *The Day the Chinese Attacked: Korea, 1950*. New York: McGraw Hill, 1990, 104.
43. Leckie, Robert, *Conflict: The History of the Korean War: 1950–53*. New York: G. P. Putnam's Sons, 1962, 180.
44. 3rd Battalion, 8th Cavalry Regiment, War Diary, November 1950.
45. Appleman, 695.
46. *Advance Register*, Wichita, March 19, 1951.
47. Appleman, 698.
48. Tonne, 160.
49. Walter L. Mayo, Jr., interview by author, April 10, 1993.
50. Appleman, 701.
51. *New York Herald Tribune*, November 3, 1950.
52. *Advance Register*, March 9, 1951.
53. Tonne, 157.
54. William Mayer to Peter Susko, February 28, 1988.
55. 3rd Battalion, History.
56. William A. McClain to author, December 15, 1992; William A. McClain to Cletus Pottebaum, January 3, 1990.
57. Paul F. Bromser, interview by author, October 18, 1993.
58. Bromser interview.
59. 3rd Battalion, History; 8th Cavalry, Periodic Operations Report.
60. 3rd Battalion, History; 3rd Battalion, War Diary.
61. Jerry Emer to author, January 11, 1992; Knox, Donald. *The Korean War: An Oral History*. San Diego: Harcourt Brace, 1985.
62. 3rd Battalion, History.
63. Frank Peljae, interview by author, February 26, 1992.
64. Walter L. Mayo, Jr. to author, December 3, 1991.
65. McClain to Pottebaum.
66. *Advance Register*, Wichita, March 9, 1951.
67. Tibor Rubin to author, January 28, 1993.
68. Herer, Michael, "Documentary of a Hero," *Extension*, June 1954.

69. Joe Ascue, interview by author, January 13, 1992.
70. 3rd Battalion, History.
71. William Bryant, interview by author, November 30, 1991.
72. 3rd Battalion, History.
73. John R. Ritter to author, undated.
74. Rev. Richard A. Mallory to Military Ordinate, August 21, 1951.
75. Mayo interview.
76. Herbert A. Miller to author, January 18, 1993; Hanssen interview.
77. 3rd Battalion, History.
78. Bromser interview; Walter L. Mayo, Jr. to author, August 17, 1994.
79. Appleman, 707.

CHAPTER 2
GROWING UP ON A FARM

1. *The WPA Guide to 1930s Kansas.* Lawrence, Kansas: University Press of Kansas, 1984, 69.
2. *WPA Guide,* 72.
3. Schruben, Francis W., *Kansas in Turmoil, 1930–1936.* Columbia, Mo.: University of Missouri Press, 1969, 47.
4. Eugene and Helen Kapaun, interview by author, April 28, 1992.
5. Stevenson, Burton, ed., *The Home Book of Quotations.* New York: Dodd, Mead & Company, 1964.
6. Monsignor Arthur J. Tonne, interview by author, April 29, 1992.
7. Paul Meysing, statement to author, May——, 1992.
8. Martin Klenda to author, June 5, 1992.
9. Tonne interview.
10. *The Marion Review,* June 18, 1941.
11. Eugene and Helen Kapaun interview.
12. Tonne, 11.
13. Paul Meysing, interview by author, April 29, 1992.
14. Victoria Melcher to author, June 6, 1992.
15. Tonne interview.
16. Melcher letter.
17. Melcher letter.
18. M. Benda to author, June 1, 1992.
19. Klenda to author.
20. Benda to author.
21. Benda to author.
22. Klenda to author.
23. Amelia Vinduska to author, January 31, 1992.
24. Sister M. Vitalia Winter to author, February 16, 1992.
25. Melcher to author.
26. Benda to author.
27. Eugene and Helen Kapaun interview.
28. Benda to author.
29. Emil Kapaun, diary.
30. Kapaun diary.
31. Winter to author.
32. Kapaun diary.

CHAPTER 3
BECOMING A PRIEST

1. Kapaun diary.
2. Rev. Quentin Kathol, O.S.B., to author, May 20, 1992.

3. *Morning Star*, Conception High School and College, Missouri.
4. *Morning Star*.
5. Kapaun diary.
6. Eugene and Helen Kapaun interview.
7. Meysing interview.
8. Winter to author.
9. Kathol to author.
10. Op. cit., Kapaun diary.
11. William M. Lorenz to author, July 15, 1992.
12. Rev. Fred M. Tuzicka, interview by author, February 9, 1995.
13. Recollection of Rev. Walter Heeney, O.S.B., furnished to author by Rev. Quentin Kathol, O.S.B., May 20, 1992.
14. Meysing interview.
15. Recollection of Rev. Malachy Riley, O.S.B., furnished to author by Rev. Quentin Kathol, O.S.B., May 20, 1992.
16. *Morning Star*.
17. Kathol to author.
18. Patsy Meysing Waner to author, January 6, 1992.
19. Meysing interview.
20. Meysing interview.
21. Margie Krotz Stegeman to author, August 4, 1995.
22. Meysing interview.
23. Eugene and Helen Kapaun interview.
24. Tonne interview.
25. *Kansas in Turmoil*, 47.
26. Emil Kapaun to Bishop Augustus Schwerter, July 8, 1934.
27. Rev. Martin Picke, O.S.B., to Rev. Arthur Tonne, April 7, 1954.
28. *Morning Star*.
29. Eugene and Helen Kapaun interview.
30. Sister M. Virgilia Winter to Rev. Arthur Tonne, January 8, 1954.
31. Rev. Bede Scholz, O.S.B. to Rev. Arthur Tonne, March 30, 1954.
32. Monsignor Aloysius. F. Preisner to author, March 5, 1992.
33. Monsignor Aloysius F. Preisner, talk given at dedication of Kapaun-Mt. Carmel High School, Wichita, undated.
34. Kapaun to Emil Melcher, February 1, 1938.
35. Kapaun to Emil Melcher, February 17, 1938.
36. Kapaun to Melcher, February 17, 1938.
37. Emil Kapaun to Emil and Victoria Melcher, March 2, 1938.
38. Kapaun to Emil and Victoria Melcher, May 1, 1938.
39. Kapaun to Emil and Victoria Melcher, October 10, 1938.
40. Kapaun to Emil and Victoria Melcher, November 25, 1938.
41. Preisner talk.
42. Kapaun to Melcher, May 1, 1938.
43. Kapaun to Melcher, November 25, 1938.
44. Kapaun to Emil and Victoria Melcher, April 14, 1940.
45. Sister Dominica Buchholz, interview by author, February 13, 1992.
46. *The Marion Review*, Marion, Kansas, June 18, 1940.
47. Kapaun to Emil and Victoria Melcher, April 5, 1939.
48. Kapaun to Melcher, October 10, 1938.
49. Eugene and Helen Kapaun interview.
50. Meysing interview.
51. Tonne, 64.
52. Meysing interview.
53. Eugene and Helen Kapaun interview.
54. Kapaun diary.

55. Kapaun diary.
56. Kapaun to Bishop Winkelmann, February 18, 1942.
57. 2 Macc. 7:1–42.
58. Kapaun to Gerald Franta, October 19, 1942.
59. Kapaun to Franta, November 30, 1942.
60. Kapaun sermon given at Herington Army Base, Kansas, October 24, 1943.
61. Kapaun, notes as teacher at St. John Nepomucene Church, Pilsen, Kansas.

CHAPTER 4

INTO THE ARMY

1. Rose Gleason, interview by author, May 1, 1992.
2. Tonne interview.
3. Tonne, 76.
4. Kapaun to Franta, September 10, 1944.
5. Office of Chief of Chaplains, U.S. Army, "The Regimental or Unit Chaplain," Tech Cir. No. 4, March 1, 1942.
6. *Kapaun Herald*, Kapaun High School, Wichita, Kansas, undated.
7. Tonne, 88.
8. Emil Kapaun to Bishop Augustus Winkelmann, June 1, 1945.
9. Maxine Svitak, interview by author, April 29, 1992.
10. Kapaun to Winkelmann, June 1, 1945.
11. Kapaun to Winkelmann, November 1, 1945.
12. Headquarters, U.S. Forces India Burma Theater, Chaplain's Report (Emil Kapaun), October, 1945.
13. John D. Donnelly, interview by author, March 28, 1993; Kapaun to Winkelmann, March 1, 1946.
14. Kapaun to Emil and Victoria Melcher, November 27, 1945.
15. Donnelly interview.
16. Emil Kapaun to Bishop Augustus Winkelmann, January 3, 1946.
17. Kapaun to Sklenar, February 3, 1946.
18. Tonne, 99.
19. Kapaun to Emmet A. Blaes, February 26, 1947.
20. Tonne, 103.
21. Tonne, 106.

CHAPTER 5

BACK INTO UNIFORM

1. Virginia Mozouch to author, October 25, 1992.
2. Anita Pechanic to author, January 17, 1992.
3. Eugene and Helen Kapaun interview.
4. Tonne, 108.
5. Frank J. Spicka to author, June 24, 1992.
6. Eugene and Helen Kapaun interview.
7. Tuzicka interview.
8. Mozouch letter.
9. Eugene and Helen Kapaun interview.
10. Op. cit., Confidence in Battle, 49.
11. Leonard W. Schneider to Rev. Arthur J. Tonne, January 31, 1954.
12. Kapaun to Carroll, September 1, 1948.
13. Kapaun to Tuzicka, September 20, 1948.
14. Kapaun to Tuzicka, September 20, 1948.
15. Kapaun to Tuzicka, November 17, 1948.
16. Kapaun to Eugene and Helen Kapaun, December 6, 1948.

17. Kapaun to Tuzicka, January 30, 1949.
18. Kapaun to Eugene and Helen Kapaun, December 6, 1948.
19. Kapaun to Tuzicka, November 17, 1948.
20. Kapaun to Eugene and Helen Kapaun, June 24, 1949.
21. Walter J. Mullen, Jr. to author, March 6, 1993.
22. Kapaun to John and Virginia Mozouch, November 14, 1949.
23. Kapaun to John Mozouch, September 5, 1949.
24. Kapaun to Uncle Jim and Aunt Anna, June 30, 1949.
25. Kapaun to Eugene and Helen Kapaun, January 26, 1949.
26. Kapaun to Mozouch, September 5, 1949.
27. Kapaun to John and Virginia Mazouch, December 22, 1949.
28. Sister M. Loyola to Rev. Arthur J. Tonne, February 25, 1954.
29. Eugene and Helen Kapaun interview.
30. Kapaun to Eugene and Helen Kapaun, January 15, 1950.
31. Kapaun to Meysing, January 3, 1950.
32. Symonds, F. Addington, *Christianity in Action.* Surrey, England: The World's Work, Ltd., 1955, 120.
33. Anthony Pecoraro to unnamed addressee, November 16, 1989.

CHAPTER 6

GOING TO WAR

1. Blair, 48.
2. Zellers, Larry, *In Enemy Hands: A Prisoner in North Korea.* Lexington: The University Press of Kentucky, 1991, 94–100.
3. Tonne, 126.
4. Kapaun to Eugene and Helen Kapaun, February 25, 1950.
5. Kapaun to Meysing, March 10, 1950.
6. Kapaun to Eugene and Helen Kapaun, February 25, 1950.
7. Kapaun to Monsignor Sklenar, June 21, 1950.
8. Phil Moore, interview by author, March 2, 1993.
9. Emil Kapaun to Eugene and Helen Kapaun, May 30, 1950.
10. Kapaun to Meysing, March 10, 1950.
11. Monthly Report of Chaplain (Emil Kapaun) to Military Ordinate, March——, 1950.
12. 8th Cavalry Regiment, report of Catholic Chaplains' Fund, May 1950.
13. Monthly Report of Chaplain, March——, 1950.
14. Kapaun to Tuzicka, April 13, 1950.
15. Kapaun to Eugene and Helen Kapaun, May 4, 1950.
16. Kapaun to Eugene and Helen Kapaun, April 9, 1950.
17. Matthew 5:1–12.
18. U.S. Far East Radio Network, talks by Emil Kapaun, April 17–22, 1950.
19. Kapaun to Eugene and Helen Kapaun, May 30, 1950.
20. Tonne, 131.
21. Westover, John G., *Combat Support in Korea.* Washington: Center for Military History, U.S. Army, 1987, 142.
22. Schnable, James F., *U.S. Army in the Korean War: Policy and Direction: The First Year.* Washington: Office of Chief of Military History, 1972, 86.
23. Appleman, 196.
24. Tonne, 136.
25. Tonne, 136.

CHAPTER 7

THE STRUGGLE IN KOREA

1. Kapaun to Eugene and Helen Kapaun, July 15, 1950.
2. Dunn, Si, *The First Cavalry Division: A Historical Overview 1921–93.* Dallas: Taylor Publishing Company, 1984.

3. Westover, 143.
4. Westover, 143.
5. Dowe, Raymond M., Jr., *The Ordeal of Chaplain Kapaun. Saturday Evening Post.* January 16, 1954.
6. Jack Stegall, interview by author, November 21, 1993.
7. Kapaun to Enos and Elizabeth Kapaun, July 29, 1950.
8. Tonne, 149.
9. Kapaun to unnamed addressee, July 29, 1950.
10. Zellers, 159.
11. Kapaun to Eugene and Helen Kapaun, August 8, 1950.
12. Leckie, 90.
13. Elmer Palmer, interview by author, February 27, 1992.
14. Tonne, 137.
15. Kapaun to Enos and Elizabeth Kapaun, August 7, 1950.
16. Tonne, 183.
17. Frank DelGregg, interview by author, March 4, 1992.
18. *Kansas City Star*, September 8, 1953.
19. Palmer interview.
20. Venzke, 82.
21. Thomas Horrigan, M.D. to author, January 18, 1993.
22. Mayo interview.
23. McClain to Pottebaum.
24. Horrigan to author.
25. Kapaun to Enos and Elizabeth Kapaun, August 8, 1950.
26. Kapaun to Sklenar, August 12, 1950.
27. Tonne, 156.
28. Robert G. Wixom to author, February 13, 1992; Mack to author.
29. Kapaun to Enos and Elizabeth Kapaun, August 8, 1950.
30. DiCerchio interview.
31. Leo F. McNamee to author, March 23, 1993.
32. William A. McClain to author, December 15, 1992.
33. Filmore A. McAbee to author, December 14, 1992.
34. Headquarters, 1st Cavalry Division, September 2, 1950, Award of Bronze Star to Emil J. Kapaun.
35. Tibor Rubin to author, January 28, 1993.
36. Douglass Hall, interview by author, February 27, 1992.
37. DiCerchio interview.
38. Kapaun to Rev. Joseph ———, August 18, 1950.
39. Ernest Terrell, Jr. to author, May 12, 1993.
40. Palmer interview.
41. Mayo interview.
42. Horrigan to author.
43. Bromser interview.
44. Carl T. Wohlbier to author, February 15, 1992.
45. Hall interview.
46. Hall interview.
47. Wohlbier to author.
48. DelGregg interview.
49. Mack to author.
50. Dowe, *Saturday Evening Post.*
51. Tonne, 137.
52. Tonne, 138.
53. Kapaun to Monsignor John Sklenar, August 12, 1950.
54. Symonds, 121.
55. Kapaun to Eugene and Helen Kapaun, August 12, 1950.

56. Walter L. Mayo, Jr., talk, undated, 1983.
57. Kapaun to Rev. Joseph ———.
58. Bong, Baik, *Kim Il Sung: Biography II* Tokyo: Mirasisha, 1970, 302.
59. Appleman, 254.
60. Kapaun to Enos and Elizabeth Kapaun, August 7, 1950.
61. Symonds, 121.
62. Kapaun to Father Joseph ———.
63. Appleman, 347.
64. Westover, 146.
65. Appleman, 362.
66. Kapaun to Eugene and Helen Kapaun, September 25, 1950.
67. Appleman, 562.
68. Blair, 259.

CHAPTER 8

A REVERSAL OF FORTUNE

1. Appleman, 572.
2. White, William Lindsay, *The Captives of Korea.* Westport., Conn.: Scribner's Sons, 1957, 27.
3. Breuer, William B., *Shadow Warriors: The Covert War in Korea.* New York: John Wiley & Sons, Inc., 1996, 153.
4. Venske, 77.
5. Kapaun to Eugene and Helen Kapaun, September 25, 1950.
6. Tonne, 143.
7. Tonne, 145.
8. White, 71.
9. Leo F. McNamee to author, March 23, 1993.
10. Eugene and Helen Kapaun interview.
11. Rev. Aloysious M. Knier to author, June 27, 1992.
12. ATIS Enemy Documents, Issue 29.
13. White, 74.
14. Spurr, 151.
15. Ascue interview.
16. Clarence Anderson, M.D., affidavit, December 7, 1953.
17. Joseph O'Connor, statement, November 12, 1953.
18. Palmer interview.
19. Joel Adams, affidavit, February 11, 1954.
20. Edward Adams, affidavit, June 3, 1954.
21. Tonne, 193.
22. Crosbie, Philip, *Pencilling Prisoners.* Melbourne: The Hawthorn Press, 1954, 124.
23. Anderson, Major Clarence and others, "Medical Experiences in Communist POW Camps in Korea," *Journal of the American Medical Association* 156, no. 2 (September 11, 1954):120–22.
24. Anderson affidavit.
25. Mayo talk, 1983.
26. Henry Pedicone, interview by author, December 15, 1992.
27. Eric Phillips statement, January 29, 1954.
28. White, 47.
29. Anderson, "Medical Experiences."
30. Mayo interview.
31. White, 47.
32. Mayo talk, 1983.
33. White, 48.

34. McClain to Pottebaum.
35. Mallory letter.
36. Robert Morrison to author, February 23, 1992.
37. Walter L. Mayo, Jr., statement, undated.
38. Mayo, talk, 1983.
39. War Crimes Division, Judge Advocate Section, Korean Communications Zone, U.S. Army, *Operation Little Switch, supplementary to Interim Historical Report (June 30, 1953)*, November 1, 1953.
40. Mayo statement.
41. Morrison letter.
42. Anderson statement.
43. Philip Henry Peterson, statement, December 23, 1953.
44. *Saturday Evening Post.*
45. *Saturday Evening Post.*
46. Mayo interview.

CHAPTER 9

THE VALLEY

1. Raymond M. Dowe, Jr., statement, November 25, 1953.
2. Sidney Esensten, M.D. to author, November 15, 1991.
3. Pedicone interview.
4. Mayo talk, 1983.
5. Zellers, 71.
6. Crosbie, 84–87.
7. White, 75.
8. Dowe statement.
9. Tonne, 187.
10. Mayo interview.
11. Tonne, 158.
12. Dowe statement.
13. Anderson statement.
14. Pedicone interview.
15. Luke 23:39–43.
16. Robert Sheppard statement, March 11, 1951.
17. *Kansas City Star*, September 8, 1953.
18. Pedicone interview.
19. Sidney Esensten, M.D. to Marie Martin, February 7, 1989.
20. Anderson, "Medical Experiences."
21. Esensten to author, November 15, 1991.
22. Esensten to author, November 15, 1991.
23. Mayo interview.
24. McClain to author.
25. Esensten to author, November 15, 1991.
26. Esensten to author, November 15, 1991.
27. David F. MacGhee to Marie Martin, February 6, 1989.
28. Esensten to author, November 15, 1991.
29. Pedicone interview.
30. Symonds, 130.
31. Fehrenbach, T. R., *This Kind of War.* New York: Grosset & Dunlop, 1969, 546.
32. Anderson, "Medical Experiences."
33. Kinkead, Eugene, *In Every War But One.* New York, W. W. Norton & Company, 1959, 146.
34. Anderson, "Medical Experiences."

35. Sidney Esensten, M.D. to author, August 29, 1994.
36. Zellers, 130–134.
37. Kinkead, 148–149.
38. Dowe statement.
39. *Saturday Evening Post.*
40. McAbee to author.
41. Esensten to author, November 15, 1991.
42. White, 85.
43. Walter L. Mayo, Jr., talk, 1963.
44. Esensten to author, November 15, 1991.
45. Esensten to author, August 29, 1994.
46. Anderson statement.
47. Dowe statement.
48. Dowe statement.

CHAPTER 10
CAMP NO. 5

1. Joseph Magnant, statement, November 11, 1953.
2. Magnant statement; Mayo interview.
3. Rees, David, *Korea: The Limited War.* New York, St. Martin's Press, 1964, 329–333.
4. Mayo talk, 1963.
5. Kinkead, 153.
6. Esensten to Pottebaum.
7. Anderson, "Medical Experiences."
8. Mayo talk, 1983.
9. Dowe statement.
10. McClain to author.
11. Mayo talk, 1983.
12. *Post Standard*, Syracuse, August 18, 1953.
13. Jones, Francis S., *No Rice for Rebels.* London: The Bodley Head, 1956, 40.
14. Deane, Philip, *I was a Captive in Korea.* New York: Norton, 1953, 149.
15. *Post Standard.*
16. *Collier's*, January 22, 1954.
17. *Collier's.*
18. Kinkead, 99.
19. Tonne, 198.
20. *Collier's.*
21. *Post Standard.*
22. Mayo talk, 1983.
23. Mayo talk.
24. Mayo talk.
25. *Post Standard.*
26. *Saturday Evening Post.*
27. Mayo talk, 1983.
28. Mayo interview.
29. McClain to Pottebaum.
30. Mayo talk, 1983.
31. Tonne, 172.
32. John N. McLaughlin to author, March 23, 1992.
33. Esensten to author, November 15, 1991.
34. *Saturday Evening Post.*
35. Tonne, 196.

36. McClain to author.
37. Mayo interview.
38. Dowe statement.
39. Pedicone interview.
40. Magnant statement.
41. McClain to Pottebaum.
42. Anderson, "Medical Experiences."
43. McClain to author.
44. Anderson, "Medical Experiences."
45. Esensten to author, August 29, 1994.
46. White, 86.
47. Anderson, "Medical Experiences."
48. William R. Shadish, M.D. to author, December 28, 1991.
49. Tonne, 188.
50. Operation Little Switch.
51. W. W. Smith, interview by author, January 9, 1992.
52. Mayo talk, 1983.
53. Sidney Esensten, M.D., statement, January 14, 1954.
54. Crosbie, 64.
55. McClain to Martin.
56. *Saturday Evening Post.*
57. McClain to author.
58. Lawrence V. Bach to author, January 14, 1992.
59. Jones, 213.
60. *Advance Register*, Wichita, October 16, 1953.
61. McClain to Pottebaum.
62. Rees, 333.
63. Mayo statement.
64. *Saturday Evening Post.*
65. Esensten to author, November 15, 1991.

CHAPTER 11
THE DYING PLACE

1. MacGhee to Martin.
2. Smith interview.
3. Miller to author.
4. Theo Baudin to Cletus J. Pottebaum, January 23, 1993.
5. Phillips statement.
6. Esensten to author.
7. Edwin Smith, statement, November 12, 1953.
8. Anthony Farrar-Hockley, *Echoes of War: The Edge of the Sword.* London: Buchan & Enright, Publishers, 1954.
9. McClain to author.
10. Tonne, 193.
11. Esensten to author, November 15, 1991.
12. Esensten to author, November 15, 1991.
13. McLaughlin to author.
14. Esensten to author, November 15, 1991.
15. Phillips statement.
16. McLaughlin to author.
17. *Saturday Evening Post.*
18. Carl Kopischkie to Monsignor Arthur J. Tonne, February 28, 1987.
19. Esensten to author, November 15, 1991.

20. Esensten to author, November 15, 1991.
21. Symonds, 130.
22. Esensten to Pottebaum.
23. McGhee to Martin.
24. Esensten to Pottebaum.
25. Esensten to author, November 15, 1991.
26. Bromser interview.
27. Mayo talk, 1983.
28. Tonne, 175.
29. Walter Bray, interview by author, March 2, 1992.
30. Baudin to Pottebaum.
31. Bray interview.
32. Dowe statement.
33. *Kansas City Star*.
34. Bromser interview.
35. Ps. 23:4.
36. Dowe statement.
37. Esensten to author, November 15, 1991.
38. *Advance Register*, October 16, 1953.
39. Mayo interview.
40. Esensten to author, November 15, 1991.
41. Pelser, Frederick and Pelser, Marcia E., *Freedom Bridge*. Vacaville, Calif.: The Fremar Press, 1984.
42. McLaughlin to author.
43. Tonne, 201.
44. Kapaun notes.
45. Luke 23:34.
46. Dowe statement.
47. Stegall interview.
48. Ascue interview.
49. Smith interview.
50. Smith interview.
51. White, 89.
52. Tonne, 195.
53. Ascue interview.
54. *Saturday Evening Post*.

EPILOGUE

1. Military Ordinate of the U.S.A. to Bishop Mark K. Carroll, November 23, 1950.
2. Helen Kapaun, interview by author, September 26, 1996.
3. Tonne, 213.
4. 8th U.S. Army, Korea, August 18, 1951, General Orders 562, Distinguished Service Cross Award to Emil J. Kapaun.
5. Tonne, 213.
6. *Marine Corps Gazette*, May 1988; Tonne, 208.
7. War Department, Washington, D.C. to Enos Kapaun, July 12, 1953.
8. *Marion County Record*, September 19, 1990.
9. Helen Kapaun, interview by author, September 28, 1996.
10. Department of the Army to Enos Kapaun, January 1, 1955.
11. Didde Printing Company to Columbia Pictures Company, March 16, 1955.
12. *Marion County Record*, September 19, 1990.
13. Esensten to Pottebaum, November 14, 1989.

14. McClain to Pottebaum, January 3, 1990.
15. Dowe, *Saturday Evening Post.*
16. Tonne, 199.
17. Tonne, 159.
18. Tonne, 189.

BIBLIOGRAPHY

LETTERS AND STATEMENTS

Achee, Edward, affidavit, June 3, 1954, Record Group 153 (Records of the Office of the Adjutant General), Entry 183, "Big Switch Investigation Reports," National Archives and Records Administration, College Park, Md. (hereafter NARA).

Adams, Joel R., affidavit, February 11, 1954, NARA.

Allen, Rev. Thomas, to Emil Kapaun, June 12, 1934 (author file copy).

Anderson, Clarence, M.D., affidavit, December 7, 1953 (NARA).

Baudin, Theo, to Colonel Cletus J. Pottebaum, USAF, retired, January 23, 1993 (author file copy).

Cahill, Rev. Thomas to Bishop Mark Carroll, undated (author file copy).

Carroll, Bishop Mark, to Emil Kapaun, October 13, 1950 (author file copy).

Department of the Army, Office of the Adjutant General to Enos Kapaun. January 4, 1955 (author file copy).

Didde Printing Company to Columbia Pictures Company, March 16, 1955 (author file copy).

Donnigan, George J., to Rev. Arthur J. Tonne, February 2, 1954 (author file copy).

Dowe, Raymond M., statements, October 16, 1953; November 25, 1953 (NARA).

Esensten, Sidney, M.D., statement, January 14, 1954 (NARA).

———, to Marie Martin, February 7, 1989 (author file copy).

———, to Cletus J. Pottebaum, November 14, 1989 (author file copy).

Fiske, Rev. Martin, O.S.B., to Rev. Arthur J. Tonne, April 7, 1954 (author file copy).

Gannon, John P. to Rev. Dolan, S.J., undated (author file copy).

Huel, Corporal Henry A. to Lieutenant Vincent J. Hohan, February 27, 1944 (author file copy).

Jablonovsky, Rev. John Cyril to Rev. Arthur J. Tonne, November 4, 1989 (author file copy).

Kapaun, Emil to Victor Bina, December 30, 1946, March 11, 1947 (author file copies).

———, to Emmet A. Blaes, February 26, 1947 (author file copy).

———, to Bishop Mark Carroll, September 1, 1948 (author file copy).

———, to Sister M. Euphrasia, February 28, 1947 (author file copy).

———, to Gerald Franta, October 20, 1942; November 30, 1942; March 30, 1943; September 10, 1944; October 28, 1944 (author file copies).

———, to Rev. Joseph Goracy, October 12, 1950 (author file copy).

———, to Enos and Elizabeth Kapaun, July 29, 1950; August 7, 1950; August 8, 1950; August 12, 1950 (author file copies).

———, to Eugene and Helen Kapaun, November 17, 1948; December 6, 1948; January 2, 1949; January 6, 1949; March 1, 1949; April 22, 1949; June 24, 1949; October 7, 1949; November 10, 1949; January 15, 1950; January 19, 1950; February 25, 1950; March 10, 1950; April 9, 1950; May 4, 1950; May 30, 1950; July 3, 1950; July 10, 1950; July 14, 1950; August 16, 1950; September 25, 1950; October 2, 1950; October 13, 1950 (author file copies).

———, to Sister M. Alice Klenda, March 18, 1940 (author file copy).

———, to John and Virginia Mazouch, September 5, 1949; November 14, 1949; December 22, 1949 (author file copies).

———, to Emil Melcher, February 1, 1938; February 17, 1938 (author file copies).

———,to Emil Melcher and Victoria Melcher, February 21, 1938; March 2, 1938; May 1, 1938; October 10, 1938; November 25, 1938; February 19, 1939; April 5, 1939; April 14, 1939; February 2, 1941 (author file copies).

———, to Joseph Meysing, January 3, 1950; March 10, 1950 (author file copies).

———, to Fred Moffitt, October 12, 1950 (author file copy).

———, to Bishop Augustus Schwerter, July 8, 1934 (author file copy).

———, to Rev. John Sklenar, February 3, 1946; April 10, 1950; June 21, 1950; August 12, 1950 (author file copies).

———,to Uncle Jim and Aunt Anna, June 6, 1945; August 30, 1949 (author file copies).

———, to Rev. Fred Tuzicka, September 20, 1948; November 17, 1948; January 30, 1949; November 14, 1949; April 13, 1950; October 14, 1950 (author file copies).

———, to Bishop Christian Winkelmann, April 6, 1940; February 18, 1942; June 1, 1945; November 1, 1945; January 3, 1946; February 1, 1946; March 1, 1946 (author file copies).

———, to Rev. Joseph ———, August 18, 1950 (author file copy).

———, to unnamed addresses, April 14, 1950; June 5, 1950; July 29, 1950; August 31, 1950; October 4, 1950 (author file copies).

Kaschko, Harold, affidavit, December 29, 1953 (NARA).

Killian, William, statement, November 30, 1953 (NARA).

Kopischkie, Carl, to Rev. Arthur J. Tonne, February 27, 1987 (author file copy).

Loyola, Sister M. to Rev. Arthur J. Tonne, February 25, 1954 (author file copy).

MacGhee, David F., statement, April 13, 1954 (NARA).

———, to Marie Martin, February 6, 1989 (author file copy).

Magnant, Joseph, statement, November 11, 1953 (NARA).

Mallory, Rev. Richard A. to Military Ordinate, August 21, 1951 (author file copy).

Mayer, William to Peter Susko, February 28, 1988 (author file copy).

Mayo, Walter L. Jr., statement, undated (NARA).

McClain, William to Cletus Pottebaum, January 3, 1990 (author file copy).

Meysing, Paul, statement, May ———,1992 (author file copy).

Military Ordinate of the United States to Bishop Mark K. Carroll, November 23, 1950 (author file copy).

Miller, Elmer to Carlos Fraser, November 6, 1950 (author file copy).

Moffat, David Livingstone to George P. Foster, undated (author file copy).

———, to Phil Moore, October 4, 1985 (author file copy).

Nardella, Ralph, statement, December 28, 1953 (NARA).

O'Connor, Joseph, statement, November 12, 1953 (NARA).

———, to Enos and Elizabeth Kapaun, Easter 1954 (author file copy).

Pecoraro, Anthony to unnamed addressee, November 16, 1989 (author file copy).

Pedicone, Henry, statement, December 1, 1953 (NARA).

Peterson, Philip Henry, statement, December 23, 1953 (NARA).

Phillips, Eric, statement, January 29, 1954 (NARA).

Picke, Rev. Martin, O.S.B., to Rev. Arthur J. Tonne, April 7, 1954 (author file copy).

Schmitt, Rev. Martin to Emil J. Kapaun, June 23, 1945 (author file copy).

Schneider, Leonard W. to Rev. Arthur J. Tonne, January 31, 1954 (author file copy).

Scholz, Rev. Bede, O.S.B., to Rev. Arthur J. Tonne, March 30, 1954 (author file copy).

Shaw, Eugene David to Elizabeth Kapaun, May 18, 1954 (author file copy).

Sheppard, Robert, statement, March 11, 1951 (NARA).

Sklenar, Rev. John M., statement, June 21, 1934 (author file copy).

Smith, Edwin, statement, November 12, 1953 (NARA).

Smolen, Joseph, affidavit, December 31, 1953 (NARA).

Stanley, Milford, statement, November 30, 1954 (NARA).

Teahan, Rev. Eugene to Emil Kapaun, June 22, 1945 (author file copy).

Unnamed soldier at Herington, Kansas Army base to Emil Kapaun, February 27, 1944 (author file copy).

Vandusky, Ray, statement, undated (author file copy).

Walsh, Rev. Raphael, O.S.B., to Rev. Arthur J. Tonne, February 22, 1954 (author file copy).

Winkelmann, Bishop Christian to Emil Kapaun, February 29, 1942 (author file copy).

Winter, Sister M. Virgilia to Rev. Arthur J. Tonne, February 8, 1954 (author file copy).

LETTERS TO AUTHOR

Axman, Sister Claudia, February 13, 1992.

Bach, Lawrence V., January 14, 1992.

Benda, M., June 1, 1992.

Emer, Jerry, January 11, 1992.

Esensten, Sidney, M.D., October 21, 1991; November 15, 1991; August 29, 1994.

Hilary, Sister, January 28, 1992.

Horrigan, Thomas, M.D., January 18, 1993.

Hupp, Monsignor Robert C., September 24, 1992.

Hussman, Monsignor George A., June 29, 1992.

Jennings, R., February 13, 1992; December 15, 1992.

Kapaun, Eugene and Helen, September 7, 1993.

Kaschko, Harold, January 21, 1992.

Kathol, Rev. Quentin, O.S.B., May 20, 1992.

Klenda, Martin, June 5, 1992.

Knier, Rev. Aloysius M., June 27, 1992.

Lorenz, William M., July 15, 1992.

Mack, Robert, November 14, 1991; December 3, 1991.

Mayo, Walter L., Jr., April 14, 1993; August 17, 1994.

McAbee, Filmore A., December 14, 1992.

McClain, William A., December 15, 1992.

McLaughlin, General John N., March 23, 1992.

McNamee, Leo F., March 23, 1993.

Melcher, Victoria, June 6, 1992.

Miller, Herbert A., January 18, 1993.
Miller, John A., March 8, 1993.
Morrison, Robert, February 23, 1992.
Mozouch, Virginia, October 25, 1992.
Mullen, Walter J., Jr., March 6, 1993.
John R. Ondrias, July 13, 1994.
Paladin, ———, November 5, 1991.
Pechanic, Anna, January 17, 1992.
Preisner, Monsignor A. F., March 5, 1992.
Ritter, John R., undated.
Rubin, Tibor, January 28, 1993.
Shadish, William R., M.D., December 28, 1991.
Spicka, Frank J., June 24, 1992.
Stegeman, Margie Krotz, August 4, 1995.
Terrell, Ernest, Jr., May 12, 1993.
Vsetecka, Leonard J., December 14, 1993.
Vinduska, Amelia, January 31, 1992.
Waner, Patsy Meysing, January 6, 1992.
Winter, Sister M. Vitalia, February 16, 1992; February 17, 1992.
Wixom, Robert, February 13, 1992.
Whitsitt, Gayle, June 12, 1992.
Wohlbier, Carl T., February 15, 1992.

INTERVIEWS BY AUTHOR

Anderson, Clarence, M.D., August 24, 1993 (telephone interview, notes in author file [naf]).
Ascue, Joseph, January 13, 1992 (telephone, naf).
Barry James, May 29, 1994, (telephone, naf).
Bray, Walter, March 2, 1992 (telephone, naf).
Bromser, Paul F., October 18, 1993 (telephone, naf).
Bryant, William, November 30, 1991 (telephone, naf).
Buchholz, Sister Dominica, February 13, 1992 (telephone, naf).
Coon, Harley, January 18, 1992 (telephone, naf).
DelGregg, Frank, March 4, 1992 (telephone, naf).
DiCerchio, John D., January 8, 1992 (telephone, naf).
Donnelly, John, March 28, 1993 (telephone, naf).
Gleason, Rose, May 1, 1992 (telephone, naf).
Hall, Douglass, February 27, 1992 (telephone, naf).
Hanssen, Cyrille W., May 24, 1993 (telephone, naf).
Eugene and Helen Kapaun, April 28, 1992 (Colwich, Kansas interview, naf).
Kapaun, Helen, September 26, 1996 (telephone, naf).
Latham, General Willard, November 15, 1991 (telephone, naf).
Malone, Monsignor Quentin J., February 10, 1992 (Brookville, N.Y. interview, naf).

Mayo, Walter L., Jr., April 10, 1993 (Falls Church, Va. interview, naf).

McNamara, Eugene, August 31, 1993 (telephone, naf).

Meysing, Paul, April 29, 1992 (Marion, Kansas interview, naf).

Moore, Phil, March 2, 1993 (telephone, naf).

Murray, Joseph, February 23, 1992 (telephone, naf).

Palmer, Elmer, May 24, 1993 (telephone, naf).

Pedicone, Henry, December 15, 1992 (telephone, naf).

Peljae, Frank, February 26, 1992 (telephone, naf).

Smith, W. W., January 9, 1992.

Stegall, Jack L., November 21, 1993 (telephone, naf).

Summers, Don, February 13, 1992 (telephone, naf).

Svitak, Maxine, April 29, 1992 (Pilsen, Kansas interview, naf).

Tonne, Monsignor Arthur, April 29, 1992 (Marion, Kansas interview, naf).

Tuzicka, Rev. Fred, February 9, 1995 (telephone, naf).

BOOKS

Alexander, Bevin. *Korea: The First War We Lost*. New York: Hippocrene Books, 1986.

Appleman, Roy. *South to the Naktong, North to the Yalu*. Washington: Center for Military History, U.S. Army, 1986.

Beech, Keyes. *Tokyo and Points East*. Garden City, N.Y.: Doubleday, 1954.

Biderman, Albert. *March to Calumny*. New York: MacMillan, 1963.

Blair, Clay. *The Forgotten War*. New York: TimesBooks, 1987.

Bong, Baik. *Kim Il Sung: Biography (II)*. Tokyo: Miraisha, 1970.

Breuer, William B. *Shadow Warriors: The Covert War in Korea*. New York: John Wiley & Sons, Inc., 1996.

Collins, J. Lawton. *War in Peacetime: The History and Lessons of Korea*. Boston: Houghton Mifflin Company, 1969.

Crosbie, Philip. *Pencilling Prisoners*. Melbourne: The Hawthorn Press, 1954.

Davies, S. J. *In Spite of Dungeons*. London: Hodder and Stoughton, 1954.

Deane, Philip. *I was a Captive in Korea*. New York: Norton, 1953.

Detzer, David. *Thunder of the Captains*. New York: Thomas Y. Crowell Company, 1977.

Dunn, Si. *The First Cavalry Division: A Historical Overview 1921–83*. Dallas: Taylor Publishing Company, 1984.

Farrar-Hockley, Anthony. *Echoes of War: The Edge of the Sword*. London: Buchan & Enright, 1954.

Fehrenbach, T. R. *This Kind of War*. New York: MacMillan, 1963.

———. *The Fight for Korea: From the War of 1950 to the Pueblo Incident*. New York: Grosset & Dunlop, 1969.

1st Cavalry Division: Korea, June, 1950 to January, 1952. Atlanta: Albert Love Press, undated.

George, Alexander L. *The Chinese Communist Party in Action: The Korean War and Its Aftermath*. New York: Columbia University Press, 1967.

Gough, Terrance J. *U.S. Army Mobilization and Logistics in the Korean War*. Washington: Center for Military History, U.S. Army, 1987.

Gittings, John. *The Role of the Chinese Army*. London: Oxford University Press, 1967.

Goulden, Joseph C. *Korea: The Untold Story*. New York: TimesBooks, 1982.

Griffiths, Samuel B., II. *The Chinese People's Liberation Army*. New York: McGraw-Hill, 1967.

Hastings, Max. *The Korean War*. New York: Simon and Schuster, 1987.

Heller, Francis B. *The Korean War: A 25-Year Perspective*. Lawrence, Kansas: The Regents Press of Kansas, 1977.

Hoyt, Edwin P. *The Day the Chinese Attacked: Korea, 1950*. New York: McGraw-Hill, 1990.

Hoyt, Edwin P. *The Bloody Road to Panmunjon*. New York: Stein and Day Publishers, 1985.

Hunter, Edward. *Brainwashing: The Story of the Men Who Defied It*. New York: Farrar, Straus & Cudahy, 1956.

Jones, Francis S. *No Rice for Rebels*. London: The Bodley Head, 1956.

Karig, Walter, Malcolm W. Cagle, and Frank Manson. *Battle Report: The War in Korea*. New York: Rinehart and Company, 1952.

Kim Il Sung. *Biography (II)*. Tokyo: Miraisha, 1970.

Kinkead, Eugene. *In Every War But One*. New York: W. W. Norton & Company, 1959.

Knox, Donald. *The Korean War: An Oral History*. San Diego: Harcourt Brace, 1985.

Knox, Donald and Alfred Coppel. *The Korean War: Uncertain Victory*. San Diego: Harcourt Brace Jovanovich, 1988.

Leckie, Robert. *Conflict: The History of the Korean War 1950–53*. New York: G. P. Putnam's Sons, 1962.

MacDonald, Callum A. *Korea: The War Before Vietnam*. New York: The Free Press, 1986.

Marshall, S. L. A. *The River and the Gauntlet*. New York: William Morrow & Company, 1953.

Mossman, Billy C. *United States Army in the Korean War, Ebb and Flow*. Washington: Center for Military History, 1990.

Office of Chief of Military History, Department of the Army. *Korea 1950*. Washington: U.S. Government Printing Office, 1952.

Paige, Glenn D. *The Korean Decision*. New York: The Free Press, 1968.

Paik Sun Yup. *From Pusan to Panmunjon*. Washington: Brassey's (U.S.), Inc., 1992.

Pelser, Frederick and Marcia E. Pelser. *Freedom Bridge*. Vacaville, Calif., The Fremar Press, 1984.

Poats, Rutherford M. *Decision in Korea*. New York: The McBride Company, 1954.

Rees, David. *Korea: The Limited War*. New York: St. Martin's Press, 1964.

Ridgway, Matthew B. *The Korean War*. Garden City, N.Y.: Doubleday, 1967.

Sandler, Stanley, ed. *The Korean War, An Encyclopedia*. New York: Garland Publishing, Inc., 1995.

Schnable, James F. *U.S. Army in the Korean War: Policy and Direction: The First Year*. Washington: U.S. Government Printing Office, 1972.

Schruben, Francis W. *Kansas in Turmoil: 1930–1936*. Columbia, Mo.: University of Missouri Press, 1969.

A Handbook of Korea. Seoul: International Publishing House, 1987.

Smith, Robert. *MacArthur in Korea: The Naked Emporer*. New York: Simon and Schuster, 1982.

Spurr, Russell. *Enter the Dragon: China's Undeclared War Against the U.S. in Korea 1950–51*. New York: Newmarket Press, 1988.

Stevenson, Burton, ed. *The Home Book of Quotations*. New York: Dodd, Mead & Company, 1964.

Summers, Harry G., Jr., ed. *Korean War Almanac*. New York: Facts On File, Inc., 1990.

Symonds, F. Addington. *Christianity in Action*. Surrey, England: The World's Work, Ltd., 1955.

Thornton, John W., Jr. *Believed to Be Alive*. Middlebury, Vt.: Paul S. Eriksson, 1981.

Toland, John. *In Mortal Combat*. New York: William Morrow and Company, Inc., 1991.

Tonne, Father Arthur. *The Story of Chaplain Kapaun: Patriot Priest of the Korean Conflict*. Emporia, Kansas: Didde Publishers, 1954.

Venzke, Roger R. *Confidence in Battle, Inspiration in Peace: The United States Army Chaplaincy, 1945–1975*. Washington: Office of the Chief of Chaplains, 1977.

Westover, John G. *Combat Support in Korea*. Washington: Center for Military History, U.S. Army, 1987.

White, William Lindsay. *The Captives of Korea*. Westport, Conn.: Scribner's Sons, 1957.

Whiting, Allen S. *China Crosses the Yalu: The Decision to Enter the Korean War*. New York: MacMillan, 1960.

Work Projects Administration. *The WPA Guide for 1930s Kansas.* Lawrence, Kansas: University Press of Kansas, 1939.

Zellers, Larry. *In Enemy Hands: A Prisoner in North Korea.* Lexington, Ky.: The University Press of Kentucky, 1991.

PERIODICALS AND OTHER PUBLICATIONS

Advance Register. Wichita, Kansas March 9, 1951; October 16, 1951; May 18, 1991.

Altar and Home. Conception Abbey, Missouri, December, 1952.

Anderson, Clarence L. and others. Medical Experiences in Communist POW Camps in Korea. *Journal of the American Medical Association,* September 11, 1954.

Chaplain's Newsletter, Archdiocese of the Military Services, U.S.A., June 1993.

Colliers. January 22, 1954.

Dowe, Raymond M., Jr. The Ordeal of Chaplain Kapaun. *Saturday Evening Post,* January 16, 1954.

Herer, Michael. *Documentary of a Hero.* Extension, June 1954.

Joyce, John M. *The Intrepid Shepherd of Pyoktong.* The Retired Officer, November 1983.

Kanhistique. Kansas History and Antiques, May 1992.

Kansas City Star. September 8, 1993.

Kapaun Herald. Kapaun High School, Wichita, Kansas, undated.

Marine Corps Gazette. May 1988.

Marion County Record. Marion, Kansas, December 1, 1955; September 19, 1990.

Morning Star. Conception College, Mo. October 6, 1933; November 17, 1933; April 6, 1934; April 3, 1936; April 24, 1936.

New York Herald Tribune. November 3, 1950; November 4, 1950.

New York Times. October 21, 1950; November 4, 1950; February 26, 1992.

News Herald. Hutchinson, Kansas June 7, 1954.

Our Sunday Visitor. Huntington, Ind., January 2, 1955.

Post Standard. Syracuse, N.Y., August 18, 1953.

Review. Marion, Kansas, June 18, 1940.

Trooper Staff. 8th Cavalry Regiment, Tokyo, July 1, 1950.

Wichita Beacon. Wichita, Kansas, August 1, 1950; September 9, 1953.

Wichita Eagle. Wichita, Kansas, September 3, 1953; May 28, 1989.

Wichita Eagle and Beacon. Wichita, Kansas, April 15, 1979.

Wrubben, W. H. *American Prisoners of War in Korea: A Second Look at the 'Something New in History' Theme.* American Quarterly, Spring 1970.

U.S. GOVERNMENT AND MISCELLANEOUS DOCUMENTS

ATIS Enemy Documents, Issues 11, 29 and 47.

Carroll, Mark, talk at Pilsen, Kansas, October 18, 1952, author file copy.

8th U.S. Army, Korea, August 18, 1951, General Orders 652, Distinguished Service Cross Award to Emil J. Kapaun.

8th Cavalry Regiment, Unit Historical Report, September 1950, Record Group 407, NARA.

———. Periodic Operations Report, November 1 to November 13, 1950, Record Group 53, NARA.

———. Report of Catholic Chaplains Fund, May 1950.

Headquarters, 1st Cavalry Division, September 2, 1950, Award of Bronze Star to Emil J. Kapaun.

Kapaun, Emil, diary, 1929–1935, extracts, author file copy.

———. records at School 15, Marion County, Kansas, 1930, author file copy.

———. transcripts and other records from Conception College High School and Conception College, Mo., author file copy.

———. transcript from Kenrick Seminary, St. Louis, Mo., author file copy.

———. sermons given at St. John Nepomucene Church, Pilsen, Kansas on Easter 1941 and April 30, 1943, and notes as teacher, author file copies.

———. sermons given at Herington Army base, Herington, Kansas, April 25, 1943; May 9, 1943; October 24, 1943; author file copies.

———. Monthly Report of Chaplain to Headquarters, U.S. Forces in India, Burma Theater, 1945–46, author file copies.

Kathol, Quentin, O.S.B., abstracts from interviews with Rev. Walter Heeney, O.S.B.; Rev. Anselem Coopersmith, O.S.B.; Rev. Malachy Riley, O.S.B.; Rev. Luke Becker, O.S.B.; Rev. Louis Meyer, O.S.B.; Rev. Ambrose Sperandio, O.S.B.; Rev. Placid Immegart, O.S.B.; Rev. Lawrence Gidley, O.S.B.; and Rev. Gilbert Stack, O.S.B., May 1992, author file copies.

Martin, Marie. *The Hero Behind Barbed Wire: Chaplain Kapaun.* Undated, unpublished, author file copy.

Mayo, Walter L., Jr., talk, undated, 1963, author file copy.

———. talk, undated, 1983, author file copy.

Office of Chief of Chaplains, U.S. Army. *The Regimental or Unit Chaplain.* Tech Cir. No. 4, March 1, 1942.

Preisner, Aloysius F., talk given at dedication of Kapaun-Mt. Carmel High School, Wichita, Kansas, undated, author file copy.

Records of the Office of Chief of Chaplains, U.S. Army, Record Group 247, NARA.

That War in Korea. Chicago: Films Incorporated. Undated, video-cassette.

3rd Battalion, 8th Cavalry Regiment, History, October 30, 1950, to November 5, 1950.

————. War Diary, November 1950.

————. Unit Journal, November 1950.

U.S. Department of Defense, Washington: *POW: The Fight Continues After the Battle.* The Report of the Secretary of Defense's Advisory Committee on Prisoners of War, August 1955.

U.S. Far East Radio Network, talks by Emil Kapaun, April 17–22, 1950, author file copy.

War Crimes Division, Judge Advocate Section, Korean Communications Zone. Operation Little Switch, supplementary to Interim Historical Report, June 30, 1953; November 1, 1953.

————. Operation Big Switch, supplementary to Interim Historical Report, Operation Little Switch, November 1, 1953; February 29, 1954.

INDEX

ABOUT THE AUTHOR

A former newspaper reporter, WILLIAM L. MAHER served in the Counter Intelligence Corps in Tokyo during the Korean War. He holds a Juris Doctor degree from Georgetown University and is the Village Justice of Brookville, New York.

— COVER ILLUSTRATION —
Emil Kapaun at the time of ordination as priest.
Les Broadstreet, Wichita

Emil Kapaun (right front) assisting soldier off the battlefield in Korea.
U.S. Army Photo

WHITE MANE PUBLISHING CO., INC.

To Request a Catalog Please Write to:
WHITE MANE PUBLISHING COMPANY, INC.
P.O. Box 708 • Shippensburg, PA 17257
e-mail: marketing@whitemane.com

Breinigsville, PA USA
17 September 2009
224227BV00004B/1/P